LIGHT CAR PATROLS, 1916-19

LIGHT CAR PATROLS, 1916-19

WAR AND EXPLORATION IN EGYPT AND LIBYA WITH THE MODEL T FORD

A Memoir by Captain Claud H. Williams

1/1st Pembroke Yeomanry, attached No. 5 Light Car Patrol

With Introduction and History of the Patrols by Russell McGuirk

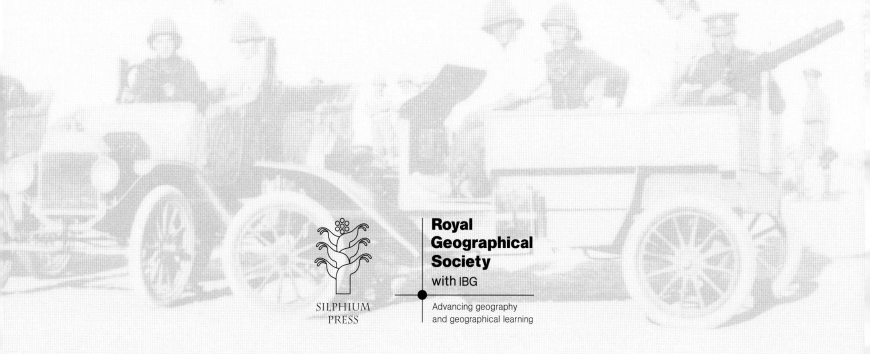

SILPHIUM PRESS

Royal Geographical Society
with IBG

Advancing geography
and geographical learning

Produced by Silphium Books, an imprint of
The Society for Libyan Studies
c/o The Institute of Archaeology
31–34 Gordon Square
London WC1H 0PY

www.societyforlibyanstudies.org

Cover design and layout: Chris Bell, cbdesign

ISBN 978-1-900971-96-6

CONTENTS

GLOSSARY

Libyan Desert: Located in the northeast part of the Sahara Desert, the Libyan Desert may be loosely defined as that part of the Sahara west of the Nile, including all of Egypt's Western Desert, northern Sudan and extending across Libya. Others would limit its extension into Libya to the most arid part of the Libyan province of Cyrenaica.

Western Desert: The Egyptian desert west of the Nile up to the Libyan and Sudanese borders.

Light Car: A term used in Great Britain before the First World War for an automobile of various engine capacities, but at the time usually less than 1.5 litres (90 cubic inches). During the war the Model T Ford, with its 2.9 litre engine (177 cubic inches) was termed a Light Car by the British Army by comparison with the much more powerful Rolls-Royce. (See 'LC' in Abbreviations Used.)

Yeomanry: British regional cavalry, usually part-time, in the Territorial Force. (The TF was the volunteer reserve component of the British Army from 1908 to 1920.)

ABBREVIATIONS USED

AOC — Army Ordnance Corps

ASC — Army Service Corps. In 1918, the name changed to Royal Army Service Corps

AACS — Australian Armoured Car Section

CGS — Chief of the General Staff

C-in-C — Commander in Chief

DQMG — Deputy Quartermaster-General

GHQ — General Headquarters

GOC — General Officer Commanding

GS — General Staff

EEF — Egyptian Expeditionary Force

FDA — Frontier Districts Administration

ICC — Imperial Camel Corps

LACB — Light Armoured Car Brigade. This was a unit of armoured Rolls-Royces under the Motor Section of the Machine Gun Corps.

LC — Although part of the registration number of British Army motor vehicles, this does not stand for 'Light Car'. L and LC were used to designate vehicles in the Mediterranean area.

LCP — Light Car Patrol

LRDG — Long Range Desert Group

MGC — Machine Gun Corps

MO — Medical Officer

NCO — Non-Commissioned Officer

OC — Officer Commanding

RGS — The Royal Geographical Society

WDA — Water Dump 'A'. Temporary Water Dumps 'B' and 'C' were set up for the Kufra Reconnaissance Scheme.

WFF — Western Frontier Force. In 1917, this became the **Western Desert Force** (and later Delta Force). **Southern Section** refers to that part of the Western Desert Force with headquarters at Hindaw in the Dakhla Oasis.

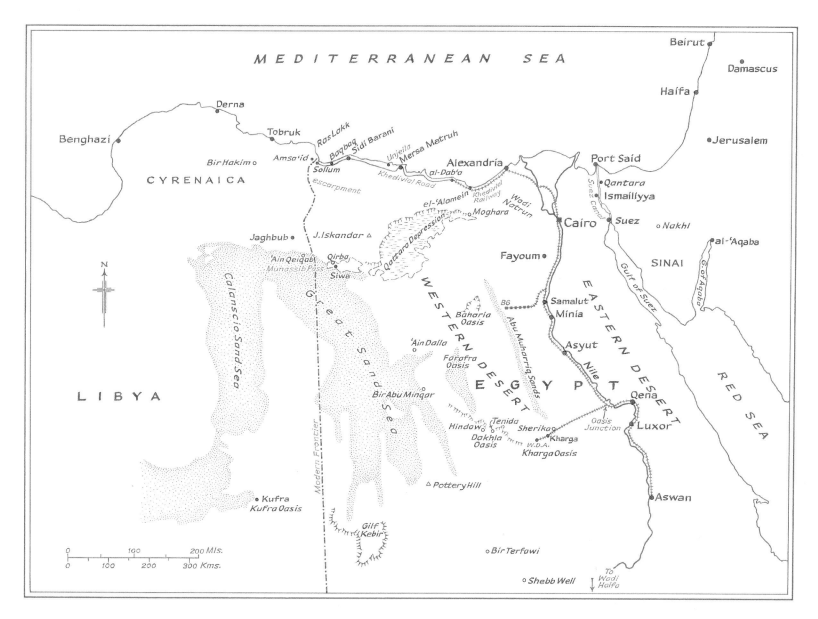

Map of Libya and Egypt

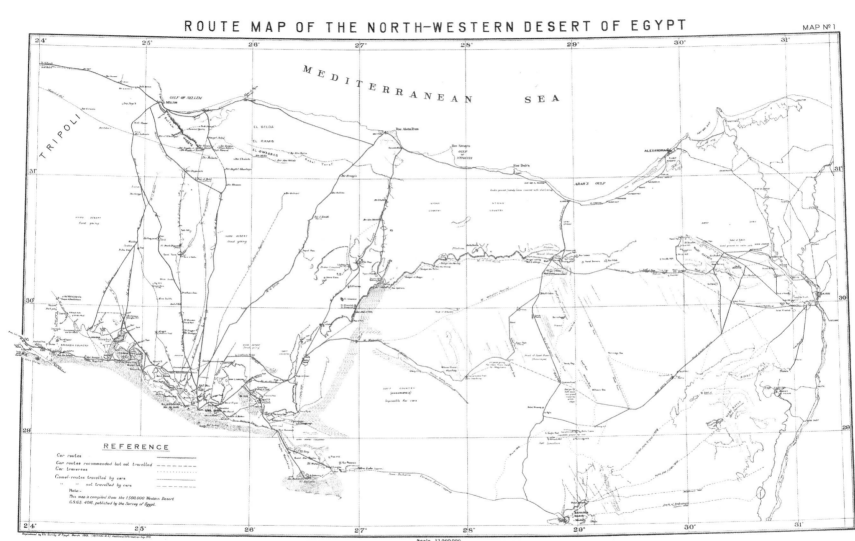

MEDITERRANEAN SEA

TRIPOLI

REFERENCE

Car routes
Car routes recommended but not travelled
Car traverses
Camel-routes travelled by cars
   "   "   not travelled by cars

Note:—
This map is compiled from the 1:500,000 Western Desert
G.S.G.S. 4011, published by the Survey of Egypt.

Scale 1:1,000,000

MILES 0   10   20   30   40   50   60   70   80 MILES

KILOMETRES 0 10 20 30 40 50 60 70 80 90 100 KILOMETRES

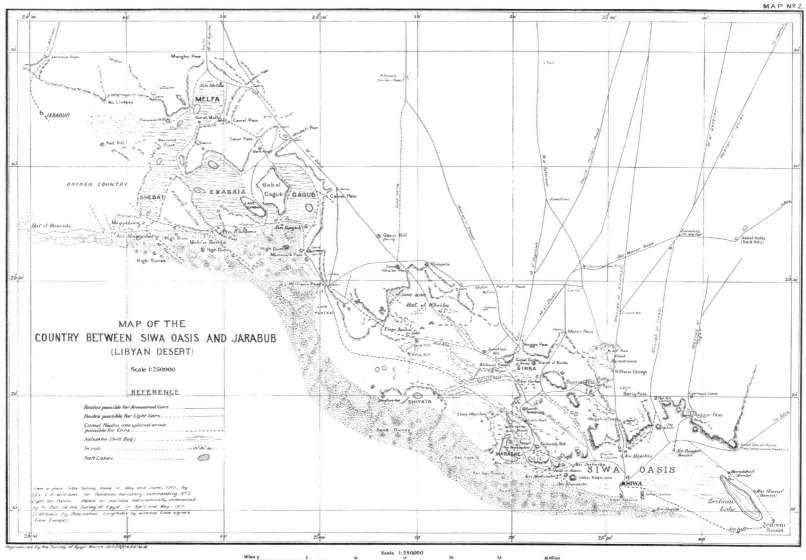

MAP OF THE
COUNTRY BETWEEN SIWA OASIS AND JARABUB
(LIBYAN DESERT)

Scale 1:250000

REFERENCE

Routes possible for Armoured Cars
Routes possible for Light Cars
Camel Routes unexplored or not
possible for Cars
Sabakha (Salt Bog)
Scrub
Salt Lakes

From a plane-table Survey made in May and June, 1917, by
2nd C.H. Williams, 1st Pembroke Yeomanry Commanding Nº 5
Light Car Patrol. Based on positions astronomically determined
by Mr. Ball, of the Survey of Egypt, in April and May, 1917.
(Latitudes by Observation. Longitudes by wireless time-signals
from Europe).

Reproduced by the Survey of Egypt March 1919 (18)0484'M.A)

Scale 1:250000

Miles
Kilometres

PART ONE

INTRODUCTION BY RUSSELL McGUIRK

INTRODUCTION

The scene should sound familiar:

> *Egypt has been invaded; thousands of British and colonial soldiers are rushed to the Western Desert to stop the enemy before he can get to the Nile Valley; a tiny force of volunteers, organized into motor patrols, carries out extraordinary journeys deep inside the desert.*

This meagre sketch clearly refers to momentous events preceding the Battle of el-Alamein. The story of that epic two-year struggle for Egypt, beginning with the Italian invasion from Libya up to the defeat of the German army dangerously close to the Nile, has been told and re-told in minute detail, popularised through television and film, to the point where mere mention of the words 'Western Desert' is enough to imply the Western Desert of Egypt and bring to mind visions of Rommel and Panzer tanks, Montgomery and the 8th Army—and, of course, the cars of the Long Range Desert Group wreaking havoc behind enemy lines. But if these dramatic events during the Second World War are common knowledge, it is extraordinary that so few of us are aware that the same three-line scene perfectly depicts events in the same desert during the Great War. The invasion in that case occurred in 1915. The cars were three dozen Model T Fords known as the Light Car Patrols.

For three years the Light Cars ranged widely over the Western Desert, first as part of military operations against the Turkish-led Sanusi army from neighbouring Libya; and later to chart much of that wilderness, the size of Sweden, for the first time. How can we know so much about war and exploration in the Western Desert, yet so little about the Light Car Patrols, the true pioneers of desert motoring?

The most famous of the desert explorers to use motor cars, Ralph Bagnold, acknowledged that his own astonishing achievements in the 1920s and '30s with Model T and Model A Fords were based on the work of the Light Car Patrols during the First World War. In the opening pages of *Libyan Sands* (1935) he regrets that no one has told their story:

> The history of the desert motor-car in Egypt is oddly discontinuous. Introduced into the country early in the Great War by the British Army, it was found that the Ford car, even the Model T of twenty years ago, was capable of supplanting the camel in certain areas, notably in the western desert, and in 1916 a tiny force of Light Car Patrols, armed with machine guns, guarded the whole 800-mile frontier against a possible recrudescence of the Senussi menace. These patrols covered great distances of unknown waterless and lifeless country as a normal routine, they took part in the final capture of Siwa Oasis from the Senussi, and among other things they succeeded in mapping, with the aid of speedometer readings and compass bearings, a great part of the northern desert, with its ranges of sand dunes, between the Nile and Siwa. Their exploits, with the crude vehicles they had, were astonishing... As far as I can trace, no one has ever written up the history of the Light Car Patrols. It is a pity, for there was nothing like them before.[1]

Bagnold went on to found the above-mentioned Long Range Desert Group during the Second World War, having been given the task because he convinced General Wavell that the British in Egypt needed something 'corresponding to the Light Car Patrols'[2] which could give warning of impending attack from the west. The LRDG proved to be far more than simply a motorized alarm system against invasion, but its forerunners were the Light Car Patrols.

The first historian of the Long Range Desert Group was W.B. Kennedy Shaw, who, before joining the LRDG, had been a member of Bagnold's team of amateur explorers between the two world wars. Shaw's history opens with a reference to a confidential publication entitled *Report on the Military Geography of the North Western Desert of Egypt*, by Captain Claud H. Williams, who had been the commanding officer of

---

[1] Bagnold, R. (1935), *Libyan Sands*, pp. 16-17.
[2] Bagnold, R. (1990), Sand, Wind and War, p. 14 (cited by Goudie (2008), *Wheels across the Desert*).

Opposite: Off-loading a Model T Ford at Port Said.

No. 5 Light Car Patrol. Williams' 'Military Geography' was written for the British Army in 1918–19 for the purpose of preserving the special knowledge acquired by the patrols which might be of military value in the future. Naturally, this document was made available to the LRDG in the early 1940s.[3]

When Shaw's *Long Range Desert Group*[4] first appeared in 1945, the author of the 'Military Geography' was 69 years old and managing his large sheep farm in New Zealand. Seeing his name and service with the Light Cars mentioned on the first page of Shaw's book, Williams sent the author the manuscript of a memoir about his service in the first war entitled 'Light Car Patrols in the Libyan Desert'. With Williams' permission, Shaw presented the manuscript to the Royal Geographical Society in London. That memoir, which forms Part II of the present volume, is a unique first-hand account of the work of the Light Car Patrols.

It is fitting that the RGS should be the repository for Williams' account. The Society's involvement in desert exploration, in particular exploration of the Libyan Desert, is long and distinguished. Indeed, in the second quarter of the 20th century no fewer than five of the Society's annually awarded Founder's Medals were presented to explorers of the Libyan Desert—Major Bagnold among them in 1935—while the Society's *Geographical Journal* is simply unrivalled for articles by distinguished desert explorers.

In addition to the manuscript of 'Light Car Patrols in the Libyan Desert', the RGS also holds a rare copy of Williams' *Report on the Military Geography of the North Western Desert of Egypt* (classified by the British Government as 'confidential' until 1963[5]), as well as an unpublished typescript entitled 'Handbook for Patrol Officers in Western Egypt', written by a certain Dr John Ball, whose name will appear frequently in these pages. It also has a collection of contemporary maps produced by the Survey of Egypt and based on the work of the Light Car Patrols. We shall see that Light Car officers had different strengths, but one of Claud Williams' particular talents lay in his mastery of surveying techniques. As often as not, his name appears on these maps as the officer responsible for the information they contain.

---

[3] *Report on the Military Geography of the North Western Desert of Egypt* was meant to replace an earlier volume, *Military Notes on Western Egypt*, hastily put together by Dr John Ball in 1916.
[4] Shaw, W.B. Kennedy (1945), *Long Range Desert Group: The Story of its Work in Libya, 1940–1943*.
[5] Williams used to relate how, after the two world wars, he asked the HMSO for a replacement copy because his own author's copy was falling apart—only to be told that his request was impossible to grant as the material was 'classified'.

THE MODEL T FORD

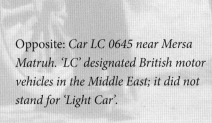

Opposite: *Car LC 0645 near Mersa Matruh. 'LC' designated British motor vehicles in the Middle East; it did not stand for 'Light Car'.*

It is no exaggeration to say that the Light Car Patrols were only possible because of the unique qualities of the Model T Ford. At the start of the Sanusi campaign in late 1915, the British Army relied mainly on two types of motor car: the Rolls-Royce and the Ford. The Rolls-Royces were mainly armoured cars, few in number but self-evidently formidable against the horse and camel-mounted Sanusi. Needless to say, they were a source of great pride to the British.

The Model T Ford was at the other end of the automotive 'social scale' entirely. Its primary function at the beginning of the campaign was to serve as handmaiden to the Rolls-Royce. It was chosen because it was inexpensive and despite the fact that the British, since the start of the war, had taken a dim view of Henry Ford's outspoken pacifism. From the very beginning of the fighting Ford had worked fervently to keep the United States out of the war, vowing that the internationally popular Model T Ford would not be used by either side. In early December 1915, as the military campaign in the Western Desert was getting under way—and, incidentally, as the millionth Model T was trundling off the assembly line in Detroit—Henry Ford was sailing around the North Sea in his 'Peace Ship', still hoping 'to get the boys home by Christmas'. Britain at the time was in trouble both on the Western Front and at Gallipoli; casualties were horrendous and, consequently, pacifism was abhorred by the vast majority of the British population—indeed it took either uncommon courage or great cowardice to be a pacifist or a conscientious objector in the country, and not a few expressing those principles ended up in prison, like mathematician-philosopher Bertrand Russell. Ford's determination to keep his automobile out of the war did not prevail.

There was already a Ford assembly plant in Manchester, and the British government was able to purchase some 19,000 Model T Fords in the course of the war, and more than one thousand wound up in Egypt before it was over.

With the first threat of Sanusi invasion on Egypt's western frontier British Army Headquarters ordered an Emergency Squadron of Rolls-Royce armoured cars and Model T Fords to Sollum, a coastal town on the Egyptian side of the Libyan border. The track was in bad condition, and the Rolls-Royces—the pride and joy of British automotive engineering—got stuck. That would not have been particularly noteworthy given the state of the track but for the fact that the handmaidens drove on past and continued all the way to Sollum. Thereafter, examples of this one-upmanship by the Fords occurred repeatedly. The Rolls-Royces were unbeatable where the ground was flat and hard, but where surface conditions were bad due to mud, sand, rock—and even swamp, as we shall see—the Fords were more reliable.

What qualities made the Model T Ford so ideal for desert patrols?

- Its revolutionary design was uncommonly simple. By the start of the war the assembly time for a single Ford at Highland Park, near Detroit, was an incredible 93 minutes! For the British Army this structural simplicity meant that maintenance and service, both at the workshop and in the field, were relatively easy.

- It was rugged. The car's frame and running gear were both fashioned from an alloy known as vanadium steel, with tensile strength unprecedented in automotive manufacturing.

- It had high ground clearance and was light-weight. The Ford and the Rolls-Royce had the same 10-inch clearance, but the armour-plated Rolls weighed over four times the 1200lb unarmoured Ford. The latter was even lighter when stripped down for desert work. The Ford's weight was evenly distributed, which made it well-balanced. This characteristic enabled the vehicle to be used on perilous escarpment tracks and (especially for Bagnold ten years later) even on steep sand dunes.

- The Ford was inexpensive and so were replacement parts. Spare part availability was a matter of concern in Egypt. With the sinking of just two ships, HMT *Titian* and HMT *Waterfels*, nearly 500 cases of spares bound for Egypt—nearly all for Fords—were lost. Despite the risks entailed in having to order them from England, Ford parts were cheaper to replace in Egypt than those of other motor cars. A story told by a senior transport officer in the Royal Army Service Corps[6] suggests that desert workshops had ample spares for the Ford. The Corps kept meticulous records, and at one point an officer was baffled when the number of Model T Fords in the Sollum region exceeded by one the number on his inventory. It turned out that an enthusiastic Australian at the area workshop had collected enough spare parts to assemble a new car, which he did![7]

There is no shortage of archival testimony concerning the Model T's superior performance in the Western Desert. At any one time there were seldom more than three dozen Fords with the Light Car Patrols, but there were hundreds more, all individually numbered, in other units. An officer working near Baharia Oasis with the Motor Section of the Machine Gun Corps reported, for example, that to drive on very broken terrain his unit had mounted guns on both Studebakers and Fords, and that 'the Studebakers were not a great success... [but] the Fords were excellent and able to cover any sort of ground and were of the very greatest use'.[8] The general surprise and admiration concerning the qualities of the Model T Ford can be summed up in this comment by a soldier being driven around by a Light Car driver from Siwa Camp:

---

[6] Badcock, G. E. (1925), A History of the Transport Services of the Egyptian Expeditionary Force, p. 306.

[7] For readers interested in a brief summary of technical detail, suffice it to say that the Model T had a 177 cubic inch, 2.9 litre, engine with 4-cylinders and 2 side-valves per cylinder. Block and crankcase were cast as a single piece with a detachable head. The engine, which was started with a hand-crank, produced 20 horsepower at 1600 rpm. The vehicle was rear-wheel drive with two forward speeds and reverse. Transmission control was by means of three foot pedals and a lever to the right of the driver's seat. The pedal on the left was used to engage the gear, while maintaining it in middle position put the car in neutral. By pushing the lever forward and taking his foot off the left pedal, the driver entered high gear. The middle pedal was for reverse. The right-hand pedal was for braking. On a good surface normal cruising speed was 35 to 40 miles per hour (56–64 kilometres per hour), and top speed on a good road was about 45 mph (72 km/h).

[8] WO 95/4443, letter in the MGC file.

'We whirled round impossible corners on a road that was not a road, fell over small precipices, ran over boulders, and generally achieved the impossible.'[9]

Claud Williams was, of course, second to none in expressing his appreciation of the Model T Ford and, as one might expect, 'Light Car Patrols in the Libyan Desert' has numerous insightful and humorous anecdotes about the car. In fact, Williams provides a light-hearted but intelligent record of virtually all aspects of the patrolmen's daily life and work. Readers may notice, however, that he does not say much about friends and fellow-soldiers, even when they are the subject of a particular story. When one of his men is wounded stopping a caravan, when another performs an unbelievable feat of navigation in a sandstorm, Williams tells the story but leaves the persons involved nameless, only occasionally going so far as to refer, for example, to '... my friend L.' Fortunately, in this first published edition of the memoir it has been possible to identify most of the principal characters left anonymous in the original text. This sort of minor clarification of the text has been done with footnotes: Williams' own text is left virtually unchanged. In the history of the Patrols which follows, care has been taken, where possible, to provide background information to events touched upon by Williams but where historical context or amplification might be helpful. The history is meant to supplement the memoir and vice versa.

It is hoped that this volume will go some way in meeting Bagnold's challenge to tell the story of the Light Car Patrols and to give the Patrolmen their rightful place among the great explorers of the Western Desert.

---

[9] Briggs, Martin S. (1918), *Through Egypt in War-Time*, p. 150.

HISTORY OF THE LIGHT CAR PATROLS IN EGYPT AND LIBYA

BY RUSSELL McGUIRK

BACKGROUND

Before the First World War, there were no motor cars in the Western Desert. The Egyptian Coastguard Camel Corps regularly policed its northern region, their principal task being to suppress the smuggling of drugs, tobacco and firearms. This contraband entered Egypt from Libya or was landed on the northern coast, and all of it was run to the Nile Valley by smugglers' caravans. The coastguards were also responsible for controlling tribal feuds and settling personal disputes among the Bedouin. Otherwise, there was little government interference in the daily lives of the desert Arabs.

Apart from the Fayoum Oasis, which is near Cairo and was connected to the Nile Valley by light railway, there are five major oases in the Western Desert, all of which feature in the story of the Light Car Patrols. Siwa is near the Libyan frontier, about 180 miles (290 km) southwest of the coastal town of Mersa Matruh. Before the war the fastest way to get from Matruh to Siwa was on the back of a racing camel, and the trip would take five or six days. By 1917, the Fords could easily exceed 100 miles (161 km) in a day on the same journey. The other four large oases, all in the middle of the desert, are Baharia, Farafra, Dakhla and Kharga. The last mentioned, like Fayoum, had commercial links with the Nile Valley and could be reached by train, but the three outlying oases of Baharia, Farafra and Dakhla had few visitors.

By the end of the first year of the war the Egyptian Coastguard had acquired several Model T Fords for use along the northern coast. Coastguard stations existed at regular intervals, the main ones being at al-Dab'a (100 miles (161 km) west of Alexandria),

Above: A detachment of the Egyptian Coastguard Camel Corps in the Western Desert.
Opposite: *The light railway from the Nile Valley to Kharga.*

Der Kampf um den Suezkanal

ENVER PASCHA

German postcard illustrating the Turkish attack on the Suez Canal in February 1915. Enver Pasha was the Ottoman Minister of War.

Mersa Matruh, Sidi Barani and Sollum. A rail line ran from Alexandria to al-Dab'a, and west of that point the coastguards had scraped a dirt track known as the 'Khedivial Road', which continued all the way to Sollum.

When war suddenly erupted in the Western Desert in November 1915, British forces in the country were concentrated near the Suez Canal. The Turks had attacked the Canal from across Sinai in February of that year and, while the attempt was foiled, Intelligence expected them to try again. The British were wrong-footed when Egypt was suddenly invaded from Libya by the Turkish-supported army of an Islamic sect known as the Sanusi Brotherhood. Its leader was Sayyid Ahmad al-Sharif, called the Grand Sanusi. As the Light Car Patrols were formed as a result of this conflict, a brief review of its main events up to the formation of the Light Car Patrols is relevant to this history.

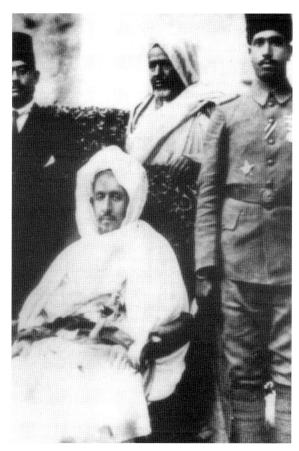

Below: *Al-Sayyid Ahmad al-Sharif al-Sanusi, known as the Grand Sanusi (seated). Standing beside him is Muhammad Saleh Harb, an officer in the Egyptian Coastguard who deserted in late 1915 and joined the Sanusi Army. He led the Sanusi force that occupied Egypt's central oases in February 1916.*

Above: *Following the northern coastline, the 'Khedivial Road' went from al-Dab'a, west of Alexandria, to Sollum, on the Libyan border. Here, two British officers in a Ford Light Car with two Western Desert Arabs.*

THE SANUSI INVASION

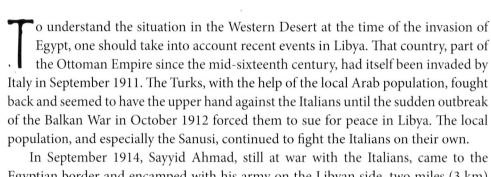

To understand the situation in the Western Desert at the time of the invasion of Egypt, one should take into account recent events in Libya. That country, part of the Ottoman Empire since the mid-sixteenth century, had itself been invaded by Italy in September 1911. The Turks, with the help of the local Arab population, fought back and seemed to have the upper hand against the Italians until the sudden outbreak of the Balkan War in October 1912 forced them to sue for peace in Libya. The local population, and especially the Sanusi, continued to fight the Italians on their own.

In September 1914, Sayyid Ahmad, still at war with the Italians, came to the Egyptian border and encamped with his army on the Libyan side, two miles (3 km) west of Sollum. A year later he was still there. Initially, his relations with the British in Egypt were good, but in the spring of 1915, the situation changed when (i) the allies landed on Gallipoli (threatening Constantinople, the seat of the Caliphate) and (ii) Italy (the Sanusi's great enemy) joined the world war on the side of the allies. Consequently, Sayyid Ahmad began to accept financial and military assistance from Turkey. Turkish soldiers began to appear in ever greater numbers on the frontier, and British ties with the Sanusi came under strain. Hostilities became inevitable on 5 November 1915, when a German U-boat torpedoed the British steamer HMS *Tara* and delivered ninety-two survivors into the hands of Turkish officers on the Libyan side of the border. The same U-boat then surfaced off Sollum, attacked two Coastguard cruisers at anchor in the bay, and shelled the British camp.

The British were caught completely off guard. The commander of the British Army in Egypt was Lieutenant-General John Maxwell, a protégé of Minister of War Lord

Opposite: *The British camp at Sollum. The camp and the two Coastguard schooners in the bay were attacked by a German U-boat on 5 November 1915.*

The view from the house in Rashida village, Dakhla Oasis, where the Grand Sanusi stayed from April to October 1916. Photo taken by Lt Lindsay.

Kitchener. He responded to the crisis by ordering the above-mentioned Emergency Squadron to bolster British defences along the coast between Mersa Matruh and Sollum and followed this up by sending to Matruh a full 'Western Frontier Force' to defend Egypt in case of invasion.

As the six Rolls-Royce armoured cars and twelve Model T Fords of the Emergency Squadron moved west from the railhead at al-Dab'a, vehicles were assigned to protect Mersa Matruh and Sidi Barani. The remaining cars attempted to carry on to Sollum, and it was during this stage of their mission that the armoured cars were brought to a standstill, while the Fords succeeded in getting through. Two weeks after the German attack, with Sanusi warriors now agitating to invade Egypt, the British withdrew from Sollum and Sidi Barani, and the men from those outposts fell back on Mersa Matruh. With the British gone, the Sanusi army marched unopposed into Egypt and took possession of the entire coastal region west of Mersa Matruh, while Matruh itself became the forward base of the British and colonial troops of the Western Frontier Force (WFF).

Two days before the British withdrew from Sollum, a low-ranking but already influential intelligence officer named T.E. Lawrence visited the local commander there to assess the situation on the border for British Army HQ in Cairo. However, Lawrence's mission came too late, and the situation deteriorated so quickly that withdrawal was the only option.

Over the next few months the WFF fought four battles with the Sanusi, gradually pushing them back towards Libya. The last of these clashes (26 February 1916) was at al-'Aqaqir, near Sidi Barani. The Sanusi army, overpowered and forced to retreat, withdrew to Siwa—still within Egypt, but near enough the border for it to escape

Above and left: *Bimbashi Leo Royle, Egyptian Coastguard Camel Corps, at Girba before the war.*

into Libya if threatened. At this point the British assumed the campaign was virtually over, but they were wrong. The bulk of the Sanusi army suddenly went not to Libya, but southeast, deep into the Egyptian desert, where it occupied the central oases of Dakhla, Farafra and Baharia. In April Ahmad al-Sharif followed his army and set up headquarters at Dakhla.

One can well imagine the frustration felt at British Headquarters at this startling development. The Sanusi were not defeated; they had moved to the very centre of Egypt! Just as the fighting in the north seemed about to end, a new front would now have to be opened in the middle of a largely unknown and very inhospitable desert. In this manner was the stage set for the story of the Light Car Patrols.

Meanwhile, the campaign in the north was not quite over. When the British reoccupied Sollum (14 March), they received information that the *Tara* crew were being held at Bir Hakim. This place, virtually featureless apart from a good well, was deep inside Libya. Although it did not appear on WFF maps, two Arab guides were found who said they knew where it was. But was a rescue possible? In the direction indicated by the guides there were no roads, the desert was completely uncharted, and Sanusi or Turkish forces might be anywhere in the area.

Any rescue attempt inside the enemy heartland would obviously depend on the armoured cars. The Emergency Squadron had been withdrawn by this time, but another armoured car detachment, commanded by the Duke of Westminster, had taken its place. The decision whether or not to attempt the rescue was down to three men: the WFF commander, General Peyton; the Duke of Westminster; and Captain Leopold Royle. The latter had previously been the Egyptian Coastguard's most experienced officer in the Western Desert. Now officially with the Royal Flying Corps, he was temporarily attached to the WFF as an Intelligence Officer. He knew that the ground was good for motor vehicles for at least fifty miles (80 km) going west, and he thought the attempt was worth making. The other two agreed.

On 17 March 1916, the Duke of Westminster and Captain Royle led a 41-car column into Libya. Ten of the vehicles were armoured cars; the rest were mostly Fords, many in the form of ambulances. In short, twelve hours after crossing into Libya the column found Bir Hakim, rescued the prisoners and returned to Egypt.

Opposite: *Pushing a Rolls-Royce out of soft sand.*

RIVALRY AT
THE WAR OFFICE

The dramatic rescue came just as General Maxwell was leaving Egypt, handing his command over to General Archibald Murray. One might assume under the circumstances that Maxwell was able to leave in triumph, but that is not what happened. A group of generals at the War Office blamed Maxwell and Kitchener for failing to foresee and pre-empt the Sanusi invasion in the first place. One of these men, Major General Arthur Lynden-Bell, was Murray's Chief of the General Staff, who wrote to his War Office colleagues, undermining Maxwell in stingingly personal attacks.

> Maxwell... is absolutely useless as a soldier and for over a year has done absolutely nothing towards the defence of Egypt... He is supposed to have some marvellous knowledge of Egyptian affairs![10]

Lynden-Bell was equally dismissive of the Cairo Intelligence Department run by Gilbert Clayton with such men as Aubrey Herbert (a Member of Parliament and, remarkably, a Turcophile), George Lloyd (also an MP and future High Commissioner to Egypt), Leonard Woolley (later a renowned archaeologist), and the ever-controversial T.E. Lawrence.

---

[10] IWM, Papers of Maj. Gen. Sir Arthur Lynden-Bell, undated letter to Maj. Gen. Callwell.

We were told that the Egyptian Intelligence was most astonishingly efficient and that the astounding work they had done should be talked of with bated breath... an absolute myth![11]

In fact, all these men, from Kitchener to Lawrence, were experts insofar as they spoke either Arabic or Turkish and had spent years in the Middle East, while Lynden-Bell knew little about the region in which he had now arrived. Maxwell's handling of the Sanusi problem had obviously failed, but it had been cleared at every step with the War Office; and while Lynden-Bell's criticism was unfair, the departure of Maxwell and the advent of men who opposed him meant a complete change of policy for maintaining the security of the Western Desert. In the formulating of this new policy Lynden-Bell himself took the lead. Middle East expert or not, he became the prime mover behind the Light Car Patrols.

Major General Arthur Lynden-Bell, Chief of the General Staff, who founded the Light Car Patrols.

---

[11] Ibid., letter to Gen. F. B. Maurice, 16 January 1916. Generals Callwell and Maurice served successively as Director of Military Operations at the War Office in London.

THE FORMATION OF THE LIGHT CAR PATROLS

As the campaign against the Sanusi was drawing to a close in the north, Lynden-Bell began to argue (i) that the vast majority of British and colonial soldiers in Egypt should be withdrawn from the Western Desert, either to be sent to France or allocated to the up-coming push against the Turks in Sinai and Palestine; (ii) that the remaining Sanusi were containable where they were and unlikely, at this stage, to cause trouble among Egyptians in the Nile Valley; and (iii) that what was needed against them now were 'small, handy, mobile columns'.[12] What Lynden-Bell originally had in mind was a combination of camel corps and aeroplanes. But no sooner had several dozen Fords participated in the dash into Libya to rescue the *Tara* crew, than a new idea suddenly began to circulate round British Army Headquarters. What could be smaller, handier, or more mobile than a Model T Ford? By 23 March an enthusiastic Lynden-Bell was already setting up a new local[13] unit of Ford 'Light Cars' and writing to the Quartermaster General's office to appropriate every Ford that could possibly be spared:

> In view of the very great use which the Ford cars have proved for patrol work and other work of similar nature in the Western Desert, I am very anxious to collect as many of these cars as can possibly be spared from other duties with a view to forming a Light Car Scout Corps.

[12] Ibid., cf. letters Lynden-Bell to Gen. Maurice, 28 February 1916 and Gen. Maurice to Lynden-Bell, 11 March 1916.
[13] The Light Car Patrols remained a 'local' formation for over a year. They were placed under Machine Gun Corps (Motors) in late summer 1917.

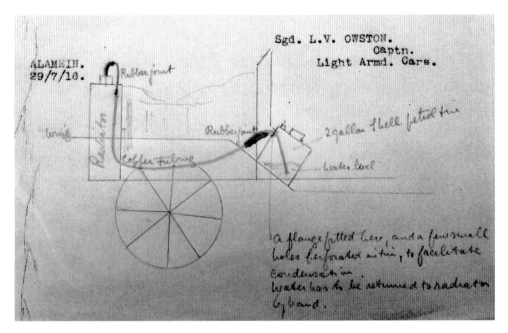

ALAMEIN.
29/7/16.

Rubber joint

Radiator

Coffer Fuel box

Rubber joint

Sgd. L.V. OWSTON.
Captn.
Light Armd. Cars.

2 gallon Shell petrol tin

water level

A flange fitted here, and a few small holes perforated in tin, to facilitate condensation.
Water has to be returned to radiator by hand.

Left: *Owston sketch of Model T condenser system.*
Below: *Leycester Varley Owston, Commander of the Light Armoured Car Brigade in the Western Desert from spring 1916.*

Judging by the appearance of the front gate, GHQ could certainly dispense with the use of these Ford cars or most of them,[14] and I imagine that the same is true of other staffs. Possibly you know of Ford cars being used on other than staff duties, which could also be replaced by some other type, or could be made available by a more rigid economy of cars.

Please let me have your views as soon as possible; what I should like would be from 30 to 40 cars.[15]

---

[14] General Headquarters were located in the luxurious Savoy Hotel at Midan Suleiman Pasha (today's Tal'at Harb). Lynden-Bell's comment implies that Staff officers had a tendency to leave their Ford cars parked near the front gate.
[15] National Archives, WO 95/4361, letter from Lynden-Bell to DQMG of 26 March 1916.

A week later the new formation of Light Car Patrols was already taking shape. The Quartermaster General summarily called in Fords from around Cairo and the Canal Zone, and these were adapted for desert driving.

Headquarters considered various permutations for the force, finally deciding on six patrols of six Fords each, one of which would be used to carry baggage, ammunition and supplies. They also, provisionally, asked for two cars to be fitted with box bodies for mounting a machine gun in the back, and it soon became standard to have at least several gun-mounted cars in each patrol.

No. 5 Patrol at Wadi Natrun, June 1916. Claud Williams is standing behind the Ford boxcar (far right), second to the left of the man with the machine gun.

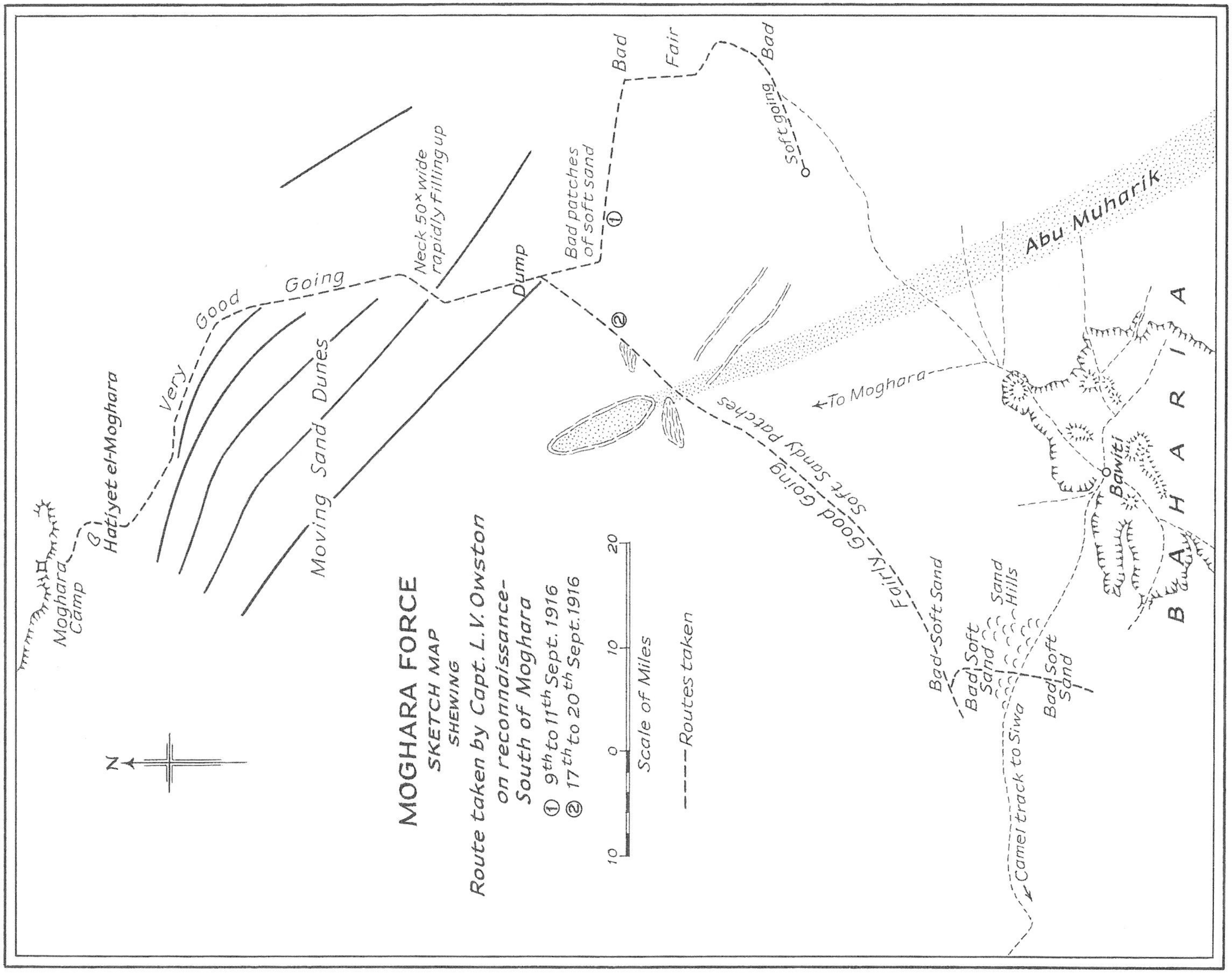

MOGHARA FORCE
SKETCH MAP
SHEWING
Route taken by Capt. L.V. Owston
on reconnaissance
South of Moghara
① 9th to 11th Sept. 1916
② 17th to 20th Sept.1916

Scale of Miles

------- Routes taken

N

Moghara Camp

Hatiyet el-Moghara

Very Good Going

Moving Sand Dunes

Neck 50× wide rapidly filling up

Dump

Bad patches of soft sand

①

②

Bad

Fair

Bad

Soft going

Abu Muharik

To Moghara

Good Going Soft Sandy patches

Fair(ly)

Bad-Soft Sand

Bad Soft Sand

Sand Hills

Bad Soft Sand

Bawiti

B A H A R I A

Camel track to Siwa

Above: *Car of No. 4 Patrol, with Lewis Gun mounted forward.*
© *Imperial War Museum (HU 92031).*
Opposite: *Major L.V. Owston (far left) and men of the Light Armoured Car Brigade, with a Model T Ford. When the Light Car Patrols were first being formed Owston was given the job of testing Fords to get optimum performance in off-road desert conditions.*

Soon after the *Tara* crew rescue the WFF's armoured car brigade was again changed. The Duke of Westminster's unit was replaced by another, this one commanded by Captain Leycester Owston. Over the next year Owston would work closely with the Light Car Patrols, but his first service for the new force was to carry out tests on Fords to optimize their performance in desert conditions. In the summer of 1916 he devised a condenser system for preventing radiator water from boiling over and being lost. He and his men took four Fords into the desert for a fortnight and developed a method whereby copper tubing was run from the radiator cap to a two-gallon petrol tin placed on a slant near the left forward mudguard. It was not 100% effective, and the preserved water had to be returned to the radiator by hand—but it worked well enough.

Officers and men for the Light Car Patrols were selected mainly from British yeomanry assigned to duty with the Western Frontier Force, while drivers and mechanics came from the Army Service Corps. Each patrol had personnel of about thirty men, but with additional staff at the various local bases dealing with maintenance, supplies, etc., there were consistently well over 200 men in the Light Car force.[16] Interestingly, and despite the presence of at least two New Zealanders in the original six patrols, the archives give no hint of any Australians serving in the unit at this stage.[17]

---

[16] The first mention of the LCPs as a separate entity in the list of total units in Egypt (November 1916), gives a figure of 18 officers and 252 other ranks, as well as weaponry of 20 machine guns and 18 Lewis guns. (WO 33/905, No. 6155, 17 Nov. 1916).
[17] Lt A. S. Lindsay was the second New Zealander. A third, Lt W. H. P. McKenzie, was given command of the new No. 7 LCP, set up in late 1916–early 1917 for service in Sinai and Palestine.

ARRIVAL OF THE YEOMANRY

On 15 March 1916, a convoy of transport ships arrived at Alexandria carrying yeomanry regiments mainly from Wales and the Welsh Border country. As they had all been 'dismounted' the previous November, they were no longer considered cavalry. The yeomen were now just hastily trained infantry, and it is fair to say they were universally disgruntled about this. Among the newly arrived regiments assigned to the Western Frontier Force were the Pembrokeshire, Denbighshire and Shropshire Yeomanries, and these three regiments provided the officers and many of the 'other ranks' for three of the six original Light Car Patrols. The commanding officers for these three patrols turned out to be long-term Light Car men, that is, they stayed with the Patrols from late spring or early summer 1916 until after the Armistice. Each was a second lieutenant in 1916; and each performed distinguished service with the Light Cars. Claud Williams, with the Pembrokeshire Yeomanry and assigned to No. 5 Patrol, was one of them. The other two were Edward Davies Moore, Shropshire Yeomanry, who served with No. 3 Patrol; and Roy Austin Davidson, Denbighshire Yeomanry, with No. 6 Patrol.

A fourth Light Car commander, Lt Alfred Stewart ('Mac') Lindsay, was already in Egypt when the others arrived. Lindsay, a New Zealander who had emigrated to Scotland, was with the Fife and Forfar Yeomanry and assigned originally to No. 1 Patrol. He was also an outstanding officer and served till after the Armistice.

Numerous other officers were accepted into the Light Cars, but served either for short periods or after the main events in the Light Car story. (All known Light Car officers are listed in Appendix 1 on page 129.)

EARLY DISTRIBUTION OF LIGHT CAR PATROLS

Above: *Officers of 1/1st Pembroke Yeomanry, Wadi Natrun, June 1915. Claud Williams is second row, third from right; Llewellyn Partridge is front row, third from left.*

Patrol No.	Officer Commanding	Regiment	Based in 1916
No. 1 LCP	2nd/Lt A.S. Lindsay	Fife & Forfar Yeo	Kharga
No. 2 LCP	2nd/Lt G.G. Lockett	Cheshire Yeo	Minia – B6 line
No. 3 LCP	2nd/Lt E.D. Moore	Shropshire Yeo	Minia – B6 line
No. 4 LCP	2nd/Lt H.N. Harding	County of London Yeo	al-Dab'a
No. 5 LCP	2nd/Lt C.H. Williams	Pembroke Yeo	Wadi Natrun
No. 6 LCP	2nd/Lt R.A. Davidson	Denbigh Yeo	Moghara

A look at Claud Williams' first few months in Egypt will illustrate what life was like for the arriving yeomen. The Pembroke Yeomanry were sent to Camp Beni Selama, an hour's train ride to the northwest of Cairo. There they passed two dreary months, their days filled with route marches, musketry practice, compass drill, and regimental parades; they attended lectures with titles such as 'The Attack', 'Defence of Isolated Posts in Egypt' and 'Patrolling the Desert'. Only very occasionally did they get the opportunity to visit Cairo on short leave. In late May, the Regiment moved to Wadi

Vehicles of No. 4 Patrol loaded on railway flatbed cars soon after the unit's arrival in Egypt. © Imperial War Museum (HU 92035).

Natrun, midway between Cairo and Alexandria and just off what is still today called the 'Desert Road'. There the prospects for finding interesting employment at first seemed as bleak as at Beni Salama, but in June recruiters for the Light Car Patrols arrived looking for volunteers, and Lt Williams jumped at the opportunity to do something useful and interesting. He wrote home a few weeks later, bursting with enthusiasm:

> I think I told you all of my new job, [commander of a] Motor Patrol with extra pay and a temporary step up. I am the only one of the lot who has a decent job. The others stew in camp & do ordinary regimental duties. I have my 48 hours out & 48 hours in, 100 miles of front to patrol, the mild excitement of stopping & examining an occasional caravan... I have with me an interpreter, a signaller with Helio & Lamps, a Lewis gunner & two other men. Four rifles & a Lewis gun. One has to be careful at night. I generally stop at sunset on high ground, have a good look round with glasses, feed, and after dark shift a mile or two & bunker down in the sand by the cars. Each takes his turn standing sentry & we get away by daylight. I know this old desert now like the road to Gisborne.[18]

---

[18] CHW's letter to his sister Violet, 5 July 1916.

EARLY ACTIVITIES, 1916

Positioning the Light Car Patrols around the Sanusi-occupied oases took place throughout the spring and summer of 1916. Along or near the northern coast, No. 4 Patrol was allocated to al-Dab'a; No. 5 to Wadi Natrun; and No. 6 covered both el-Alamein and nearby Moghara, a small oasis at the eastern end of the Qattara Depression. In the Nile Valley, Patrols Nos. 2 and 3 were sent to Minia, in preparation for an eventual move against Baharia, while No. 1 Patrol was sent further south pending the occupation of Kharga.

As early as April some Light Cars were involved in actions that earned mention in despatches. One of the Minia-based patrols captured four men, including a Turkish officer, between Baharia Oasis and the Nile Valley; No. 6 Patrol stopped two enemy supply caravans near el-Alamein.

Also in April aerial reconnaissance and local agents confirmed that there were no Sanusi in Kharga Oasis, so 1,600 British and colonial soldiers were rushed there via the existing railway, which set the stage for a move against Dakhla. Engineers immediately began to extend the Kharga railway in the direction of Dakhla, while No. 1 Patrol was sent to the railhead to protect the workers. Meanwhile, to the north, work on another light railway was begun from the Nile Valley to Baharia together with a parallel system of blockhouses near the tracks, protection being provided by Patrols No. 2 and 3.

In May and June, two incidents served to underline the hazards of using aeroplanes for desert patrolling, a fundamental component of Lynden-Bell's original plan for desert security. Near Kharga a Royal Flying Corps biplane was lifted in a sandstorm and wrecked as it hit the ground again, only the engine and propeller being salvageable.

Two weeks later, another air accident occurred in the same area, one which convincingly showed that Ford Light Cars were, at the very least, safer than aeroplanes. The occasion was a combined air and camel reconnaissance of the outskirts of Dakhla between 14 and 17 June. Lt Lindsay's No. 1 Patrol had only recently arrived in the area, and in writing the order for the move on Dakhla, the commanding officer at Kharga somewhat deprecatingly pointed out that the Light Car Patrol was to be allowed to accompany the other units, but '... no assistance is to be expected from it [!]'.[19]

'The Ridley Tragedy' by Stuart Reid.

At dawn on 14 June, a small force of Imperial Camel Corps, together with several Fords from No. 1 Patrol, left the Railhead at Kharga to set up a petrol dump near Dakhla and carry out a reconnaissance of an old caravan track, known as the 'Gubari Road', leading to the oasis. The next day two aeroplanes—with two pilots and a mechanic—left their base near the Kharga Railhead with orders to *rendez-vous* at an advanced landing site forty miles (64 km) to the west, by a point on the Gubari Road. The pilots could not find the location, however, and while they were searching, one machine had to make an emergency landing and was damaged. The three men stayed together that night, and the next morning the pilot in the undamaged biplane flew back to get help. When help arrived at the site of the forced landing, the damaged aircraft and the two stranded men were gone. For five days the area was combed

---

[19] WO 95/4442, Operation Order No. 19, 16 June 1916.

Right: *Capt. Carlyon Mason-Macfarlane,*
7th Hussars, attached Imperial Camel Corps;
killed on reconnaissance at Baharia Oasis,
September 1916. He was a close friend of
Gertrude Caton-Thompson, later the well-
known archaeologist of Kharga Oasis.
In her autobiography she revealed that she
had been profoundly in love with him. She
never married.
Below: *Lt Roy Austin Davidson, Officer*
Commanding No. 6 Patrol.

by the Camel Corps and several Fords from No. 1 Patrol. The missing men were finally found by the Light Cars, but by then the pilot had committed suicide with his revolver, and the mechanic had died of thirst. Throughout the ordeal the mechanic kept a journal, which revealed that the two men had managed to get their aeroplane into the air again until another forced landing had sealed their fate. The dead men were buried where they were found. Lt Lindsay led the burial party, and he and his men erected a cross and read the funeral service.[20] This incident had, at least, revealed the potential usefulness of the Light Cars to the British commander at Kharga, whose report stated: '... the Ford Car Patrol did excellent work'.[21]

Meanwhile, to the north, the British were approaching Baharia from three directions: from Moghara Oasis (to the north), from Wadi Natrun (to the northeast), and from the end point of the railway– blockhouse line from the Nile Valley (to the east). A force was sent to normally uninhabited Moghara, which is just over 100 miles (161 km) from Baharia. Moghara is also at the eastern end of the huge Qattara Depression, as well as being at the lower end of the 35-mile (56 km) wide gap between the Mediterranean and that Depression. Twenty-six years later Rommel's tanks would have no option but to try to pass through the gap, which made it the setting for the Battle of el-Alamein. However, the camel-mounted Sanusi were not restricted to the hard and flat ground required by the German Panzers. It was thought they would try

---

[20] Later the bodies were transferred to Cairo.
[21] WO 95/4442, Report by OC Kharga, 21 June 1916.

Left and below: *Work party from No. 1 Patrol clearing a way up the western escarpment of Kharga Oasis in preparation for the move against Dakhla Oasis, October 1916.*

to escape from Baharia by travelling west through the more difficult terrain below the Qattara Depression. Indeed, that is the route they had taken to get there in the first place—the old caravan track between Siwa and Baharia.

In September 1916, Lt Davidson's No. 6 Patrol helped Captain Owston to carry out two reconnaissances in this rough terrain south of Moghara, the objective being to discover the whereabouts and nature of the Siwa-Baharia track. Owston and his men were, of course, using their unit's four Fords and not the armoured cars. Davidson's patrol assisted by establishing an advance 'dump' of food and fuel for the expedition. The first outing was hampered by parallel lengths of sand dunes, which forced the cars to travel southeast, while their objective was to the southwest. When they finally got round the dunes, there were many patches of soft sand, which forced them to turn back.

A second attempt a week later was more successful. Owston found the track but reported that the whole area south of Moghara was unsuitable for armoured cars, or indeed for any car heavier than a Ford. In any case, no further action could be taken in this wilderness until the Sanusi made their move.

By September, there were six blockhouses in a line extending for 73 miles (117 km) from the Nile towards Baharia. The westernmost (B6) was still 28 miles (45 km) east of the oasis, but the long north-south ribbon of the Abu Muharriq Dunes lay in-between, so patrolling from B6 inside and west of the dunes was done by the Imperial Camel Corps. One ICC officer, Capt. Mason-MacFarlane, had recently made a solo five-day reconnaissance of part of Baharia Oasis itself. Several weeks later, in early September, he went back to the area with a patrol consisting of himself, one Lt Ryan, and three privates. The five men descended into the oasis with their camels and were reconnoitring near the base of the northern escarpment, when they were seen and shot at by some Sanusi half a mile (0.8 km) away. Although they managed to get back up to the plateau with their animals, the two officers then walked away from the others along the escarpment rim. While they were gone, a dozen Sanusi suddenly appeared at the top between the ICC men and their officers, who by now were out of sight. It was late afternoon, and shots were exchanged until dark, but the three men

Above top: *Alfred Stewart Lindsay.*
Above below: *Lindsay's passport photo.*
Right: *Early 20th century postcard of Cairo Citadel, where Dahman bin Hayyin was executed.*

Armoured Car at Durbar, Dakhla, October 1916.

were unable to get round the Sanusi to look for their missing officers. They spent the night in the area and the next morning headed back through the dunes. Aeroplanes were unable to find the missing men.

Two weeks later, Claud Williams and the Pembroke's Transport Officer, Major Llewellyn Partridge, took four cars from No. 5 Patrol on another reconnaissance near Baharia. Travelling from Wadi Natrun, the patrol went round the top of the Abu Muharriq Dunes and continued to within 25 miles (40 km) of the oasis. They hid their cars and waited, hoping to capture a native who might know what had become of the missing officers. Williams gives us an exciting first-hand account of what happened next (see pages 172–5), so it is necessary here to say no more than that a small Sanusi caravan did appear; the Light Cars captured it; and the camels were found to be carrying 'an assortment of automatic

Above: *British camp on the edge of Dakhla Oasis, October 1916.*
Opposite: *Paying wireless men at Sheikhs' Tombs, Dakhla.*

pistols, bombs, dynamite and some detonators'. What is of particular interest is Williams' description of the senior Sanusi officer, a clean-cut and affable Libyan with whom he quickly established good relations. This prisoner was taken to Cairo, where he was imprisoned in the old Citadel pending his trial by military court.

The friendly Libyan was Dahman bin Hayyin of the battalion of Sanusi regulars known as the *muhafizia*. Williams does not mention in his memoir that he visited this man in prison, although he did tell his sister:

> ... I must tell you that when in Cairo I found the Senoussi officer whom I captured rather miserable because he had no decent clothes, so I got a dragoman whom I know very well to help me buy him an outfit. The whole boiling from shoes to turban only cost 30/- and we went along with these things to his cell. It was the fun of the world to see him strip & jump into his new togs. When quite dressed he told my dragoman that there was only one Senoussi in Africa better dressed & that was the Grand Senoussi himself.[22]

Before Dahman's trial could take place, the bodies of Captain Mason-MacFarlane and Lt Ryan were found by No. 2 Light Car Patrol (2nd/Lt G.G. Lockett, Cheshire Yeo) at the foot of the Baharia escarpment. This confirmation of the men's fate may have

---

[22] Letter to Violet Williams, 7 November 1916.

Pte Morton (pictured right), Baharia, 20 December 1916.

influenced the court when passing sentence. The prisoners were convicted of 'attempting to enter an area occupied by British troops in the guise of non-combatants, and carrying bombs, pistols, and documents inciting to disloyalty and revolt'.[23] Two of them, including Dahman, were shot. This was a regrettable outcome to the episode. The British had not been in the habit of executing Sanusi prisoners—at least not when General Maxwell was GOC—and the Sanusi generally treated British prisoners in their hands with generosity and compassion, including the Captain of HMS *Tara*, who had escaped from the POW camp at Bir Hakim and spent a week on the lam dressed as an Arab before being recaptured.[24]

The incident of Dahman bin Hayyin's futile attempt to attack the British Army with pistols and a few sticks of dynamite has significance in the light of what was then happening inside the southern oases. The Sanusi had been occupying those areas for seven months.[25] Totally isolated and cut off from their supply lines to the west, many of their several thousand soldiers were ill, and all were hungry. With the British railway approaching Baharia, the Turkish commander there sent a message to Ahmad al-Sharif in Dakhla, saying that he could not hold Baharia without reinforcements. Also at about this time, Ahmad al-Sharif's cousin and future head of the Sanusiya (and future King of Libya), Muhammad Idris, wrote to him that there was a favourable opportunity to negotiate peace if only the Sanusi army would return to Libya. Whether or not he was convinced by his cousin's plea, Ahmad al-Sharif knew by now that his army stood no chance staying where it was. In September, he moved to Baharia and prepared to make a dash with his army back across the desert to Siwa. But as he and his commanders feared being caught in the open by the armoured and Light Cars, they decided to cover their retreat by feigning an attack in the north, hopefully giving the impression that the Sanusi army was about to attack there. Dahman's brave but pitiable gesture was part of that feint.

---

[23] *The Times*, 27 January, 1917, p. 5.
[24] This was Captain Rupert Gwatkin-Williams. Cf. his account of the Tara incident in *Prisoners of the Red Desert* (1919); also McGuirk, R. (2007), *The Sanusi's Little War*, Appendix 1.
[25] One can only speculate what the Sanusi hoped to accomplish by occupying Baharia, Dakhla and Farafra. Perhaps they hoped the defeat of the Allies at Gallipoli would free up the Turkish Army to make a second, more effective strike at Egypt from the east, whereupon they would be in a better position to strike the Nile Valley from the occupied oases.

On 20 September, No. 3 Patrol (commanded by Lt Edward Moore) discovered a way through the Abu Muharriq Dunes. Although 'Moore's Crossing', as it became known, was not suitable for heavy vehicles and ambulances, the Light Cars could now get from B6 to Baharia in a few hours.

The British had two Arab agents inside Baharia, and during the second week of October they reported that the evacuation had started, indeed that Ahmad al-Sharif himself had left the oasis on the 9th. The new WFF commander, Major-General Watson, sent all available armed vehicles in the Baharia area, 32 in total, in pursuit. Participating in the chase were Light Car Patrols 2, 3 and 5, under the overall command of Major Partridge. The pursuit was in vain, however. With just a few days' head start, the retreating army had managed to get into the Great Sand Sea and escape. As Claud Williams put it:

With natives at Baharia, Pte Morton second from right, standing, 20 December 1916.

> ...the birds had flown and all we found were the tracks of a large number of men, camels, donkeys, and a couple of mountain gnus, only a few days old. We missed our fight by those few days.[26]

Led by the Imperial Camel Corps and the Light Car Patrols, the British quickly reoccupied Baharia. Far to the south, Lindsay's No. 1 Patrol was at the heart of the move

_____
[26] CHW Memoir, see page 175.

to reoccupy Dakhla. Lindsay had located the Sanusi outposts on the south side of the oasis as early as mid-September. On 12 October, he found the enemy positions unoccupied, and within days the whole oasis was occupied by a motley British force of '5 officers, 44 other ranks, eight cars (one armoured), 14 cycles, 3 Lewis Guns, 1 machine gun, 3 camels, an Intelligence Officer and 2 native scouts'.[27] British garrisons were established in both Baharia and Dakhla, and before long the administration of the two oases was back in the hands of the civil authorities.

Also in October, Farafra was re-occupied by a small detachment of Imperial Camel Corps led by an experienced desert traveller named Wilfred Jennings Bramly, now an Intelligence Officer with the WFF. With the taking of Farafra the whole of the Western Desert was back under the control of British and Egyptian authorities—the only exception being Siwa, where Sayyid Ahmad was waiting with 1200 of his soldiers, trying to decide his next move.

The role of the Light Car Patrols in reclaiming the central oases had clearly impressed the generals in Cairo. When one of them, General Charles Dobell, was handed a command position with the Egyptian Expeditionary Force for the campaign in Sinai and Palestine, he immediately asked Headquarters to set up a new Light Car Patrol for operations east of the Suez Canal. The result was a seventh Patrol, commanded by another New Zealander, Lt W.H.P. McKenzie. No. 7 Patrol was mentioned in despatches almost as soon as it entered service with the EEF and performed with distinction throughout the eastern campaign.

Below and left: *Morton's home-made Christmas card for 1916.*
Opposite: *Rolls-Royce tender supplying Baharia camp, 17 January 1917.*

---

[27] WO 95/4442, War Diary, Sherika, 17 October 1916.

1ST AUSTRALIAN ARMOURED CAR SECTION

Before turning to the events of 1917, we must touch on a colourful and somewhat anomalous unit known as the 1st Australian Armoured Car Section,[28] whose men eventually came to play a significant role in Light Car Patrol history. The 1st AACS was the product of a few inspired Australian motor car enthusiasts, who wanted to form their own armoured car unit for service overseas. They managed to acquire three powerful vehicles and a motorcycle— all donated by private individuals. Two of the cars, a Mercedes (60hp) and a Daimler (50hp), were given custom-made armour-plating and fitted with an American Colt, air-cooled machine gun each; the third vehicle, a prestigious Belgian Minerva, was converted into a support tender. As for the motorcycle, it was an impressive sight as it was equipped with a side-car on which was mounted an accessory tripod for a machine-gun.

The Section's commander, Lt Ernest Homewood James, was a 36-year-old engineer and leading member of the group of enthusiasts who had conceived the unit and brought it to fruition; the rest of the Section was made up of thirteen hand-picked volunteers. The 1st AACS sailed from Melbourne and, surmounting heavy gales, high seas, and measles, arrived in Egypt in August 1916.[29]

---

[28] Sometimes called the 1st Australian Armoured Car Battery.
[29] For further details on 1 AACS see R. Dux, *The Benzine Lancers: Mechanicalizing the Australian Military Forces, 1901 to 1919* (Military Heraldry & Technology Section, AWM); and Finlayson, David and Cecil, Mike, 'Pioneers of Australian Armour: The Armoured Car Section and 1st Light Car Patrol' (2005), *Ironsides* (Journal of the Royal Australian Armoured Corps, Head of Corps Historical Collection).

Initially attached to the Rolls-Royce armoured cars on the Baharia blockhouse line,[30] the new arrivals also worked with No. 2 and No. 3 Light Car Patrols.

The Australians adapted well to desert patrolling by car—bush driving in Australia evidently being excellent training for tackling the Egyptian desert. But the two armoured vehicles, said to exceed 50mph on a good road, were not as efficient in the desert as the armoured Rolls-Royces and the unarmoured Fords, and spare parts for such non-standard vehicles proved very difficult to obtain.

Lt E.H. James, OC No. 1 (Australian) Light Car Patrol.

---

[30] That is, the British 11 and 12 Light Armoured Motor Batteries.

Opposite: *Taken by Captain Owston, this photo shows the British column on the way to Siwa shortly before the Battle of Girba, February 1917. General Hodgson, in command, is fourth from left.*

THE BRITISH RAID ON SIWA

In mid-January 1917, word reached Intelligence that Sayyid Ahmad was intending to leave Siwa soon for his Libyan 'capital', Jaghbub.[31] When, a week later, further information came that the Grand Sanusi's departure was imminent, General Watson thought he saw an opportunity to capture him and end the Sanusi threat once and for all. He gave orders for a motorized column—Rolls-Royces from Capt. Owston's Light Armoured Car Brigade and Light Car Patrols Nos. 4, 5 and 6, plus an additional eighty-two (!) touring cars, vans and lorries for HQ Staff, medics and signallers, and supplies of food, water, and petrol—all to assemble at Mersa Matruh as quickly as possible. The largest gathering of motor cars ever seen in the Western Desert departed for Siwa on 1 February 1917. Commanding this operation was Brigadier-General Henry Hodgson. Major Partridge was again put in overall command of the Light Cars.[32]

In the afternoon of the second day, the column set up camp twelve miles (19 km) north of the Siwa depression, while Partridge and Intelligence Officer Captain Royle, who had participated in the *Tara* crew rescue eleven months earlier and, more importantly, who knew every corner of the Siwa Oasis, went off with Claud Williams to search for a way into the depression. The pass usually taken when entering Siwa from the north had been rendered impassable by the Sanusi. Royle found a secondary pass that was undefended and usable by the armoured cars.

---

[31] If this information was correct, it tends to confirm that Sayyid Ahmad was indeed deferring to the wishes of Muhammad Idris.

[32] Partridge had often participated in Light Car expeditions, usually, but not exclusively, working with Claud Williams and No. 5 Patrol.

The next day (3 February) the column split, with most of the armoured cars and Light Car Patrols Nos. 4 and 5 descending the escarpment, while a smaller force, including No. 6 Patrol, went to block the Munassib Pass, the main way into Libya, in case the Sanusi tried to escape to the west. The support vehicles all stayed where they were.

Once inside the depression the main attack force headed towards 'Ain Girba, ten miles (16 km) north of Siwa town, where 850 Sanusi were known to be encamped.[33] The cars had to cross a large area of encrusted swamp, then rocky terrain followed by deep sand. Although two of the armoured cars were for a while mired almost to the axles, all cars eventually got through. The Sanusi were caught by surprise and forced to scramble up onto the rocks behind their camp to defend their position. Their most effective weapons for holding back the attackers were their mountain guns and machine guns, of which they had two of each.

Beginning late in the morning, the battle went on until nightfall. At one time or another six armoured cars and a dozen Light Cars were involved in the fighting, but they were unable to get near the Sanusi camp, partly because of the rough ground, but also because the Sanusi handled their mountain guns well.

When the gunfire finally abated, the silence was broken only by occasional sniping or short bursts from Sanusi machine guns. Shortly before dawn on 4 February Sanusi gunners fired a few more rounds, whereupon all was still. In the semi-darkness, the British could make out fires in the Sanusi camp and movement of men and camels. Then, at daybreak—nothing. The Sanusi had got away with their animals over a pass behind their camp. The only chance they could

Above: *Lt C.W.G. Thorpe, Suffolk Yeomanry, Officer Commanding No. 4 Patrol during the raid on Siwa, February 1917.* © *Imperial War Museum (HU 92045).*

Opposite: *Davidson at the wheel of car LC 2526.*

---

[33] The rest of Ahmad al-Sharif's army was with him in Siwa town.

Above: *No. 4 Patrol in the Siwa column, February 1917. © Imperial War Museum (HU 92038).*

Opposite: *Siwa town.*

be stopped now would be if the Munassib detachment managed to intercept them. But the 'battle' at 'Ain Girba was over. It had been, as Claud Williams calls it, 'a regular *opéra bouffe* affair: an immense amount of noise and very little blood-shed'.[34] Three British soldiers were wounded, while (according to Williams) a native doctor later reported nine Sanusi slightly wounded.

On 5 February, the British main force left for Siwa town. They were prepared for a hostile reception, but before they got there they were met by an Arab waving a white flag. The elders of the town had sent him to welcome the British to Siwa!

[34] CHW Memoir, page 176.

Llewellyn Partridge, Transport Officer for the Pembroke Yeomanry in 1916–17. He twice commanded the Light Car Patrols in operations against the Sanusi. Here, with the rank of full colonel, he has just been made an aide de camp to King George V (1926).

The Munassib force had had only limited success. The detachment's guides had trouble picking up the track to the pass; and when they finally did find it, the going was too rough for the Rolls-Royces. Lt Davidson's No. 6 Patrol got through, albeit with difficulty, and even managed to get one of its cars to the bottom of the pass. There Davidson and his men confronted an advance party of Sanusi in retreat from 'Ain Girba. Most of the Sanusi were able to clamber back up onto the plateau, where they vanished, although some set up a position on a distant hill for the purpose of signalling others to stay away from the Munassib Pass. It turned out that there was a second pass (4 miles/6 km south of Munassib) below which were high dunes, and Sayyid Ahmad and his army used this route to escape into Libya.

Llewellyn Partridge received the Distinguished Service Order for his work on General Hodgson's staff and his command of the three Patrols at Siwa.[35] Roy Davidson and Claud Williams were both awarded the Military Cross for their participation in the action at Girba and Musassib. Williams claimed he had done nothing to deserve the medal, writing to his sister: 'You will see from my photo that I look ten years older & feel it too. The last year in this howling wilderness has aged me as you see... You may notice a second [decoration]. It is the MC given for nothing at all.'[36] In fact, what Williams had done was deemed vital on the day of the battle. During the fighting General Hodgson was acutely aware that his force might at any time be attacked on its left flank and rear by Sanusi arriving from Siwa town. Late in the day Williams and No. 5 Patrol were sent to clear the main pass in case a quick exit from the Depression was necessary. The Sanusi had used explosives on the track and had embedded in it slats of wood stuck through with nails. Williams and his men cleared all this away and repaired the damaged track so that even the armoured cars would have no trouble getting back to the plateau, and this work was mentioned in a despatch by General Archibald Murray describing the action of 3 February 1917.[37] General Murray went on to praise the accomplishments of the Light Cars and the armoured cars during the last nine months of the Sanusi campaign.

[35] 'For conspicuous gallantry and devotion to duty. He displayed great judgement and skill in the leadership of his three light car patrols and showed inexhaustible resource in overcoming the most serious physical obstacles. Later in action proved self a dashing and competent leader.'
[36] CHW to his sister Violet, 3 October 1918. The first decoration had been the Egyptian 'Order of the Nile'.
[37] Supplement to the *London Gazette*, 6 July 1917, p. 6762.

I have already referred to the excellent work of the armoured cars and light car patrols on the western front. Their mobility, and the skill and energy with which they are handled, have made them an ideal arm for the western desert... It is not too much to say that the successful clearance of the western oases and the satisfactory state of affairs which now exists on the western front is due more to the dash and enterprise of the armoured car batteries and the light car patrols than to any other cause...[38]

The Sanusi campaign was now over. The actions of 3–5 February 1917 were virtually the only fighting the Light Cars saw in Egypt in the entire war. Most of the British force was now removed from the Western Desert, including the yeomanry regiments, although many of the yeomen with the Light Cars stayed on for the time being. However, Major Partridge's role with the Light Cars was over, and he departed with his Pembrokeshire Regiment. The most experienced patrol commanders—Claud Williams, Mac Lindsay, Roy Davidson and Edward Moore—were told their work in the Western Desert was not finished.

Until the departure of the yeomanry regiments the individual Patrols had tended to be based with or near the regiment of the Patrol commander, and that link was now broken. Administratively homeless for some months, in September 1917 the Light Car Patrols were finally placed within the Motors section of the Machine Gun Corps.

---

[38] CHW letter of 3 October 1918.

EXPLORATION AND SURVEY WORK

In considering the exploration and survey work of the Light Car Patrols in the Western Desert, we should first take account of the state of geographical knowledge of that region at the outbreak of war in 1914. An Egyptian government department known as the Survey of Egypt had been established in 1898 with the aim of surveying all the inhabited regions of Egypt and as much of the adjacent desert as possible. Consequently, and in a remarkably short time, topographical surveys were made of most of the large oases of the Western Desert: Kharga (1900), Dakhla (1901), Farafra (1901), Baharia (1903), and the Fayoum (1905). Conspicuously absent from this list is Siwa, where the survey work was delayed for political reasons. In the first decade of the 20th century there was no border between Egypt and Libya, and this state of affairs existed because both countries were part of the Ottoman Empire. At the time, British authorities in Cairo found it expedient to take a relaxed approach to matters concerning the 'western frontier'.

Knowledge of the Western Desert outside its oases grew over the years—albeit slowly—thanks to a small number of intrepid Europeans, who moved about that wilderness via the old caravan routes. The greatest of these explorers was the German Gerhard Rohlfs, whose expeditions by camel in the 1870s amounted to thousands of miles back and forth across the Libyan Desert from Tripoli on the far side of Libya to the Nile Valley. One of the most spectacular of Rohlfs' trips was from Dakhla, west to the Great Sand Sea, then north through the dunes for 300 miles (483 km) all the way to Siwa. Other noteworthy names include Wilfred Jennings-Bramly—the same who led the camel corps to Farafra in 1916—who had been to Siwa in 1896 (via Moghara and Qara) and again in 1898 (via Farafra); and W.J. Harding King, who explored Farafra and Abu Minqar, and then in 1911 marched 200 miles (322 km) from Dakhla in the direction of 'Uweinat at the south-west corner of Egypt. These men and others collected topographical information and sketched route maps.

In addition, information was collected by the European officers of the Egyptian Coastguard Camel Corps as they tried to find and close down smugglers' routes across Egypt. As a young coastguard, in 1907–8, Leo Royle spent six months, without a break, patrolling by camel from Siwa to 'Ain Dalla, and even to Abu Minqar, over 200 miles (322 km) south of the Mediterranean coast. One of Royle's objectives was to investigate the possibility that a route existed from Libya's Kufra Oasis through the middle of the Sand Sea to Abu Minqar, ostensibly used by smugglers, but he was unable to confirm its existence. The Coastguards had also been from one end of the large Qattara Depression to the other—indeed, armed coastguards were permanently stationed at the western and eastern ends of the Depression to stop smugglers passing through it. The Coastguards travelled throughout the northern part of the desert, and officers were encouraged to send new geographical information to Coastguard Headquarters in Cairo, where a large wall-map was regularly up-dated.

Nevertheless, when the Sanusi crisis began, 95% of the Western Desert as a whole was still *terra incognita*. The British were fortunate that most of the war against the Sanusi was waged within twenty miles (32 km) of the Mediterranean coastline, usually within easy reach of the 'Khedivial Road'. The British Army wanted better maps, and so did the Survey of Egypt. On the Sinai front, the Topographical Section of the Army's Intelligence Branch worked closely with the Royal Flying Corps. Certain areas east of the Suez Canal had been mapped to high standard by using aerial photographs, controlled by ordinary field survey methods. However, on the western front the RFC seldom had more than two or three aeroplanes at a time; and, as we have seen, they had already lost one machine in a dust storm, and suffered two fatalities when another went astray. The job of carrying on the survey of the Western Desert was, therefore, assigned to the Light Car Patrols.

Above: *Dr John Ball (1872–1941), British geologist and geographer with the Survey of Egypt. He wrote the 'Handbook for Patrol Officers in Western Egypt' and occasionally accompanied Light Car Patrols on journeys to explore and map the desert. In 1926 he won the Victoria Gold Medal of the Royal Geographical Society for his contributions to scientific geography.*

Right: *Claud Williams surveying the desert with his theodolite. Dr John Ball called Williams the best of the Light Car Patrol surveyors.*
Opposite: *No. 6 Light Car Patrol, commanded by Lt Roy Davidson.*

At this point a new and extraordinary character enters the story: Dr John Ball of the Survey of Egypt. Forty-four years old in 1916, he had worked in Egypt for over 20 years. He had a sound understanding of technical instruments, was a superb draughtsman, and he invariably worked to a high standard. He was also short, impatient and a bit deaf.

Early in 1917, Dr Ball issued his 'handbook' of survey techniques to Light Car Patrol officers. A quick glance at it reveals the author's unrealistic expectations. The document assumes a sound mathematical knowledge, or at least the ability to acquire it quickly, and aims to instruct soldiers how to carry out closed and open traverses, triangulations, astronomical readings, and suchlike mysteries of the professional surveyor as must have provoked more than a few wry comments from the patrolmen.

Right: *'All after a bite', a light-hearted sketch by mechanic Harold Morton (No. 2 Patrol).*
Below: *Private Harold Morton, mechanic, assigned to No. 2 Patrol. Photo taken at Baharia Oasis, 17 January 1917.*

The latter thought they knew what to expect when they volunteered to join the patrols: probably to be shot at by hostile Bedouin; certainly to be in danger of running out of water or petrol far from base, or being caught in a sandstorm that might blow continuously for two or three days. They had taken on those dangers and, in the process, learned how to travel for days in uncharted desert and get back to base again safely. They did this routinely. That they should now be required to become professional-level surveyors some of them apparently did not take very seriously. Dr Ball's friend, C.S. Jarvis (of whom more later), wrote years afterwards that the map-maker had 'the very poorest opinion of the soldier as a topographer...'. Jarvis

Left: *Rolls-Royce armoured cars pass No. 4 Patrol in the Western Desert.*
© *Imperial War Museum (HU 92042).*
Below: *Quail shooting near Matruh. Lindsay is on left.*

went on to say, however, that Dr Ball 'makes an exception in the case of [Captain] Williams'.[39] In fact, sources indicate that other officers were also good at this work, including Llewellyn Partridge, Roy Davidson, Mac Lindsay and the latter's second-in-command late in the war, Sydney Fairman.

But Claud Williams, in particular, impressed Dr Ball. Within a few months of becoming a patrol officer Williams thought up and applied a brilliant but simple solution to the problem of compass readings being distorted by the metal of the cars. Tired of having to

---

[39] Jarvis, Major C.S. (1938), *Desert and Delta*, p. 88.

stop the vehicle and move ten yards away from it every time he needed to take a reading, Williams realised that a small vertical rod on a horizontal plate fixed to the dash-board would cast a shadow, which could be used to set a relatively straight course. A third necessary element of this improvised 'sundial compass' was a piece of metal like a compass-needle, which rotated stiffly round the base of the rod, and which could be moved to any position by hand, thereby making possible a relatively constant relation between shadow, needle and the desired course. The evidence for Williams' impressive contribution to desert navigation with motor cars is a

Above: Sandy conditions, southern zone.
Left: 'This was taken after a breakdown of the car on the right. I came out on the other and had just concluded when the officer snapped me. He has given me this. Charlie Chaplin with the white mug—that's me.' (Pte Morton).
Opposite: Lindsay (in the car) and unidentified fellow officer hunting at Wadi Majid, near Matruh, 1916. The previous Christmas Day, a battle had been fought here between the WFF and the Sanusi army.

Left: *'A lovely desert scene. All rock and soft sand. The rear wheel is down to the hub in soft sand. Waiting for a push.'* (Pte Morton). Opposite: *Lt Sydney Fairman who, as second-in-command of No. 4 Patrol, served with Mac Lindsay. Taken at Mersa Matruh, date unknown.*

single sentence written by Dr Ball: 'The employment of a sun-dial attached to the motor car as an aid in traversing, first introduced by Lieut. Williams, has met with great success in the Western Desert.'[40] Writing many years after the First World War Claud Williams revealed that the original version of his sundial compass had been 'a nail in a board'.[41]

---

[40] Ball, Dr John (1917), 'Handbook for Patrol Officers' (unpublished). For more information on the sundial compass see pages 127 and 249 For information about Bagnold's later elaboration of the sun-compass refer to his article (with Harding King and Douglas Newbold) 'Journeys in the Libyan Desert 1929 and 1930', *Geographical Journal*, Vol. 78, No. 6 (December, 1931), especially Appendix 1 (by Newbold), which mentions Ball's 'Handbook' and the earlier WWI version of the sun-compass as well as giving a detailed description of the Bagnold's version.
[41] Cf. 'Conclusion', page 249.

AUSTRALIAN MOVE TO NO. 1 LIGHT CAR PATROL

In early December 1916, the Australians gave up the three cars which they had brought from Melbourne and were sent to the new railhead west of Kharga, known as Water Dump 'A'. There, they took over the six Fords, the Lewis Guns—and indeed the very name of the original No. 1 Light Car Patrol.[42] The 1st Australian Armoured Car Section ceased to exist. To their disappointment the Australians found their 'new' cars so battered and broken as to be scarcely usable as they were. Fortunately, spare parts for Fords were abundant (thanks to the Army's Mechanical Transport units), and, as patrol commander James wrote, his men '...worked night and day for the next couple of weeks overhauling and reconditioning the vehicles...'.[43]

The Australians had a flair for desert travel. A mere three weeks after taking over the Fords they were exploring old caravan routes south of Dakhla. They followed one of these, the Darb al-Terfawi, all the way to the wells at al-Shebb, just north of Egypt's border with Sudan. From James' account it is clear they had not yet been introduced to Claud Williams' sundial compass.

> We travelled mostly by the aid of the compass, but discovered that the instrument was very much affected by the magnetos of the motors and, consequently, had continually to be checked by stopping the cars and [taking it] some distance away from the engine...[44]

---

[42] Archives in Britain, and especially in Australia, often refer to the Ford-equipped unit as the No. 1 (Australian) Light Car Patrol. E.H. James was promoted to the rank of captain on 1/1/1917.
[43] James, Capt. E. H., 'The Motor Patrol', Australian War Memorial 224/MS. 209, transcribed and published on the website of The Australian Light Horse Studies Centre.
[44] Ibid.

They explored a range of hills to the east of al-Shebb, discovered passes, and made their way back to Dakhla by an entirely different route, having spent four days and nights in uncharted desert.

In early January 1917, the Australians were ordered to move further west, where they were to explore the possibility of communication links between the several oases most distant from the Nile. They apparently interpreted these orders as an invitation to try to get to the Sanusi-occupied oasis of Kufra, 450 miles (724 km) west of Dakhla, beyond the Egyptian frontier—in other words, inside hostile Libya. When one considers that Ahmad al-Sharif was not defeated until the following month, the Australians' plan seems totally madcap. Nevertheless, what they accomplished is impressive.

The armoured Daimler called 'Gentle Annie', armed with a Colt machine gun (model 1895). The headlamps could be positioned lower down on the front of the vehicle (as in this photo) or higher up either side of the windscreen (as in photograph page 73).

Opposite: *Vehicles of the 1st Australian Armoured Car Section on arrival in Egypt, August 1916 (Camp Moascar, near Ismailia, mid-way along the Suez Canal). The two armoured cars are (to the right) a British Daimler (50hp) and (middle) a Mercedes (60hp), both with an external chain drive. The other car (left) is a Belgian Minerva, converted into a supply tender. The motorcycle is a 2-cylinder New Hudson (6hp) with a flat sidecar onto which a machine gun could be fitted.*

James tells the story as follows:

We decided to try the Kufra Oasis first. It was reported that no Europeans had ever reached this oasis. There was certainly no caravan route to the west [from] Dakhla Oasis...[45] The well-known explorer Harding-King had made an expedition in 1911 to the southwest of Dakhla for 200 miles in the direction of Kufra but had to return on account of the very heavy country and complete absence of water.

We determined to make our route further north than west. We spent a week making a dump in the desert about 80 miles out from our last camp. We buried stocks of petrol and water... also supplies of bully beef and biscuit here, as this was to be our jumping off point... Water & petrol would be the governing factors of the journey, and in order not to waste any of the precious liquid in the radiators of the cars, we fitted condensers to the radiator caps and closed up the overflow pipes. The condensed water being caught in a 2 gallon petrol can be returned at intervals to the radiator again...

Having completed our dump and got everything ready, we made a start with three Ford Cars and a crew of two men on each. Two Motor Cyclist Despatch Riders accompanied the Patrol in order to keep up communications.

Every ounce that was not necessary was taken off the vehicles. For instance, the cars had no bodies at all. The seats consisted of ration & ammunition boxes; the cushions were the men's blankets. Two of the cars were stripped of the Lewis Gun mountings. This meant that only one car was really armed, but each car was provided with a rifle, and the crews all had their revolvers.

All the cars at the start were... overloaded... It was intended to [leave] one of the cars as an advanced dump at a point about 200 miles from our objective and make the final dash with two cars and a cyclist.

After leaving the last well, ...Bir Sheikh Muhammad, ...the desert begun to change for the worse. Hitherto the sand, although perhaps soft underneath, generally had a hard crust. This meant that once a car got a start it could usually keep going. The

---

[45] It subsequently became clear there was such a route.

Above: *Men of the 1st Australian Armoured Car Section hauling 'Gentle Annie' through sand east of Baharia, 1916. Left to right: Sergt. A. Lloyd, Cpl. N. Bisset, Lt Holloway (Imperial Army), Lt E.H. James, Driver Oscar Hymen, Sergt I. Young (inside car), Cpl. G.F. Morgan, Sergt H. Creek, Cpl. W.P. Thompson.*

crew would run along and push until a speed of 6 or 8 miles per hour was reached and then jump up on to the step. The nature of the ground was now quite different and seemed to be composed of very fine drift sand on the surface to a depth of about six inches. This meant very heavy going in low gear which of course was the very thing we wished to avoid, as it meant increased petrol and water consumption and reduced speed. However, we found that if one car led the way in low gear, the others could follow in the tracks it made running in top gear as the going was much easier for the following cars. Each car now took its turn half-hourly to make the road and the cyclists travelled out on either flank to ascertain if there was any improvement in the ground. Unfortunately there was no sign of improvement and after about 80 miles of this gruelling work one of the cars smashed its differential. We transferred some of the stores to the other two cars and pushed on, abandoning the disabled vehicle. We travelled for another day under similar ...conditions when a second car caved in under the strain. Things now began to look serious. The two cyclists were sent ahead to a high hill on the horizon to try out the country, and they returned that night to state that there was no improvement, so it was reluctantly decided to abandon the ...attempt as there were over 200 miles to go... The second car was temporarily repaired and the patrol returned to the well at Bir Sheikh Muhammad just as the last water can was emptied.

The cars returned along the old tracks in less than half the time taken in the outgoing journey... We towed in the remaining broken car about a week later...[46]

When the Australians returned to base, they wrote in their War Diary that they had been patrolling in the direction of Farafra, as per their orders, making no mention of the fact that their real objective had been Kufra. Had they actually succeeded in reaching that oasis, one cannot help but wonder what they would have done then, and what they would have written in the War Diary when they got back. Nevertheless, it was an astonishing example of initiative and resourcefulness. Four months later No. 1 Light Car Patrol and its Australian crew left Egypt and spent the rest of the war fighting the Turks in Sinai, Palestine and Syria.

---

[46] James, Capt. E.H., op. cit.

'LT E.D. MOORE'

Enthusiasts for the great explorations by Ahmed Hassanein Bey, Prince Kemal el-Din, Ralph Bagnold, et al.—at least those who have pored over Western Desert maps of the 1920s and '30s—may have found their attention drawn to a line meandering from Dakhla to the vicinity of the great plateau known as the Gilf Kebir in Egypt's far southwest, along with the caption 'Dr John Ball and Lt E.D. Moore, 1917'. What Moore's initials stood for had been long forgotten, and the year is in fact wrong—the journey was made in February 1918—but anyone looking at such a map understood that he and Dr Ball had made the first journey by motor car to that forbidding region, indeed all the way to the Gilf Kebir itself. Consequently, 'Lt E.D. Moore' is the only Light Car Patrol officer other than Claud Williams whose name a few geographers and historians of our time might still recognize. The key to a fuller identification of this, till now, elusive soldier was the letters 'MC' that began to appear after his name in the *Army Lists* late in the war. His Military Cross citation names him as Lt Edward Davies Moore. From the Welsh Border country, he was 33-years-old when earned his place with Dr Ball on those old maps.[47]

Lt Moore's ability to get the most out of his Fords had first become apparent when he successfully led his patrol through the Abu Muharriq dunes (near Baharia) in September 1916. The following spring he was sent to the southern zone, where he initially patrolled between Kharga and the godforsaken location to the west of

[47] Moore was born in Kerry Newtown, Montgomeryshire in 1884, the family farm being a few miles away, across the border, at Brampton Bryan, north Herefordshire. He joined the Shropshire Yeomanry in 1914 and was quickly promoted to Sergeant; in February 1915 he received further promotion from the ranks.

Left: *Work party from No. 1 Patrol on the western side of Kharga Depression, October 1916.*

that oasis called Water Dump 'A', or WDA. By autumn 1917 he was patrolling the environs of Dakhla; from there he and his men patrolled north most of the way to Siwa, skirting the Great Sand Sea, to Abu Minqar and 'Ain Dalla; and south to al-Shebb near the Sudanese border. The more No. 3 Patrol achieved, the more information the Army demanded.

Right: *Lt E.D. Moore*

THE KUFRA RECONNAISSANCE SCHEME

By December 1917, Lt Moore and his men were feeling the strain of having spent half a year exploring one of the remotest and most inhospitable stretches of desert in the world. He asked to have No. 3 Patrol recalled; the Army's answer was that the Patrol had to carry on until the area reconnaissance was finished.[48] The reason for this response became apparent before the end of the month. Intelligence had picked up a rumour that Sayyid Ahmad was making for Kufra, and the possibility that a desert track existed from that oasis into southwest Egypt therefore assumed new importance. Western Desert commanders informed GHQ Cairo that, given the experience and expertise of the Light Car Patrols, they thought there would be 'no insuperable difficulties' in carrying out a reconnaissance all the way to Kufra by going below the Sand Sea. The Australians had tried to approach Kufra by heading north from Dakhla, hoping (like Royle before the war) to find a track through the sand. A year later, the Army was interested in finding a way through to Kufra in the completely uncharted southwest.

If the Light Cars found such a route and succeeded in reaching the vicinity of the oasis, the distance from Dakhla would be about 450 miles (724 km), so any such expedition would have to be supplied for a journey of a thousand miles or more. It would be an unprecedented undertaking.

Planning the expedition was assigned to a General Staff officer in Cairo, Captain Charles Hodgson. The venture had not yet been approved by Headquarters,

---

[48] WO 95/4439, Delta and Western Force, entry 6 December 1917.

but Hodgson asked Dr Ball if he would like to go along, assuming the Army sanctioned the project. Always ready to travel into unknown territory, Ball of course accepted.

Shortly after Christmas 1917, Hodgson went to Kharga to meet with Lt Moore and two other likely participants in the expedition, Bimbashi Armstrong (an Intelligence Officer who had been with Lindsay at Dakhla a year earlier) and the ASC officer in charge of Light Car Patrol drivers and mechanics. Moore and Armstrong agreed that the plans were feasible in principle and helped Hodgson to work out the final details, which the latter took back to Cairo pending final approval. In the meantime, No. 3 Patrol began collecting supplies for two new dumps to be set up beyond Water Dump 'A'.

On 10 January 1918, Headquarters approved an expedition as far as the eastern edge of Kufra Oasis; Dr Ball would indeed be part of the team; and the Italians had given permission for the light cars to enter Libya on condition that one of their officers went as well.

At this point Ball could scarcely hide his excitement. He asked the Army to make arrangements so that he could pick up 'Eiffel Tower Time' when he got to Kufra… he would need a long wave radio. There was no such radio in Egypt, said the Army. Well then, there was a good wireless at Hindaw in Dakhla Oasis—could he take that one, and could the communications men now using it start practising nightly picking up Paris time until he got there? No, said the Army, the radio at Hindaw could not be made available. A normal medium-range wireless was offered, all that was needed for the signaller to relay messages to base. Like maritime navigators of old, Ball would have to rely on a chronometer to establish points of longitude for his map-making.

When clearance for the Scheme arrived, Moore and his men had already left to set up the two new dumps. Time was critical. The sandstorm season was beginning, and it would only get worse as the weeks passed. In fact, a severe storm blew up on 11 January as the patrolmen were working on Dump 'B', and two Fords had to be left out in the desert. The cars were soon recovered, but their engines had to be stripped down and necessary spare parts had taken longer than usual to obtain. This delayed the start of the reconnaissance by a fortnight. The latest possible departure was now held to be mid-February.

At Moore's request preparations were made for two Fords to be sent to Water Dump 'A' with a view to moving one or both to Dumps 'B' and/or 'C' once the expedition had moved beyond recall. This would afford better security and provide potential communication by wireless with the Kufra-bound patrol in an emergency.

The team was gathering; nearly everything was ready—and on the last day of January 1918 Cairo headquarters wired that the Kufra Reconnaissance Scheme was cancelled! The reasons for this decision are not evident. Had HQ been un-nerved by the sandstorm that had hampered work at Water Dump 'B' on the 11th? Were the Italians now being awkward about the Patrol entering what was supposed to be Italian territory? The decision is inexplicable—not so much because surviving documents do not give us an explanation, as because once the Scheme was cancelled, the expedition went ahead anyway, and its destination was still Kufra! It is not clear from surviving documents if the whole team went as originally planned. Certainly, John Ball went; whether Armstrong and the Italian officer went as well is not evident. However the expedition was now constituted, its purpose was entered clearly in the record: 'to use up Dumps 'B' and 'C' and reconnoitre the large dunes west of Dump 'C' with a view to finding a way through to Kufra.'[49]

The Patrol left Hindaw on 14 February 1918. The cars went via the little oasis town of Mut and headed south-south-east along the track to Bir Terfawi and al-Shebb, skirting a long strip of dunes that forced them miles out of their way. At a point some fifty miles (80 km) south of Mut the dunes finally ran out, enabling the cars to turn west. There followed hours of relatively easy going, but the terrain then turned to soft sand, occasionally punctuated here and there with sandstone hills. No. 3 Patrol had been here already, of course, to establish the two dumps that would guarantee supplies of water and petrol when they finally did enter the *terra incognita* beyond advance Dump 'C'. About a hundred miles (161 km) after turning off the Bir Terfawi track, they stopped by a prominent and isolated sandstone hill. No. 3 Patrol had been to the

---

[49] WO 95/4111, entry 14 February 1918.

site before, because the track to Dump 'C' passed right by it. Did Moore know what was there and think the good doctor would be interested? It is impossible to say whose idea it was to stop, but this location was destined to become a famous landmark and archaeological site. Round the base of the hill were hundreds of large earthenware jars. The pottery was mostly broken, but its presence clearly indicated that some native population of the distant past had also relied on 'water dumps' to cross the arid stretch of the desert between Kufra and Dakhla. Ball named the site 'Pottery Hill'; a few years later Prince Kemal el-Din gave it the Arabic name 'Abu Ballas'.[50]

Continuing their journey west, the Patrol could see ahead the high dunes of the Great Sand Sea, extending northwards hundreds of miles all the way to Siwa. While the many parallel lines of dunes continue their southward journey beyond this point, there—in 1918, at least—they opened up somewhat and were passable by the Patrol. In this navigable area, twenty miles (32 km) or so west of Pottery Hill, was Water Dump 'C'. It was now 18 February 1918.

It would appear that at this point in the journey the patrol consisted of three Model T Fords, numbers 498, 553 and 680. One of these (No. 680) was the car Moore had asked to have waiting at the dump in case of emergency. The patrolmen and Dr Ball took the other two cars and reconnoitred round the base of the high dunes, driving 17 miles (27 km) to the northwest, about half of this distance being along the hard surface between two of the dunes. They camped that night and returned to Water Dump 'C' the next day. The 19th was clear, and Dr Ball stayed up late observing the stars and taking notes.

On the 20th of February, the weather turned. A sandstorm swept in, making it difficult to carry out maintenance required by car no. 498, for which a spring needed to be replaced and an oil filter changed.

The weather was better the next day. All the water cans were collected, and cars 498 and 553 continued the journey, still looking for a track that might lead to Kufra.

---

[50] In 1999 a German explorer named Carlo Bergman discovered a number of new sites with similar pottery deposits. With Abu Ballas they strongly suggest a chain of supply depots that ran between Dakhla and Gilf Kebir, and probably further on to Kufra. The University of Cologne's ACACIA Project (2002) has dated the pottery to Pharaonic times— late Old Kingdom/early First Intermediate Period.

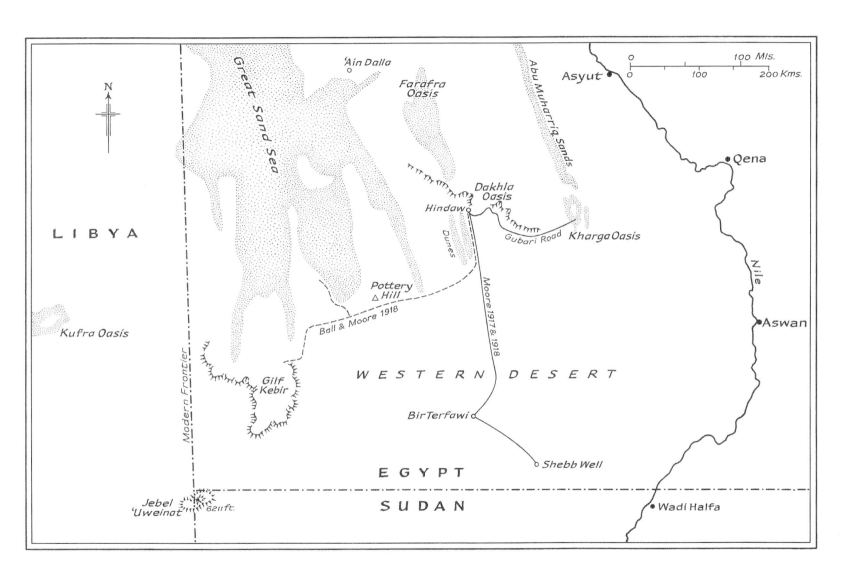

They travelled about thirty miles (48 km) west through undulating sand until they found a cairn by a sandstone bank; then they went due south into a flat sandy plain, turning southwest again by some sandstone hills. In fact, the men were approaching the Gilf Kebir, an enormous plateau that rises 300 metres from the desert floor.[51] Curiously, even the esteemed Dr Ball had no idea that he was so close to one of the most prominent features of the Libyan Desert. The northern side of the plateau has largely broken down, leaving a complex terrain of scattered limestone hills and pillars amid wide drifts of soft sand. Ralph Bagnold, who entered the area from the same direction twelve and a half years later, gives a good description of what it was like.

> Ahead low sandstone hills and peaklets could be seen, outliers of the Gilf Kebir against which the sand was piled up in dense masses. We walked to the nearest hill 2 miles away, and from there unending accumulations of sand were visible to the west, while to the south we could see no improvement… Further progress was impossible and a retreat was necessary. The sand radiated a fierce mid-day heat. We had already been working hard digging cars out of many soft patches. They were now up to their axles and had to be turned round to face the opposite direction. However, it was done in the end, and we ran back on our tracks for 8 miles till by good luck a passage was found into the next corridor to the east. Here we had better fortune and reached the hills without trouble. As anticipated, the dunes became disorganized in the hilly country and ceased altogether within 20 miles. We now threaded our way between small black rounded hills separated by flats of hard grey sand. From the top of a conspicuous 300-foot hill at the foot of which we camped that night, the country to the west and south-west as far as could be seen, that is, for at least 20 miles, appeared to be covered by a sea of tangled dunes similar to the complex variety we had just encountered.[52]

In this mysterious and dead landscape No. 3 Patrol pushed on as far as it could, but, as Bagnold's description makes clear, there was no feasible way here through to Kufra.

---

[51] The desert floor itself is, on average, 700 metres above sea level.
[52] Bagnold (1931), GJ, Vol. 78 (1). p. 27.

The cars slowly zigzagged westward until they reached a cairn atop a high hill.[53] Dr Ball took a fix on the location the best he could. It was the furthest point reached by the expedition. Moore's entry in the War Diary for the day (21 February) tells us there was another sandstorm that night. The next day they began retracing their tracks back the way they had come, finally reaching the base at Hindaw on the 24th.[54]

For once the Army recognized that No. 3 Light Car Patrol had accomplished something exceptional. General Allenby himself, now Commander-in-Chief of the Egyptian Expeditionary Force, sent his compliments to the Patrol, expressing his appreciation of its commendable work during the latest reconnaissance; and of all their excellent work since the Patrol had been stationed at Hindaw.[55] No. 3 Patrol had earned recognition but not a rest: four days after it returned from the historic journey to the edge of the Gilf Kebir, it was sent on another long journey to Al-Shebb and back.

---

[53] Lat. 23° 51' 11"; Long. 26° 29' 25"
[54] Car No. 553 had had to be left in the desert due to a broken crankshaft. Immediately upon returning to Hindaw Lt Moore sent Corporal Perry of his patrol out with 3 cars to fetch it back.
[55] WO 95/4439, War Diary 3LCP, entry 21 February 1918.

SURVEYS, PATROLS AND PAPERWORK, 1917–18

Following the Sanusi defeat at Siwa, Claud Williams spent the rest of 1917 on the move. During March and April he made regular journeys between Siwa and Mersa Matruh; in May he was instructing at Wardan Camp near Cairo; in June he patrolled out of Moghara; the height of the summer (July and August) he was at Matruh; and the rest of the year he spent between Sollum and Siwa. Davidson, also, was continually moving about the northern sector during this period, while Moore, as we have seen, was travelling extensively in the southern zone. When No. 1 Patrol was transferred to the Australians in December 1916, Lindsay went 'on leave' to the UK, returning to Egypt in February. He took over the command of No. 4 Patrol from Lt Thorpe soon after its participation in the raid on Siwa the same month. Archival information about the patrol is meagre for 1917, but No. 4 Patrol appears to have been based mainly at Siwa, with occasional visits to Sollum and Matruh. It often worked in tandem with Williams' No. 5 Patrol, as in their joint expedition to Jebel Iskandar (described by Williams in Chap. V of his memoir and by fellow-participant C.S. Jarvis in Appendix 3).

Although disappointed not to accompany his regiment when it left Egypt, Claud Williams still found his job interesting. Writing home from Mersa Matruh in March, his mood was buoyant:

> These little valleys are simply wonderful for flowers—some little insignificant things and some quite gorgeous. A crimson poppy is plentiful and yellow ranunculus & dozens of funny little things I don't know the names of. It is the one time of the year when the desert blooms & is beautiful. The weather is getting nice & hot again now too

Left: *Ford supply column arriving at Siwa Camp.* © *Imperial War Museum (HU 92044).*

Western Frontier Force Headquarters at Mersa Matruh.

& we are into drill clothing with shorts again. Of course, in a very few weeks we shall be cursing the heat & wishing for winter again, but the change is nice, and the sea is almost warm enough for bathing again. I had a good trip last week.[56]

And from Moghara in early June:

Look on the map [and you'll see] a little string of lakes 50 miles west from Alexandria & about 50 miles in from the sea & there we are with a ring of entrenchments round us & plenty of barbed wire & as safe as in Norfolk & now the reason of my writing so hurriedly & shortly. I have got a real nice job. I take out a motor patrol into the desert— 2 Ford cars, 7 men & we go South, East or West or North circling round picking tracks through the sand, bivouac where I choose when it gets dusk, cook a scratch meal & so on. It is all compass work & there are of course no roads, just the unlimited desert, low

Light Car Patrol camp at Mersa Matruh.

---

[56] Letter home, 23 March 1917.

hills & light valleys all exactly the same, many of them soft sand & the cars stick & must be pushed out. I am out sometimes all night, sometimes 2 or 3 or 4 seeing no-one but the odd Bedouin whose pass has to be examined. I just got in this morning & start out again at 6 o'clock tomorrow morning & the mail goes tomorrow & I must go to bed... I got the job because I understand surveying a little & have been ordered to ferret out feasible routes to other posts 50 to 100 miles away. It is a peach of a job...[57]

In May 1917, GHQ in Cairo announced that the yeomen still with the Light Cars (other than the officers) would soon be replaced by men from the Garrison Battalions. Williams' habitual good mood vanished as the Army began to reassign his best patrolmen.

Now that the rough of the work is done on this side they are taking away my active young fellows & giving me [class] 'B' men to man the patrol. I was furious about it all for they absolutely refused to let me go back to the regiment... They spoke very prettily about it all. They... said I was too valuable a man to leave this part of the country... I am wanted to train the new men & a lot of rot like that...[58]

He was still disgruntled two weeks later:

Did I tell you I had 8 days in Cairo a few weeks ago... I was helping for a few days at a School of Instruction for budding patrol officers. Now I have two budding officers attached to me here [Matruh] for instruction. I am utterly & heartily fed up brim full. All I want is to get back to the regiment...[59]

Apart from 'ferreting out' new routes, the patrolmen still had to police the desert. The Bedouin of the Western Desert, mainly of the Awlad 'Ali tribe, were not only pro-Sanusi; they had actually formed a regiment in the Sanusi army and had fought against the British throughout the campaign. Even in peacetime they were inveterate smugglers. The

[57] Letter home, 2 June 1917.
[58] Letter home from Matruh, 10 July 1917.
[59] Letter home from Matruh, 28 July 1917.

Opposite: *Men of No. 4 Patrol on the plateau at Sollum; behind them are the car workshops.*
Below: *No. 2 Patrol at Oases Junction (Nile Valley north of Luxor) on 5 August 1917. The Patrol is being moved from Kharga Oasis, Southern Sector, to Mersa Matruh on the northern coast.*

Light Car Patrols had, therefore, to assume the pre-war responsibilities of the Egyptian Coastguard, which meant checking caravans for arms and other contraband. Many of the patrols made were into Libya and were sometimes carried out jointly with the Italians, no doubt hampering British efforts to pacify the local population. For example, in July 1917 the Light Car Patrols in the north were told they were to help the Navy by looking for possible enemy submarine landing sites all along the coast from al-'Umayyid, near Alexandria, all the way to Ras al-Milh, beyond Tobruk (in Cyrenaica).

At the end of August Claud Williams and No. 5 Patrol left Matruh for Sollum. He was clearly in better spirits when he wrote home a few weeks later:

> As for me I am as fit as usual and have got a nice brand new strip of desert neither more nor less sandy and stony than the other old strips; but here there is some mild excitement chasing convoys. Some of the blighters don't like being caught and put up a bit of a fight, but the rattle of a Lewis gun sends their arms down and their hands up... I have

not needed to shoot anyone down yet though we shot one poor old chap through the arm, quite an accident as I had told the fellows to shoot wide. We are going out tomorrow & shall be 10 days without a wash or a shave... This trip I am going to see the moon from half full waxing to half full waning for these camel convoys travel at night. We lose more than we catch for they travel wonderfully quickly & tracking is sometimes slow. I followed one lot for 45 miles last week and then lost their tracks in stony desert. There is no chance of any other job for me until the next war, so there is not one chance in a million of my being killed for these Bedouins are badly armed and could not hit a room from inside it. The camp we are in here (when we are in and not out in fact...) I have lived in for 6 days during the last 25 [and it] is rather nice. My tent is on a little shelf of rock, all the tent ropes fastened to heavy stones, for pegs won't drive and right below is the Mediterranean only a mile away but over 600 feet below and on the little flat strip between the sea and the cliff are the rows of tents of the Garrison and the camel-lines, and it is not at all bad to look at.[60]

In fact, he was soon to realize that pursuing armed caravans was more dangerous than he had thought:

I stuck out on the job for 12 days and roped in 4 convoys, having a most interesting chase after 3 of them, 25 miles over stony country in one case. I then came in for a wash and a change & left Woodall, my 2nd, to carry on till I got out again. He got onto some tracks straight away & when he came up with the convoy, they played a trick on him, holding up their hands & then, when the cars got close up, the blighters suddenly grubbed some rifles up out of the sand and opened fire. There were only 4 of the natives, but they fairly riddled one car and got my sergeant twice through the arm. However, our men soon did them in— killed 3 & wounded one—destroyed camels and loads & came in. The riddled car had a broken wheel and 2 bullets in the crank-case (holes plugged with corks to keep the oil in). In all it was a good fortnight's work for we got 5 lots in all—20 prisoners, 75 camels with their loads and not one got past.[61]

[60] Letter home from Sollum, 22 September 1917.
[61] Letter home, 7 October 1917.

In the same letter occurs an interesting reference to the use of carrier pigeons by the Patrols. Williams says they were a great success. 'They home unfailingly and travel as much as a hundred miles in an hour or two. They are rather an amusement, too, of course.'

In October 1917, Williams and Lindsay were promoted to the rank of captain. For several months GHQ had been considering the possibility of attaching the Light Car Patrols to the Light Armoured Car Brigade. Major Owston, who had commanded the LACB for a year and a half, had left for Palestine the previous month, his place being taken by Captain Mangles MC, who had been with Lt Davidson at the Munassib Pass. Brigadier-General Yorke, commanding the coastal sector, argued against GHQ's suggestion for the Light Cars, saying it was unworkable both from administrative and tactical points of view. An alternative scheme was adopted whereby the three Patrols in the coastal sector were to be grouped together, with one of the three commanders being given overall responsibility for the group. Claud Williams was given the senior command, although there was still an expectation that a higher-ranked officer would be appointed sooner or later. The link between the LCPs and the LACB remained informal.

Top right: *'Some climb. A splendid illustration of the ground we have to traverse.' (Pte Morton, far left).*
Bottom right: *'Topping a hill. A back view taken from the last car. Notice the soft nature of the ground.' (Pte Morton).*

Meanwhile, the relentless relocation of the Light Car yeomen continued. By autumn there were barely two dozen left, and even they were told they would be back with their regiments within 90 days.

Everything is gradually being taken away from the West Front except the Light Cars. It is what I was afraid of from the beginning. The Light Cars are the cheapest & easiest means of keeping a very long desert frontier safe, and gradually the armoured cars are being pushed away to the other fronts. I suppose in the end we shall follow. My own position now is very much improved as I have a dozen cars[62] and 50 men, but I must say I hate the added responsibility. I am not made for a soldier & am too old to learn & moreover 18 months of this job have made me into a sort of specialist. I am quite useless for any other work. I shall get rather a shock someday if I am bumped into anything else.[63]

At the end of November Williams was still hoping to be relieved of his administrative work so that he could get back to full-time patrolling.

Fact is we are getting this light car force organised now and are hoping to get a senior officer put over the lot of us in which case one's importance would not be so pronounced. At present I am OC detachment at this camp near the sea & I have detachments of several units under me, which make up the Garrison of the fort [just above the escarpment at Sollum] & the same will apply when I go to Siwa next week... I'm a horribly busy person now, doing work I hate & I can't get out into the desert, but thank God next week I get away to the back of beyond & no generals or Staff officers... but if a field officer is appointed it would not be nearly so difficult to get away. What do you people think of the Palestine show? My old Regt was right in it & several old friends have gone under, but the casualties were not so very great.[64]

---

[62] Nos 5 and 6 LCP on the Sollum-Siwa axis. The six cars of No. 4 Patrol were temporarily at coastal HQ at Matruh.
[63] Letter home, 4 November 1917.
[64] Letter home, 26 November 1917.

Williams spent Christmas 1917 at Siwa, and his wish for a senior officer to come and take away his paperwork was not answered.

Who would have thought of another Xmas in Egypt. Well, this one I am spending near Siwa & not a bad place either. In a way this camp is unique being further from its base and with a thinner line of communication than any other in the war area, but here fortunately there are no enemies, only potential enemies. The camp is out on the clean high desert and the cold is intense. One cannot get warm of an evening, so one dines & then goes to bed. Still the days are pleasant. I think it is the contrast to the summer that makes me feel the cold so much for we have only had ice here once, but the mess hut is built for summer heat & is not suited for winter. It is built of a kind of reed matting locally made & the wind whistles through. The GOC was up the other day & we put him in the draughtiest corner of the mess, but with the result that a large E.P. tent[65] is coming up next week. I have just had a day down in the oasis with the M.O. [Medical Officer]. We lunched with the Sheikh of a village about 4 miles from Siwa. A most extraordinary place, built on a solid rock hill. There are still remains of an old Roman Wall in the place. There is only one entrance through a sort of tunnel cut in the solid rock & we climbed interminable flights of rude stairs cut in the rock with hovels on either side. The Sheikh's house was right at the top, perhaps 300 ft above the level of the palm groves. The view from the top was extraordinarily fine. We had taken our own lunch, but we had tea from the old buffer & some excellent dates. Dates are the staple industry of this oasis & the palm groves are very pretty. One can get dates anywhere and everywhere...

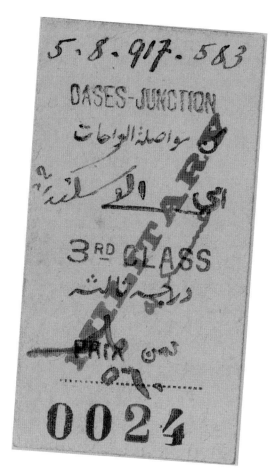

Oases Junction railway ticket.

---

[65] English Privates' Tent: it was made of multiple layers of white cloth, was 22' by 16' and had two stout poles and a ridge pole.

MILITARY MISSION TO MUHAMMAD IDRIS

In January 1918, Williams was informed that some of the Light Cars would be escorting a 'Military Mission' to the new pro-British head of the Sanusi brotherhood in Cyrenaica, Sayyid Muhammad Idris al-Sanusi, a cousin of the defeated Sayyid Ahmad.

I'm expecting orders any day to shift out on this journey (mission political) to our Bedouin friends in the West. I shall probably be away 3 weeks... I'm horribly busy with this matter. On a journey of this description there is no end to the mass of detail that has to be personally supervised & inspected. Our column is 22 cars & a possible journey of 1200 miles means an infinity of spares, tools, tyres, petrol oil, food & a million or two other matters that don't worry anyone when there is a garage & a petrol store every few miles. We go self-contained in petrol, rations, water, spare parts, oil etc., except for some petrol which we have shipped to an Italian port. Water means enquiry into the condition of numerous wells in different parts. All is arranged now except the date of starting which may be tomorrow & may be in 3 or 4 days' time. Orders will come from Rome & London about this.[66]

Over the next few months the mission seemed several times about to happen, only to be put off again. Meanwhile, Williams finished a detailed map of the area around Siwa, which he had been working on since the previous spring. Soon the collection of data, as least, was finished:

---

[66] Letter home, 13 January 1918.

I've done my old map at last with a final journey of 5 days and have located the last native trade route of any importance and the last wells of any importance. The one advantage it gets me is that I'm off to Cairo tomorrow to help them get a print off it at the Map Office.[67]

In April 1918, Williams made two trips into Libya with fellow Light Car Patrol commanders. The first, with Lindsay (No. 4 Patrol), was a circuitous journey to the west of Jaghbub for reconnaissance and topographical work. The ground was very rough and Williams' 'dear old car' finally broke down for good.

We were out seven days and ran just 600 miles over all sorts of country. We discovered several new brands of mosquitoes with awls for proboscis, new stone, stonier than ordinary stone and more of it and new sand, softer and more car-boggy than any before & finally had to abandon my dear old car which has run over 30,000 miles all by its lonesome 100 miles from home with a broken crank shaft.[68]

Two weeks later he was back in Libya, this time with Davidson (No. 6 Patrol), escorting a visiting Italian car patrol home.

In May, the Military Mission seemed to come alive again, and Williams drove a senior British officer into Libya to make arrangements with the Italians.

I have just returned from a little trip west. The GOC[69] took me along—or rather I took him along—to visit our 'Eyetalian' allies & make arrangements for a big journey in which I shall make my debut as a pukka commanding officer. It is rather exciting as it means 1200 miles. The Italians gave us no end of a time. We were met 10 miles outside their forts by a few cars and 3 Aeroplanes flying low and for the day we were there we were not allowed a moment's rest except an hour after *déjeuner*. We were banqueted 14 times in one day and photographed 18 times; attended a gala

---

[67] Letter home, 29 January 1918.
[68] Letter home, 12 April 1918.
[69] Brig.-Gen. Ralph Yorke, GOC Coastal Section, WFF. Also referred to below as 'the General'.

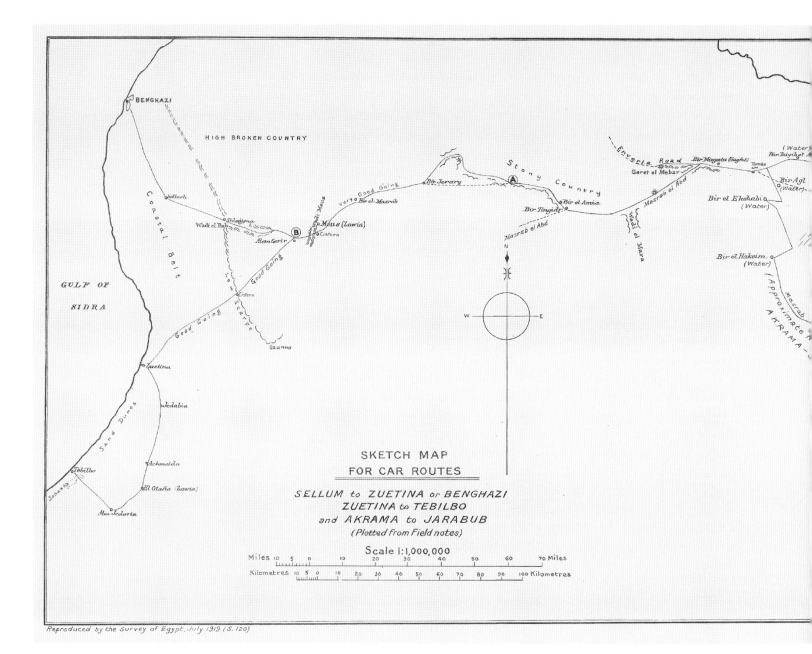

BENGHAZI

HIGH BROKEN COUNTRY

Stony Country

Enverta Road

(Water)
Bir Traiyib el A

Bir Magata (Bagfet)
Tombs
Garet el Mebar

Bir Agl
(Water)

Bir Jerary

Ⓐ

Bir el Amia

Bir el Masrab

Sollach

Bir el Ekshahia
(Water)

Coastal Belt

Shlegima
Wadi el Bab

Msus (Zawia)

Ⓑ
Cistern

Bir Tingidr

Masrab el Abd

Wadi el Mara

Masrab el Abd

Alem Gerir

N

Bir el Hakeim
(Water)

Masrab

GULF OF

SIDRA

Cistern
Low Scarpe
Good Going

Approximate AKRAMA

Good Going

W   E

Saunno

Zuetina

Sand Dunes

Jedabia

SKETCH MAP
FOR CAR ROUTES

Achmeida

Tebilbo

El Gtafia (Zawia)

SELLUM to ZUETINA or BENGHAZI
ZUETINA to TEBILBO
and AKRAMA to JARABUB
(Plotted from Field notes)

Sebakha

Abu Jedaria

Scale 1:1,000,000

Miles 10 5 0   10   20   30   40   50   60   70 Miles

Kilometres 10 5 0   10   20   30   40   50   60   70   80   90   100 Kilometres

Reproduced by the Survey of Egypt, July 1919. (S.120)

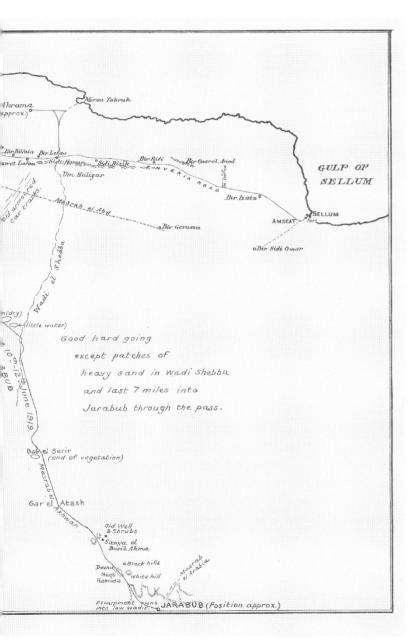

performance at the theatre & listened to the General make innumerable speeches in execrable French...[70]

Just as he was finishing this letter he heard that the journey had been postponed again. It finally took place in July.

Claud Williams devotes a chapter of 'Light Car Patrols in the Libyan Desert' to this 3-week-long journey to see Sayyid Idris. The objectives of the Mission were kept highly secret, but Williams' responsibility was to get the party there and back safely. As is clear from his own account, when the column was not moving, much of his time was spent socializing with the Italians or visiting local sights of interest.

The Mission was headed by two men with whom Williams had worked in the past: Major Mervyn MacDonnell and Captain Leopold Royle. Both were old hands in Arab affairs and spoke Arabic well. MacDonnell had been seven years in the Sudan Civil Service, followed by six in Cairo, where he and his family had a house on Gezira Island. From 1915 he worked in the same Intelligence Office as T.E. Lawrence. The two became friends, and when, in July 1916, MacDonnell fell ill with acute appendicitis while his family was away, Lawrence moved into the house to look after him. MacDonnell was operated on in Cairo and sent to England to recuperate. In 1917 MacDonnell was at Siwa with Royle and was wounded at the Battle of Girba. He was an administrator by nature, and it may be assumed he had a sound command of the political matters under discussion with Idris.

Leo Royle did not like administration or office work of any kind. For fourteen years he had chased smugglers with

---

[70] Letter home, 25 May 1918.

Sayyid Muhammad Idris al-Sanusi.

the Coastguard Camel Corps. In 1913 his Western Desert expertise and personal acquaintanceship with the headmen of the tribes on both sides of the frontier led to his becoming liaison between the British Agency in Cairo and the Grand Sanusi, Sayyid Ahmad al-Sharif. His was, in fact, Britain's Sanusi expert, and his work was commended by both Lord Kitchener and British Foreign Secretary Sir Edward Grey. When the world war began, Royle joined the Royal Flying Corps, in which he served over Sinai first as an observer and later as a pilot. Nevertheless, his flying career was constantly interrupted by orders that he help out in the Western Desert. We have seen that he was vital to the success of the *Tara* crew rescue; and that he was an Intelligence Officer with the British force at Siwa. Indeed, since the start of the war he had probably spent as much time helping the Western Frontier Force as he had with his RFC unit on the eastern front.

In July 1918, Claud Williams was in command of eight Light Cars (six from No. 5 Patrol and two from No. 2 Patrol) forming part of the Military Mission's escort. Sayyid Idris was then at the Libyan town of Zuetina, south of Benghazi and some 500 miles (805 km) west of Sollum. His cousin, Sayyid Ahmad al-Sharif, was still in Libya, but his authority as head of the Sanusi Brotherhood had been vastly eroded by his military defeat. Contrary to the rumour early in the year, he had not gone to Kufra; he had fled from one place to another—from Jaghbub to Jalo, from there to Tripolitania and Fezzan; and while the Military Mission was still in Libya, he embarked on a German U-boat in the Gulf of Sirte and went to Istanbul. Idris was now in effect the religious and political leader of Libya's eastern province of Cyrenaica.

In Tripolitania, west of Cyrenaica, the Brotherhood had far less influence. There, a powerful tribal chief named Ramadan al-Suwayhli was still receiving arms from the Turks and the Germans. The British viewed al-Suwayhli as a threat to Sayyid Idris, and the objective of the Mission was to bolster the latter's position in his own country.

The Italians feature prominently in Williams' account of the Mission, mainly as generous hosts. It should be remembered that, however divided the Libyans were during this period, the one thing they all had in common was dislike of the Italians. Seven years had passed since the Italian invasion of Libya, and the invaders had failed to subdue the Libyans on their own. A consequence of the British defeat of the Sanusi army was that the Italian position in the country had been immeasurably strengthened.

When the Military Mission was over and the cars safely back in Egypt,[71] Williams sent home a light-hearted and enthusiastic letter about the journey which supplements chapter VIII of his memoir.

> I got back yesterday after [nearly] 4 weeks. The big journey… was quite successful. We did not fire a shot, and this fact is sufficient to prove that the war is over on this front. We travelled in all just 1200 miles… We met the famous Sanusi [Sayyid Idris], and dined and lunched with him… The Italians gave us the time of our lives & I now find it hard to lunch or dine on less than 10 courses or with fewer than 4 varieties of wine and 6 of liqueurs, a block of ice and a good cigar!
>
> …Benghazi, the Italian sea port, was nice. A good hotel & beds. We were 3 days there. Curiously enough, there is a peach of a little art museum there… The Venus of Cyrene, now in the Borghese in Rome, was unearthed there, but there is a cast of the statue in the Benghazi Museum, but they have returned the originals of many other priceless things and it is a perfect gem of a collection.[72] I never enjoyed anything more in my life than looking at some of these statues.
>
> We hope that the result of our journey will be to close up this front.[73]

There is a sad postscript to this event. A week after the journey was over, Leo Royle died when his SE5a biplane crashed in Palestine. Fellow pilots flying near him at the time said his aeroplane was hit by German fighters, but conditions were cloudy and the precise circumstances of the crash were never officially determined. As for Mervyn MacDonnell, after the war he became Governor of Western Desert Province (a position previously held by Royle) and went on to become the League of Nation's High Commissioner of Danzig.

---

[71] The Mission reached Sollum, 8 August 1918.
[72] The original Venus of Cyrene was returned by Italy in 2008.
[73] Letter home, 12 August 1918.

THE ARMISTICE

By mid-September, Williams and No. 5 Patrol were back in Siwa, where they remained for the rest of 1918. His main task during this period was to finish the draft of his *Report on the Military Geography of the North-Western Desert of Egypt*. When not writing, he was often complaining that he and his men were still stuck on the frontier.

All of us are getting a bit fed up… Three years of desert is too much for anyone![74]

A letter dated a month later shows him less restrained on this subject—though doubtless his unfettered anger is tongue-in-cheek and meant to amuse his sister.

See the date! The location is SIWA CAMP! The Hun is running; the Turk is whipped; Bulgaria is down and out… [Millions] of people are chasing the rummy Hun or the rummy Turk, and the date is 18.10.18, and the location is SIWA CAMP!!

…Three months ago I went and saw the powers that be in Cairo. Then I came back here and wrote a very careful report[75] pointing out the date and the locality, and drawing attention to the fact that we have been in the Libyan Desert for 2½ years and that the men were mutinous and the officers were mentally deteriorating. I begged that, at all events, two out of the six patrols should be shifted to

[74] Letter home, 12 September 1918.
[75] See Appendix 4, Letter 4.

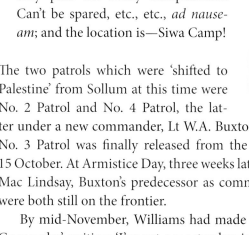

Palestine temporarily, simply to save the reason of men and officers. Well, they thought well of the matter and shifted two patrols... from Sollum. [And so] the location is still Siwa Camp. As soon as I heard it, I buzzed off in a dinky Ford to know the reason why. They were most awfully kind and sympathetic, and they paid me many compliments. Can't be spared, etc., etc., *ad nauseam*; and the location is—Siwa Camp!

The two patrols which were 'shifted to Palestine' from Sollum at this time were No. 2 Patrol and No. 4 Patrol, the latter under a new commander, Lt W.A. Buxton. Also in mid-October Edward Moore's No. 3 Patrol was finally released from the southern zone and departed Egypt on 15 October. At Armistice Day, three weeks later, all three patrols were actually in Syria. Mac Lindsay, Buxton's predecessor as commander No. 4 Patrol, and Roy Davidson were both still on the frontier.

By mid-November, Williams had made considerable progress with his 'Military Geography', writing: 'I've got a most voluminous report written up for the [Egyptian] Government, and if we remain another three or four weeks the whole job will be nicely rounded off.'[76] In the same letter (his first after Armistice Day) he expresses excitement about an invitation to see Siwa and the surrounding country—including the Great Sand Sea—from the air.

In mid-December, Williams heard that his departure from the Western Desert was imminent.

Photo of Siwa taken by Williams when he was assisting the RAF, December 1918.

---

[76] Letter home, 20 November 1918.

I have just got orders to prepare things for evacuation after Xmas. I shall, I think, be able to apply for leave to England... I don't altogether like to hurry about getting free until the men are sort of in process of being demobilised, but with Siwa Camp done, there is nothing left. I want a few weeks in Cairo to get all my notes recorded, and then I shall be glad to shake the dust of this country off my feet... One feels very unsettled with no war on... Thank God, I shall get into a flannel suit—ultra-civilian—and a stiff collar, and a bowler or straw cap... and be free again.

Opposite: *Lt Fairman, Alexandria, September 1918.*
Below: *Lindsay (right) with biplane in the Western Desert.*

Group photo of No. 2 Patrol taken in Syria late 1918. Lt R.A. Hamilton (with dog) was the fifth and last commander of this Patrol. Harold Morton, promoted to sergeant, is seated middle row, far right.

The promised aeroplane ride took place on the last day of 1918.

> We flew at 10,000 ft for 80 miles out west and 80 miles back, and were away from Camp only two hours. I went in order to point out landmarks to some RAF[77] [men] who have been sent to photograph the country. I don't mind telling you that it was near about the finest experience of my life. The whole of a marvellously intricate country—hills, gullies, passes, lakes, sand and a few villages—spread out below one like a most beautiful picture map.

Williams left Siwa for the last time two days later, but his stay in Cairo proved to be longer than the 'few weeks' he had anticipated. In his last letter from Egypt, on stationery from the Shepheard's Hotel, dated 2 February 1919, he wrote:

[77] The Royal Flying Corps was renamed the Royal Air Force on 1 April 1918.

I'm bogged in Cairo, writing up the Western Desert. I'm writing about 10 hour a day, tearing up for 2 hours a day; writing again for a further 10 hours, reading it for 4, tearing up, writing, reading, sprinkling commas throughout, scratching then out again and chasing up a few colons for duty. Between whiles, I go out and purchase a book on grammar, a dictionary, a thesaurus and a few little things like that; and spend the remaining daylight hours in studying them. Seriously, I hate the sight of pen and ink, so this is just a note. I want to make a good job of my report, which is for publication, and I've got to see it through the press before I can leave Egypt.

In the event, Williams would remain in Egypt until 17 May 1919, and what kept him there so long was the Egyptian 'revolution' which erupted in March of that year. Among the British Army units used to control rioting mobs were the Light Car Patrols.

'Aintab 12.5.19. This is our demob band… I don't suppose that you can discover your humble [servant]. If not, I am… in the white suit. Can you distinguish the bottle, the three balls, and the cars on the banner?' (Harold Morton). (Aintab is inside Turkey, 50 miles north of the Syrian city of Aleppo.)

EGYPTIAN RIOTS, 1919

When the war was over, Egyptians of all classes were in rebellious mood. General Maxwell had promised at the start of the war that Egyptians would not be involved in it—that their country would remain neutral. Maxwell was already having trouble keeping that promise, when, in March 1916, General Murray succeeded him. With the grand title General Officer Commanding-in-Chief,[78] Murray quickly made it clear he had come to Egypt to wage war, not to worry about ruffling the feelings of the Egyptian populace. Political activity was suppressed, newspapers were censored, peasant farmers were seized in their fields and dragooned into forced labour; animals, food and supplies were requisitioned. (Williams describes the grievances in greater detail.) In short, resentment against the British reached unprecedented levels, and out of that resentment arose the fortunes of an Egyptian nationalist named Saad Zaghloul.

When the war was over, Zaghloul's Wafd Party enjoyed massive popular support. He asked that he be allowed to travel to London to make the case for Egyptian independence to the British Government. The Foreign Office refused. He then asked to be permitted to attend the Peace Conference at Versailles. Again the FO said no. By now the normally compliant Egyptian Government was itself in disarray, with senior members wavering in their support of British policy. When, on 8 March 1919, Zaghloul was arrested and deported to Malta, Egypt erupted. At first there were only student demonstrations in Cairo, but these quickly escalated into

---

[78] Maxwell had been GOC British Forces in Egypt; since January 1916 Murray had been C-in-C of the Egyptian Expeditionary Force. When Maxwell departed, Murray assumed both commands.

general strikes and rioting in towns and cities across the Nile Delta. Communications were disrupted as trams were wrecked, railroads torn up and telegraph lines cut. Within a week the trouble had spread into the countryside. Totally unprepared, British authorities were facing an uprising throughout Egypt. The first fatalities occurred on 11 March in the city of Tanta, between Cairo and Alexandria, when several thousand rioters rushed the railway station, which was guarded by an armoured train: 14 killed, 91 wounded. In Cairo, three days later, armed rioters clashed with British soldiers guarded by an armoured car: 13 Egyptians killed, 30 wounded. While there were numerous incidents of the sort, the most macabre incident occurred on 18 March, when a mob boarded a train near Deirut, 240 miles (386 km) south of Cairo, murdered seven unarmed British soldiers and a prison inspector and mutilated the bodies beyond recognition. By the time order was restored in May, an estimated 800 Egyptians had been killed, as well as 31 European civilians (including numerous Greeks and Armenians) and 29 British and colonial soldiers.

When the trouble began, British High Commissioner Reginald Wingate was away at the Versailles Conference (and it is interesting to note that he had strongly advised his government to allow Zaghloul to attend that conference!). As the violence spiralled out of control, General Allenby was sent as the new High Commissioner. He arrived 25 March and arranged to meet with a delegation of Egyptian nationalists and religious authorities, with the result that Zaghloul was released and permitted to go to Paris after all. Even so, it took another two months before calm was fully restored.

The following sketch of Light Car Patrol involvement in these events is necessarily rough, reflecting a notable lack archival documentation (possibly because of the *ad hoc* nature of the security measures taken at the time).

We know that Claud Williams was still in Cairo when the disturbances began. As an eyewitness of brewing trouble and, later, as a participant in the work of the Light Car Patrols helping to restore order, he has given us an account (chapter X of his memoir) which is both sensitive to the Egyptian point of view and vividly written.

In addition to Williams, two other officers of the Light Car Patrol 'old guard' participated in the riot control: Captain Davidson, now in command of Williams' former patrol, No. 5;[79] and Captain Lindsay, now in charge of 'double' Patrol 6 & 8. In addition to these patrols, half a dozen 'Emergency' Light Car Patrols were formed, and Williams was called upon, as he puts it, 'to get several [patrols] into running order out of the wreck of a number of ambulance cars from Palestine', the officers and men being mainly provided by the Cairo Citadel garrison.[80] One of the emergency patrols was available courtesy of the RAF, which provided fourteen Model T Fords for the purpose, and it was commanded by an RAF officer.

When the demonstrations reached Alexandria No. 5 Patrol initially helped to police the streets there, but the demonstrators were mostly boisterous students and there were no incidents of violence reported. On 13 March Captain Davidson (with second-in-command, Lieutenant George Murphy, fourteen other men, six cars and four Lewis Guns) were ordered to the Fayoum Oasis. The journey was without incident and for three days there was no disorder as they patrolled the oasis. However, on 17 March a large band of Bedouin occupied several Egyptian police stations on the outskirts of the oasis, forcing the police out and seizing arms. Davidson took four cars and compelled those Bedouin who were still in the open to leave the oasis, but the police stations remained occupied. The next day the expelled Bedouin returned in force, 3000 of them, armed with rifles, swords and axes: Fayoum was under siege. The mob rushed the local government building, the *mudiria*, in the town of Medina and began firing at the troops defending it, a detachment of the 46th Punjabis. Three soldiers were killed and another wounded, whereupon the Light Cars opened fire on the intruders with their Lewis Guns. Casualties were tragically high, perhaps 100 dead, and three or four times as many wounded. Meanwhile, Fayoum remained completely cut off. The RAF had to drop food, supplies and ammunition, while the local garrison, in addition to defending the oasis, was looking after several hundred European refugees. For ten days, No. 5 Patrol made the rounds through the streets of Medina, but it seems there was no more firing. On 23 March Claud Williams was given command of an Emergency Light Car Patrol going from Cairo to Fayoum to report on conditions

---

[79] From mid-summer 1918 to February 1919 Davidson had been commanding 'double' Patrol No. 6 and 8 LCP. On 20 February Lindsay took over the command, and Davidson moved to No. 5.
[80] Those seconded to the Emergency LCPs were mainly officers from MGC (Infantry).

there and to rescue a wealthy, pro-British Egyptian, whose life was considered to be in danger. Williams reached Fayoum and was able to escort the man, whom the archives name as 'Michael' Fanous, back to Cairo.

Shortly after the Fayoum episode, No. 5 Patrol was sent to Upper Egypt where it spent much of the rest of 1919 searching villages for arms, patrolling the railway tracks and escorting senior officers. Captain Davidson left the patrol at the end of June of that year, and Lt Murphy took over command.

Lieutenant Frederick Rowland Ellis first appears in Light Car Patrol documents late in the war.[81] He served with No. 6 Patrol when it formed half of the Double Patrol 6 & 8 under Captain Lindsay's overall command, and he was commended for performing well on at least two occasions during the civil turbulence.

Lindsay's 'Bluebird' parked in front of the Shepheard's Hotel.

In mid-March, General Edward Bulfin was called to Egypt from Syria to be acting GOC of the Egyptian Expeditionary Force while Allenby was in Paris. Bulfin had no trouble getting to the Egyptian border, but it was not easy getting to Cairo with the Nile Delta in turmoil and overland travel manifestly dangerous. He managed, by train, to get to Benha, 30 miles (48 km) north of Cairo, but he could go no further. Since telegraph and telephone lines were down, an aeroplane had to fly down to Cairo to arrange for a car to go back and collect him. Ellis was then in Cairo helping Williams to assemble the Emergency Light Car Patrols. Although these were not yet fully ready

---

[81] He was apparently with No. 6 Patrol before the riots when it was half of the double patrol 6 and 8 under Davidson's overall command.

for service, he was given the task of urgently organizing an Emergency Patrol to escort and protect the car going to pick up General Bulfin. Ellis' own report of the journey to Benha and back on 16 March has survived:

> …on instructions from HQ Cairo I proceeded with my patrol to Qalyub. I noticed nothing unusual en route, but on arrival at Qalyub found the ESR[82] Station had been damaged and burned. A detachment of 1 officer and 25 other ranks were stationed there. All means of communication were severed. I sent a car back to HQ with a report to this effect; also asked for further instructions. I was ordered to proceed to Benha and ascertain the whereabouts of a train containing the Commander-in-Chief and escort him back to Cairo. About eight kilometres from Tukh saw a crowd of natives destroying railway property. As they sighted the cars they fled into adjoining fields. Shots were fired at my patrol by the natives. I dispersed the mob with machine gun fire.
>
> In places natives were endeavouring to destroy small bridges on the road.
>
> The Mamour [local government official] of Tukh informs me that serious riots had taken place during the day, and the place was in absolute chaos. I proceeded to Benha and reported to the C-in-C. My patrol returned as escort and all cars returned in good condition.[83]

Cairo was relatively quiet during the second half of March, but violence erupted again in early April. The month began with a new series of strikes. On the 3rd two Fords from one of the Emergency Patrols encountered a mob half-way down Muhammad Ali Street (which in those days ran from the Ezbekiya Gardens all the way to the Citadel).

> Two Light Cars armed with Lewis Guns were proceeding from the Governorate down Mohammed Aly Street at midday. The first car was stopped by a mob; the officer in charge, who got out to expostulate [with the crowd], was surrounded, and, to save himself, was obliged to use his revolver and keep the Car from being attacked. The second Car, which was following at a distance of 200 yards, was violently attacked with stones

---

[82] Egyptian State Railways.
[83] WO 95/4455 Force in Egypt GS Diary, March 1919, Appendix C(5).

and bottles, and he in his turn was forced to open fire. They returned to the Governorate, as it was impossible to proceed further down Mohammed Aly Street without shooting their way through.[84]

While this was happening, another car was in trouble about 500 yards away in 'Abdin Square. A certain Mr Dykes, who apparently worked undercover for the police,[85] was in the car, while a patrol of Australian Light Horsemen was attempting to break up a crowd nearby. Dykes got out of the car to help, whereupon he was shot in the back and killed. The crowd turned on the Australians, pulling two of them and their horses to the ground. Using their revolvers the men managed to escape, leaving Dykes' body to be defiled by the crowd. For several hours the mob raged out of control, and order was only restored when 100 soldiers from the 1/4th Norfolk Regiment were sent to 'Abdin Square.

Lt Ellis was clearly involved in one of these two incidents on 3 April, but the records do not specify which. All we know is that he received an MBE 'for extreme devotion in performance of military duties'; and a medal with the citation, 'for his ability in organizing a [Light] Car Patrol at short notice. He shewed great resourcefulness in bringing the Commander-in-Chief to Cairo and shewed presence of mind when confronted by a dangerous situation in Cairo on April 3rd'.

There is only negligible information about Captain Lindsay during the troubles of 1919, a fact which is particularly frustrating since he was appointed a Member of the Order of the British Empire in June of that year, suggesting that whatever he did, it was especially laudable. His MBE certificate is signed by George V.

By May, relative calm had returned to Egypt, thanks mainly to the influence of General Allenby with both the Egyptians and with his own all-too-often intractable government; and it was due to Allenby that three years later agreement was reached whereby, under certain conditions, Egypt became an 'independent sovereign state'. Those conditions, which included continued foreign control of the Suez Canal, would, of course, lead to further trouble in 1956.

---

[84] WO 95/4468, Appendix 4.
[85] Dykes worked with Bimbashi McPherson, who in turn worked for Russell Pasha, the head of police. Officially, Dykes was with the Egyptian State Railways.

ALLENBY'S VISIT TO THE WESTERN FRONTIER

In August 1919, General Allenby visited Sollum and Siwa; he even made an excursion to within 15 miles (24 km) of Jaghbub. His letter to his wife about the trip describes the geography and fauna of the region, gives the reader an interesting glimpse of his administrative problems as High Commissioner, and specifically mentions the Light Car Patrols. Thanks to the Lindsay family we have a set of superb photographs of the visit to complement the following first-hand account of the visit by the General himself.[86]

14th August 1919

My Mabel,

We've just got to the edge of the escarpment overlooking the Siwa Oasis... We reached Sollum yesterday at 7pm after a somewhat rough voyage of 26 hours. I spent most of the time in bed. We started, in motor cars, at 5am today in a thick scotch mist, which dried up in about an hour. We saw a gazelle, a hare, and a bustard; after which we went 170 miles through the most dreary and desolate desert imaginable. We have a good camp here, better than that at Palmyra. Siwa is six miles south of it, and the view across the oasis is pretty.

Opposite: *Armoured Car Detachment on the plateau between Sollum and Siwa during Allenby's visit, August 1919.*

[86] Allenby Papers, Liddell Hart Centre for Military Archives, King's College London, document 1/10/13.

Above: *General Allenby inspecting the Sollum garrison on parade, August 1919. The first seven officers on the right of the picture are Light Car Patrolmen.*
Inset: *Light Car officers (starting from the right): Lt Evans (1st), Lt Moore (5th), Capt. Ellis (6th), Capt. Lindsay (7th). Ninth from right is Lt-Col. de Lancey Forth, area commander at the time of Allenby's visit.*

Telegrams have followed me, with effect that Cranford, who was to have come out as Financial Adviser, is dead, and I am not surprised. Cheetham is ill with phlebitis and can't possibly arrive before 4 Sept. and they ask, can I wait for him? I must, of course. It is all very annoying, and I don't believe that Cheetham will find himself well enough to come out. Anyhow, I shall not be able to go away now before the end of first week in September at earliest. Clayton is, I believe, coming out at once. I have not a single adviser here now! Hope-Vere I left in bed with bad boils. He looks horribly ill. John Cecil has gone on leave. Hayter is anxious to go on leave, and so is Keown Boyd, and I think they ought both to go, but Hayter can't go till a new Financial Adviser comes out. Keown Boyd is with me, and Borthwick. Wavell was coming but could not get away at the last moment.

General Allenby (on horseback in front) during visit to Sollum, August 1919.

15 August. We went down to Siwa by car this morning and were received by all the notables with great pomp, including weird and barbaric music on divers instruments. The town is built in layers up a mound some 150 ft high, practically a series of flats built of mud, with tiny covered streets 3 ft wide. Only one or two entrances—this to protect against Bedouin raids of old. The town was partly washed down by heavy rain 100 years ago, and that part has now been re-built.

Another similar town a mile away used to wage war against Siwa, but now they live in amity. The oasis is generally salt, and there are many salt lakes and marshes. There are, however, plenty of beautiful springs of drinking water, and

these irrigate huge palm groves. A ruined temple of Jupiter Ammon exists, but only a few stones remain, covered with Egyptian and Graeco-Egyptian sculpture. There was a great population in Graeco-Roman times, but irrigation has been neglected and drainage has become blocked, so the greater part of the oasis has relapsed into salt marsh. I was presented by the mamour—an Egyptian—with a fine brass tray and an earthenware drinking bowl, and I had to buy a silver and amber necklace and a heavy silver ornament, worn, as a mark of virginity, round the neck…

The oasis is bounded on the North by a steep limestone escarpment, which is the southern edge of the flat plateau reaching to Sollum. On the south are endless dunes of heavy sand, reaching, they say, to the Sahara. Between here and Sollum it is hard sand covered with small stones, very flat and barren. Between my camp and the oasis the limestone is broken into queer-shaped hills—similar, on a large scale, to

Above: *At departure of Allenby from Sollum, 1919. Sanusi flag above the car 'courtesy of Sidi Achmed' (as Lindsay wrote in his album; he is second from left).*

Opposite: *Bluebird at Sollum, August 1919. From left to right: Capt. Ellis, Capt. Lindsay (at the wheel), Lt Moore, Lt Evans.*

the broken hills that border the Jordan. It rains seldom, not more than once in seven years or so.

17 August. We motored round the North of the oasis yesterday. Then, from the top of the escarpment, saw Jarabub (Jaghbub)—a holy town, which Europeans do not enter, but which we claim as within our sphere of influence, and the Italians also claim it– 15 miles away. We camped in the Desert—a lovely light, calm, cool & moonlit. We came on at 7.30 am and got to Sollum at 4.30 this evening. I'm stopping the night with de Lancey Forth, and we go on tomorrow evening, by yacht, to Mersa Matruh, half way to Alexandria. It has been an interesting trip, but it would not have done for you or any lady to have come. Distances too great and no conveniences. Sollum is a neat little bay, with a fairly sheltered anchorage. It is much coveted by the Italians, whose sphere of influence comes right up to our post. I had a beautiful swim this evening in calm water, which felt much more buoyant than Stanley Bay water. I think you would have been able to swim like a cork in it. The oases of the Western Desert are the old 'Islands of the Blest'—islands of fertility in a sea of sand. They are rather frauds, however, as most of their water is salt. We passed one beautiful lake yesterday—Exabia, in the Gagub [Qeiqab] oasis—brilliantly blue and green. Quite clear, but very salt and studded with little islands formed by solidified salt. It contained lots of tiny fish and some little cockles; there was a flock of 100 flamingos, and two or three ducks on it. The water was as salt almost as the Dead Sea, but, evidently, not fatal to all life. We saw four gazelle today. The Light Ford Cars, when on patrol, often run them to a standstill and then shoot them, when out of fresh meat, but they only shoot them when meat is wanted, and they are not allowed to shoot more than two on an expedition. The roads we followed are the old Camel Tracks called 'masrab' in Arabic. Hundreds of years of traffic have worn fairly smooth paths, even in the stony places, and quite heavy cars can run on them. The Light Ford Cars can go anywhere. On yesterday's expedition we used only Fords as we had to go through a bit of very bad ground. We joined the heavier cars and Mr Reid, the photographer, at lunch time today. Mr Reid took a lot of photographs at Siwa, but did not go with us yesterday.

18 August. At Sollum, inspecting; sailed at 5pm.

19 August. Reached Mersa Matruh at 7am. It is a little harbour, almost land locked. There is a little settlement; & we have a political officer & some police also. All the notables received me, and the Bedouin chiefs from 50 miles round had come in to see me. I visited one in his tent. It was carpeted and hung with beautiful rugs woven by the women. We ate excellent green figs and drank very sweet tea, flavoured with mint. He wanted to kill and eat three sheep to mark the occasion, but we refused as not having time. We sailed at 3.30pm for Alexandria. Sea fairly calm but with a swell.

20 August. We arrived this a.m. and landed at 9 o'clock. I found piles of letters, including your welcome letter of the day before you reached Marseilles, for which I thank you, my love. I have a charming letter from the Duke of Connaught, who as senior Field Marshal, welcomes me to the rank.

All love to you my darling.

Edward

AFTERMATH

The principal Light Car Patrol officers—Williams, Lindsay, Davidson and Moore—all returned to the UK by autumn 1919, and within a few months of their leaving the Patrols were disbanded. Some of the Fords were transferred to the Frontier Districts Administration, then under de Lancey Forth; others were sent to the No. 3 Armoured Car Company of the Tank Corps. As a result of the transfers most of the cars remained in the Western Desert, but the departure of the Light Car experts heralded greater danger for the novice patrolmen who replaced them. Within a year of the 3rd Armoured Car Company receiving its share of the Ford patrols, an RASC driver without the necessary desert experience, accompanied by two privates, got lost between Siwa and Sollum. C.S. Jarvis, who had been to Jebel Iskandar with Williams and Lindsay in 1917, tells the grisly tale:[87]

In 1921 an Army Light Car Patrol set out with four cars from Sollum to go to Siwa. It was in those days a fairly well-defined car track and if reasonable care were observed, there was not much risk of losing the way. About fifteen miles out from Sollum one of the cars, driven by a sergeant, developed some slight trouble and the patrol went on, telling him to follow. It was then late in the afternoon, and the intention was to run for a matter of another hour only before camping for the night. What actually happened after this has never been satisfactorily cleared up—apparently the sergeant, after he had restarted his car, ran southwards for some hours and,

[87] Jarvis, *Three Deserts*, p. 122.

failing to find the patrol, returned on his tracks to Sollum. He appears to have lost his head through terror of the desert and to have driven the car into a stone cairn by the side of the road, smashing the radiator and letting the water out. The sergeant and the two privates then started to walk into Sollum and, according to the account of the men, the sergeant became demented and shot himself. As he was only wounded, they admitted that they had fired into his head to finish him off, and ultimately they were found—at the last gasp—crawling into Sollum; a particularly ghastly detail of the tragedy being the fact that when the water bottles were emptied it was found that, in their terror of thirst, they had filled them with the blood of the dead man.

Several of the individuals in our story of the Light Car Patrols went on to play a further role in Libyan Desert exploration. In 1921 Mervyn MacDonnell, then governor of the Western Desert, went with de Lancey Forth on a journey into the Great Sand Sea. Accompanied by an FDA Camel Corps patrol, they began at Siwa and went south into the dunes for 100 miles (161 km).

In March 1923, Dr John Ball, Claude Jarvis and Sydney Fairman were part of the team with Egyptian Prince Kemal el-Din on the first of his four famous desert journeys. Using three Citroën half-track vehicles and six box Model T Fords, the expedition floundered in the dunes west of 'Pottery Hill' due to a broken axle on one of the Citroëns and had to turn back. Jarvis and Fairman had already spent an exhausting month setting up two advance dumps before the Prince and Dr Ball arrived in Dakhla to begin the real expedition. According to Jarvis, both he and Fairman were well and truly sick of the desert by the time it was over. The only redeeming feature of the whole dreadful experience was, apparently, the Prince's catering, which included 'game pie of snipe breast' and an endless supply of Napoleon brandy.

Dr Ball was also with Prince Kemal el-Din on the latter's expeditions to the west of the central oases in early 1924 and January–March 1925. Again using Citroën half-tracks and Fords, these were more successful. The 1924 journey was north from Dakhla into the Sand Sea, its climax being the rediscovery at 'Regenfeld' of a document in a bottle left by the German Gerhard Rohlfs half a century earlier. In early

Opposite and right: *'Pottery Hill', taken during Prince Kemal el-Din's 1923 expedition with Dr John Ball, Major Jarvis and Lt Fairman.*

1925 they travelled south to al-Shebb and bir Terfawi, then west to Jebel 'Uweināt, 100 miles (161 km) south of Gilf Kebir. The actual southwestern corner of Egypt is on the 6,000-foot-high 'Uweināt Mountain, where the borders of Libya, Sudan and Egypt come together. Travelling from Bir Terfawi to 'Uweināt, Dr Ball would have had a clear view of the southern half of Gilf Kebir, but he is unlikely to have realized that he had virtually reached the plateau's disintegrating northern escarpment with Lt Moore seven years earlier.[88] On his final expedition in 1926 (without Dr Ball) Prince Kemal el-Din actually went up to the plateau and skirted its cliffs. He named it al-Gilf al-Kebir, meaning 'the great barrier'.

[88] For further information about Dr Ball's participation in this and previous expeditions headed by Prince Kemal el-Din see the Prince's account 'L'exploration du Désert Libyque', La Géographie, September-October 1928, pp. 171-83; 320-36.

EPILOGUE

In 1927, the Ford Motor Company ceased to manufacture the Model T Ford—but not before the car's nineteen year production life and sales figures of over 15,000,000 had guaranteed the Model T its rightful place as the most successful motor car of its time.

Late in 1925, in the twilight of Model T production, Ralph Bagnold arrived in Cairo for the first time. A veteran of the European Western Front, he was thirty years old and an officer in the Royal Corps of Signals—and he was keen to get out of the city and explore the desert by car. He made friends with like-minded adventurers, bought a Model T Ford locally, and before long a new chapter in Libyan Desert exploration had opened.

Unquestionably, Bagnold heard about the exploits of the Light Car Patrols very soon after his arrival in Egypt. While still a novice at his new pastime, he discussed desert driving with men who knew Egypt's deserts and the dangers of driving away from the main roads and tracks. He met and received encouragement from Claude Jarvis, at that time (1926) the governor of Sinai. He drove in the Eastern Desert, between Ismailia and Cairo, with Colonel Stewart Newcombe, who had been a senior officer in Intelligence with Lawrence and MacDonnell. Most importantly, he made the acquaintance of Dr John Ball, and the latter's colleague in the Survey of Egypt, Patrick Andrew Clayton. Bagnold clearly had access to maps produced by the Survey of Egypt, which incorporated data provided by the Light Car Patrols. What is not clear is whether, at this early stage, he was given access to Claud Williams' classified Military Geography. It seems highly likely that Ball or Clayton, if not the British Army at this point, would have made it available to him.

Over the next few years Bagnold and his fellow desert enthusiasts visited many of the locations known to the Light Car Patrols, including the most remote in the Western Desert: 'Ain Dalla, Abu Minqar, al-Shebb, Bir al-Terfawi and the Gilf Kebir. By the end of the decade they were routinely climbing sand dunes with cars, although by now they had exchanged their Model T Fords for Model As. They had 'reinvented' a version of Owston's radiator condenser system, also using rubber tubing and two-gallon cans, and perfected methods for extracting cars from soft sand. As regards the famous Bagnold 'sun-compass', we may clearly assume that, through his acquaintance with John Ball, Bagnold was aware of Claud Williams' improvised 'sundial compass' and that his contribution was to refine Williams' version of the device. Bagnold's desert-driving expertise was soon such that he was able, in 1932, to lead an expedition that ranged far beyond the borders of Egypt, going deep into the Sudanese province of Darfur and modern-day Chad—and covering an incredible 6,000 miles (9,656 km) in under two months.

In the 1930s, *The Times* regularly reported the latest on Libyan Desert adventures by Bagnold, P.A. Clayton, Almasy and others, especially the hunt for the 'lost' oasis of Zerzura; and in the early '40s the public was thrilled by stories in the press about the Long Range Desert Group. One cannot help but wonder what the men of the Light Car Patrols made of the fame achieved by those who came after them, of this public fascination for a desert from which for three years they themselves had longed to escape. They may not have dreamt of going back, but they must have been proud that their own adventures had helped to make those of the next generation of Libyan Desert explorers possible.

APPENDIX 1:
LIGHT CAR PATROL ROLL OF HONOUR AND LIST OF OFFICERS

In the three and a half years the Light Car Patrols existed, no patrolmen were killed by enemy action, in Egypt or elsewhere. There were, however, two fatalities.

Private Ernest Arthur Richard Kendall, ASC driver. He died on Christmas Day 1916, when the car he was driving overturned twelve miles south of el-Alamein.

Sergeant Hudson John Watson Langley, No. 1 (Australian) Light Car Patrol. Awarded the Distinguished Conduct Medal and Bar for gallantry under fire in Palestine and Syria during 1917 and '18, Langley died of malaria in Aleppo Hospital on 2 January 1919.

OFFICERS SERVING IN EGYPT WITH THE LIGHT CAR PATROLS, 1916–19[89]

Name and highest rank while serving with the Patrols	Reg't prior to attachment to Patrols and Patrols in which he served
ADAM, Lt Fergus James (1895 –1939)	Royal Fusiliers; LCPs 2, 4 & 8.
BUXTON, Lt William Arthur (1891– ?)	Royal Welsh Fusiliers; 6LCP; OC, 4LCP (Oct. '18).
CHAPMAN, Lt H.C.	County of London Yeo; 4LCP (Jun–Nov '16).
CHAPPLE, Lt Howard Annesley	Suffolk Reg't; 3LCP (Oct. '17 to Dec. '18) invalided back to UK with malaria (Feb. '19).
DAVIDSON, Capt. Roy Austin, MC (1886–1980)	Denbigh Yeo; OC, 6LCP (Oct. '16); OC, double patrol 6 & 8 (Jul. '18); OC, 5LCP (Mar. '19).
ELLIS, Lt Frederick Rowland, MBE	2LCP; 6LCP.

[89] This list is not exhaustive. It consists of names encountered by the author during his research.

Name and highest rank while serving with the Patrols	Reg't prior to attachment to Patrols and Patrols in which he served
FAIRMAN, Lt Sydney Maurice Eward (1898–1944)	Royal Welsh Fusiliers; Imperial Camel Corps; 2LCP; 4LCP; OC, 8LCP (Jul. '18); after the war Camel Corps, FDA.
HAMILTON, Capt. Robert Claude Victor	Royal Irish Rifles; 6LCP; OC, 2LCP (Sep. '18–Apr. '19).
HARDING, Lt H.N.	County of London Yeo; OC, 4LCP (Jun. '16).
HOBSON, Capt. Eric Anthony I Iare (1894–1960)	5 Lancers; 2LCP; 4LCP (Mar. '18).
HOUGHTON, Lt Thomas Whitfield (1897–1919)	9LCP; died in Damascus.
JAMES, Capt. Ernest Homewood, MC & bar, Royal Victorian Order (1879–1960)	OC, 1st Australian Armoured Car Battery; OC, 1st (Australian) LCP.
LINDSAY, Capt. Alfred Stewart, MC, MBE, Croix de Guerre (1885–1949)	Fife and Forfar Yeo; OC, 1LCP (Jun.–Dec. '16); OC, 4LCP (Mar. '17); OC, double patrol 6 & 8.
LLEWELLYN, Capt. Griffith Robert Poyntz (1886–1972)	Glamorgan Yeo; OC, 2LCP (Dec. '16).
LOCKETT, Lt G.G.	Cheshire Yeo; OC, 2LCP (summer '16).
MOORE, Lt Edward Davies, MC, (1884–1955)	Shropshire Yeo; OC, 3LCP (Jun. '16–Sep. '19).
MORRIS, Lt Arthur George	County of London Yeo; OC, 3LCP (Sep. '19).
MURPHY, Lt George Thomas	6LCP; 5LCP (Mar '19), OC, 5LCP (Jun. '19)
NEWILL, Lt Wilfred Marston (1891– ?)	Shropshire Yeo; OC, 2LCP (Jan. '17); seconded Indian Army (Jul. '17).
PARTRIDGE, Maj. Llewellyn, DSO, (1878–1945) Légion d'Honneur, Croix de Chevalier	Pembroke Yeo; served as Pembroke Transport Officer ('16); worked with 5LCP and other patrols; commanded LCP groups Oct. '16 (nr. Baharia) and Feb. '17 (Siwa).
ROSHIER, Lt Samuel William (1889–1961)	17th Lancers; 4LCP (Aug. '18); 3LCP (Sep. '19).
SMITH, Lt P.	OC, 2LCP (briefly Jan. '17)
STANLEY, Lt H.C.	2LCP
THORPE, Lt C.W.G.	Suffolk Yeo; OC, 4LCP (Nov. '16–spring '17).
WILLIAMS, Capt. Claud Herbert, MC, (1876–1970)	Pembroke Yeo; OC, 5LCP (Jun. '16); appointed Senior Officer LCPs Western Frontier (Oct. '17); OC 2&5LCP escorting Military Mission to Benghazi (Jul. '18).
WOODALL, Lt Frederick George	Devon Regiment; 2LCP; 5LCP; 9LCP (Jul. '18).

APPENDIX 2:
DIARY OF THE MILITARY MISSION
TO SAYYID MUHAMMAD IDRIS

17/7/18 Left Sollum.

18/7/18 En route to Benghazi.

19/7/18 Arrived Solluch.

20/7/18 Arrived Benghazi. Meeting with General Moccagatta to discuss mission.

21/7/18 Conference with head of Italian Mission. Visited Police School and environs of Benghazi.

22/7/18 Visited Aerodrome. Armoured Cars, Light Car Patrols and Wireless Section inspected by General Moccagatta. Attended parade of Eritrean and Litjan troops. Visited force round Benghazi, Ordnance Workshops and Commandant of Zone. Dined with General Moccagatta.

23/7/18 Visited museum and native and Italian cavalry regiments. Farewell visit to General Moccagatta.

24/7/18 Left Benghazi 06.00, arrived Zuetina 18.30. Received by Muhammad Idris.

25/7/18 Capt. Royle paid private visit to Muhammad Idris. Joint Mission entertained to dinner by Muhammad Idris.

26/7/18 Major MacDonnell and Capt. Royle had private interviews with Muhammad Idris, who left for Ajdabia in the evening.

27/7/18 Joint Mission lunched with Muhammad Idris at Ajdabia.

28/7/18 Muhammad Idris returned from Ajdabia at 19.00.

29/7/18 Official Meeting with Muhammad Idris.

30/7/18 Presented Commander-in-Chief's gifts to Muhammad Idris and had interview.

31/7/18 Joint Mission left for Tabilbo via Ajdabia and arrived within short distance of camp same evening.

1/8/18	Inspected force at Tabilbo and started for Zuetina.
2/8/18	Arrived Zuetina 11.30.
3/8/18	Interview with Ali Pasha el Abdia.
4/8/18	Farewell meeting with Muhammad Idris. Capt. Royle took over Commander-in-Chief's presents.
5/8/18	Left Zuetina.
6/8/18	
7/8/18	En route to Sollum.
8/8/18	
8/8/18	Arrived Sollum 11.00.

APPENDIX 3:
C.S. JARVIS ON THE 'JEBEL ISKANDAR EXPEDITION'

In March 1917, Major Claude Scudamore Jarvis, 1st Devonshire Regiment, was in charge of the men guarding the perimeter of the WWF camp at Mersa Matruh. Claud Williams and Mac Lindsay may have invited Jarvis to accompany them on this reconnaissance, or perhaps Jarvis had orders to accompany them—the sources are unclear on the matter—but nearly two decades later Jarvis included the following account of the journey in his book *Three Deserts*.[90]

The only interesting thing I did during my short stay at Mersa Matruh was to accompany a desert patrol on an attempt to find a route through from two separate routes to Siwa, and to place on the map the position of the mysterious Gebel Iskander… which had never been seen by a European, but which was supposed to exist in the particularly desolate country north of Siwa…

We started off from Mersa Matruh shortly after dawn on a cold, brisk morning in March and by evening had travelled 120 miles south on the Siwa road and then westward down a steep escarpment to the lower levels of a vast canyon-like stretch of country. The going below was indescribably bad… a network of sharp limestone ridges flush with the surface and with the hollows in between filled with the finest limestone powder. This is the worst type of going one can find in the desert as it has a most disintegrating effect on the tyres, whilst the clouds of powder that arise whenever the car lurches off a limestone outcrop into a pocket of the stuff fill the

---

[90] *Three Deserts*, pp. 7–8.

eyes, nose, and mouth and add to the natural thirst one feels from the dry desert air. There was also the rather uncomfortable feeling—having descended some 500 feet down a sandy slope to the bottom of the canyon—should we ever be able to find a way a way up again to the high plateau and safety? The prospect of death from thirst in a harsh and waterless desert is not a pleasant one. Since then I have spent so much of my time in the deserts that I have forgotten the awe that one experiences on first seeing the vast stretch of empty country on all sides—the wonder of the scenery at dawn and sunset when the slanting light reveals the features of crag and escarpment in shades of mauve and purple—and last but not least the uneasy realization at the back of one's mind that if anything should go wrong with the cars, petrol, or water, one's chances of escape were slim indeed.

The following day we found Gebel Iskander—an imposing limestone massif rising some 700 feet from the floor of the canyon. From the top one looked out across a harsh and forbidding stretch of truly frightening desert shimmering in the heat haze of noon and one could understand Alexander the Great feeling appalled at the prospect. We also flushed his crow, which happened to be a raven and which, according to custom, flew off in a south-westerly direction towards Siwa, and as it was the first bird we had seen since entering the canyon we wondered if it were a direct descendant of Alexander's 'crow'.

The next day we had a truly nerve-racking time trying to find a way up out of the depression, and, having essayed an ascent to the east and north without discovering a route in any way possible, we camped that night with the creepy feeling that if no track were found on the morrow both petrol and water would run out and our prospects of getting back alive were by no means bright. The day after, however, we discovered a sandy slope up which, after six hours' pushing and hauling in terrific heat, we got the cars and that evening we ran into Mersa Matruh, stage-managing the most imperial smash during the last mile. The going was good, the patrol tired, and we were thinking more about baths and cooling drinks than driving, so that when the leading car suddenly stopped dead through failure of petrol, the second car crashed into its rear and the other two followed suit. Nobody was hurt, but three box bodies were turned into matchwood and three radiators were draped tastefully in clouds of steam over the engines and the front axles had to be seen to be believed.

APPENDIX 4:
A SELECTION OF LCP CORRESPONDENCE

1 LETTER FROM MAJOR C.W. MACLEAN TO OC, MOGHARA FORCE, CONCERNING NO. 5 LIGHT CAR PATROL

[Stamp:]
Headquarters
Western Frontier Force
19 December 1916
SR/52/24

O.C.,

Moghara Force,

EL ALAMEIN

Reference your M.F./33/S dated 17/12/16.

The attached 3 copies of a letter from the Chief of the General Staff are forwarded.

Please convey to Major Partridge and Lieut. Williams the Commander-in-Chief's approbation of the excellent work sent in by them. Perhaps you would kindly have a copy of this letter handed to the officers concerned.

C.W. Maclean[91]
Major G.S.
Western Force, E.E.F.

Talbot Block, ABBASSIA, CAIRO.

19th December 1916.

---

[91] Charles Wilberforce Maclean was married to a first cousin of Leopold Royle; he was also the father of Sir Fitzroy Maclean, author of *Eastern Approaches* (1949), who served in the Western Desert and in Yugoslavia in the Second World War.

2 LETTER FROM LYNDEN BELL CONCERNING NO. 5 LIGHT CAR PATROL

I.A. (W) 811.

G.O.C.
W.F.F.

The very interesting and useful report from O.C. No. 5 L.C. Patrol has been received and it is hoped to get the material into the map without delay.

Will you please convey to the O.C. No. 5 L.C. Patrol the C-in-C's approbation of the excellent work he has sent in.

(signed) A. Lynden Bell,
C.G.S.

G.H.Q., E.E.F.
17th December, 1916.

3 LETTER FROM BRITISH HIGH COMMISSIONER REGINALD WINGATE TO BRIG. GEN. YORKE

18th May, 1918

Dear General Yorke,

Before leaving Sollum I wish to briefly express to you my sincere thanks for your most kind reception of me in your command and my warm appreciation of my extremely interesting visit to the District which you so ably and successfully administer.

If I may say so, I consider that what has been accomplished by yourself, staff, the troops, and the administration is little short of marvellous, and there are evidences on all sides of the growing satisfaction of the inhabitants at all that has been done to help them recover from the ravages which they brought upon themselves by taking sides with the rebels against us. Whilst at the same time your Military arrangements are such as to render the various positions relatively secure against any repetition on their part or that of the enemy.

With regard to the Troops, I was specially struck with the extremely smart and soldier-like appearance of the guards of Honour and other guards both at MATRUH and SOLLUM, and I consider great credit is due to Colonel Hussey Walsh and Major Howell for the high standard of discipline and efficiency in the Battalion.

I was also much impressed with the general appearance of the men and the good work that is being done by the various sections of Royal Artillery and Royal Engineers, also by the A.S.C., A.O.C., R.A.M.C. and other Departmental units.

Where all show such keenness, it is difficult to draw distinctions, but I was specially struck with the very smart appearance on Parade and in manoeuvre of the Company of the Imperial Camel Corps under Captain Houghton, and I had also ample evidence of the thoroughly practical and workmanlike state of the Light Armoured Car Patrol[92] under Captain Williams and his Officers, N.C.O.'s and men. I had special opportunities of judging of their efficiency when they acted as escort to and from DABAA to SOLLUM.

I have never seen cleaner and more carefully laid out camps—both civil and military, whilst the disposition of the defences and the work done on them is most commendable.

It will give me the greatest pleasure to tell the Commander-in-Chief, when I next have the pleasure of seeing him, how thoroughly efficient I consider your military and civil administration to be and how much I am indebted—to yourself especially, as well as to your various officers, Staff and Regimental—for a most interesting and enjoyable visit.

Yours sincerely,
(signed) Reginald Wingate

---

[92] An error: Wingate means Light Car Patrols.

4 LETTER FROM CAPT. WILLIAMS TO MAJ. GEN. WESTERN

17/9/18

O.C. Nos 5 & 6 Light Car Patrols
to Maj. Gen. W.G.B. Western C.B.

In accordance with your permission to put the position of these patrols before you, I beg to submit the following.

L.C.P.s were formed during the middle of 1916, the personnel being found by certain Yeomanry regiments on the West Front.

The original personnel of Nos. 2,4,5,6,8 & 9 patrols have thus been working in the Lybian[93] desert for about 2½ years.

During this time work has been continuous and arduous, and men have been carefully trained for active work as patrols.

No action has occurred on this front with the exception of the SIWA fight in which L.C.P.s bore a very minor share.

All our men were originally picked from their units for quality and are good active soldiers.

When asked by higher authority to transfer to M.G.C. on the grounds of preserving the efficiency, they consented provided they remained with Light Car Patrols. This was in Sept 1917 and applications for transfer, with this proviso, were signed in Oct 1917.

For several months the question of transfer was held in abeyance and in February I applied for these Yeomanry to be allowed to return to their units rather than continue in the existing unsettled state. This course was not allowed however and in March we were informed that the transfers would go through.

Transfers were finally completed on 24/6/18, the men thus having been kept in an indefinite position for nearly 9 months, during which time they have had the chagrin of seeing their old companions gaining promotion and honour with their old units in

---

[93] [sic]

Palestine and latterly in France. [The N.C.O.s amongst them have actually been super-ceded[94] by juniors of the M.G.C. motors.]

I cite these facts to shew that they have substantial reasons for asking for a change. They feel that they did not join as non-combatants and that they cannot shew their faces in their native land, having passed through this great war without firing a shot.

On medical grounds alone these Patrols require a change. The monotony and the absence of the amenities of life, absence of excitement and the feeling of the uselessness of training, after such a long period cannot fail to have an injurious effect on their minds; and this state cannot be remedied by a few weeks in Alexandria. The foregoing applies to all ranks—officers and men.

We all feel that, given an opportunity, we would give a good account of ourselves, and carry out efficiently the purpose for which we have been training, and we do not understand the contention that Car Patrols are only of use in wide open desert. We have good guns and good gunners and cars to convey them rapidly from place to place and though open desert is of course the place where they can work to best advantage, if there is nothing doing on open desert they still have their uses in other directions.

We respectfully request that this question of changing the L.C. Patrols to an active front be given consideration and we further request that if it is decided that the West Front in Egypt is the only front on which the Patrols are required, and must continue to act, we may be informed of the decision.

We officers who were instrumental in picking the men from their former units have seen them stick with unfailing loyalty to their duty with the Patrols and we feel we owe it to them to do our best in their interests; and this must be my excuse for pushing the matter with you, Sir, in this unofficial manner, and I beg to thank you sincerely for your permission to do so. I speak not only for myself but for Capts Lindsay and Davidson who are in entire agreement with me.

C. H. Williams, Captain

---

[94] [sic]

5 LETTER FROM BRIG. GEN. YORKE TO CAPT. WILLIAMS

c/o Hopkinson Pasha
Carlton,
Ramleh,
Egypt
[undated]

Dear Williams,

As I am not coming back to Sollum, I feel I must drop you a line to thank you and the other car patrol officers for all the good work you did, whilst I was in command.

I always had, as I am sure you realised the utmost confidence in you all and was always certain, that any orders you received would be carried out in a most efficient manner, and with all your energy. And I only regret that no opportunity was given me to actually command you in action. At the same time your enterprise and energy, at all times & seasons of the year, undoubtedly had the effect of inspiring a wholesome moral lesson to any of our opponents, who may from time to time have contemplated aggressive action towards us. And after all, that was the object of [the] Force under my command. The last thing the higher authorities wanted was any trouble out our way. And I know that General Allenby appreciates what you did, not only by keeping the peace, but also the excellent cartographical work which was accomplished.

I was only sorry I could not do more for you, in the way of better organisation etc, but as you personally were in my confidence, I am sure you realise the difficulties I had to contend against. Anyhow, I had the satisfaction in knowing that you were a happy family despite many minor inconveniences, which gave you a good excuse for a friendly grouse.

I am only too grateful to you personally for your loyal support and cooperation, and I shall always look back with the utmost pleasure to the many happy days I spent with you bumping about in the old Ford car in the desert. I sincerely hope that when you come to London Town, that you will look me up in the telephone book, and we will foregather and talk over old times—Mind you do.

Well the best of luck to you all. I shall always retain most affectionate recollections of the old Car Patrols.

I am,
Yrs ever
Ralph M Yorke
G.O.C. Coastal Section

6 LETTER FROM DR JOHN BALL TO COLONEL LLEWELLYN PARTRIDGE

Survey of Egypt
Desert Surveys

Desert Survey Office,
37, Sharia El-Falaky
June 14, 1928

My dear Partridge,

You can't think how delighted I was to get a line from you. I have thought of you thousands of times since you left these parts and wondered where you were and how you were getting on. Quite a lot has come out of those old patrols with you and Brother Williams (who wrote to me a year or two ago from New Zealand and complained that the stars were all topsy-turvy over there, but he was working away with the old theodolite which you and he took out for your work and which he annexed as his trifle of loot after victory).

Do you remember walking down the Qattara Pass and taking readings of pressure for me on that little aneroid, and how we dared not accept the readings because of the instrument being lost and the consequent absence of any control? Well, I always had the feeling that <u>perhaps</u> the reading at the spring might not be so much out after all;

and when a chance offered I had the levels taken over there from Cairo by triangulation, and there turned out to be a huge depression, of which we hope to make economic use (see cutting enclosed); and by the way "Cecily Hill", which still retains its name, is one of the most important of out reference points, because you can see it from a large part of the depression.[95]

Nothing would give me greater pleasure than to see you out here again running cars over that desert. But we are not starting the real work yet, only some trial borings which will take 2 years to do, and I'm afraid there is nothing worthy of your agoing at present, to say nothing of the strong antipathy which the [Egyptian] Government is at present showing about getting any British into its service—rather, they are kicking us out as fast as they can, and I am not sure if they will keep me going after the next 2 years. If they do, it will be through fear of my making a row and the knowledge that the King of Egypt would not like it, as he and the Princes are all very keen on keeping me as long as possible.

Do drop me a line telling me what you are doing and if you found room on your tunic for the last lot of ribbons you got, for I remember your chest was tolerably covered with them already. And be sure that if any opening occurs where it might be possible to get you a congenial job in the deserts you roamed in the old days, I shall not fail to let you know of it.

With cordial regards,
Yours, sincerely,
John Ball

Note

Letters 1 through 5 are from the Williams family archives in New Zealand. Letter 6 has been provided courtesy of Mrs Mary Mill, a great niece of Llewellyn Partridge.

The author is grateful to the Williams family and Mrs Mill for permission to reproduce these letters.

---

[95] The name was actually 'Cicely Hill', after Partridge's wife.

APPENDIX 5:
CAPTAIN OWSTON'S REPORTS ON MOGHARA RECONNAISSANCE

SECRET
MF/70/S.

MOGHARA FORCE

Report on a Reconnaissance—South of Moghara, Sept. 9-11/16

Accompanying Report is a tracing from Map MOGHARA-BAHARIA, Sheet 2, Scale 1,500,000, showing the route taken as accurately as possible. If, however, more time had been expended in "plotting off" on the map, the water supply would have been used up too quickly—and the reconnaissance would not have been able to have been carried as far as it was.

Six photographs were taken during the reconnaissance, and will be forwarded as soon as finished.

Saturday, 9th Sept.

Left CAMEL POST at RAS EL BAGAR at 11 a.m. with 4 Ford Box Cars conveying 6 men, Lieut. Kenny-Leveck (Intelligence Officer) and native, 32 gallons water, 112 gallons petrol, rations for 5 days, 2 Maxims, 2,000 rounds ammunition.

The going was very good as far as point marked D at Corner of 5th Sand Dune, which was reached at 3.30 p.m. The formation was chiefly white hard sand, no grazing; and tinted spectacles very necessary as the white sand was very dazzling.

A little time was taken up in finding a way through the 4th Sand Dune. A small neck about 50 yds. wide was found, but is rapidly and visibly filling up by sand blowing from the tops of the dunes. It must be crossed with caution, as a car will sink in the middle and become partially—if not wholly—buried.

The night was spent 7 kilos. S. of Point marked D., the last 2 kilos being very bad soft clay sand.

Sunday, 10th Sept.

Our course should now have been S.W., so as to try and cut the tracks BAHARIA-SIWA, but fearing that more Sand Dunes were to come and block our way, we continued S., and when no more Sand Dunes were visible we tried to go S.W. or W., but soft clay sand prevented us. We then commenced to make a long detour E. and S.E. and S., as a long soft-sanded wadi had to be got round. We hoped to be able, eventually, to turn due W., but were unable. I did not, however, order a return to point D., so as to start afresh from there by going due W., as the water supply would not have permitted us getting very far, so I continued on the route as shown on Map, as I thought a reconnaissance E.-S.E. and S. was also necessary, so as to report whether Armoured Cars or Ford Cars could get from WADI NATRUN in this direction. On getting to the end of the route as marked on map, 30 miles N.E. of BAHARIA ESCARPMENT, I decided that we had gone far enough. The native stated that enemy outposts would be 20 miles out from BAHARIA, and as there were plenty of high points from which they could observe, I considered that it was our business not to be seen if possible. Our water supply was now just sufficient to get us home—allowing also for emergencies.

As soon as we started on the return journey, a fan flew off one of the cars—making a large gash in the radiator, which could not be soldered; another car now stopped owing to water in the petrol which was taken out in unbroken tins as issued—which is a point I should like to bring forward, as it shows carelessness at the filling base—probably due to old returned tins being filled, and water not emptied out or looked for before they are filled and soldered up. When there is an occurrence like this, it is a matter of taking down the carburettor, which takes some time. We towed the car with broken radiator about 35 kilos., until two ropes were broken owing to heavy going; we managed, however, after a considerable expenditure of water, to plug up the gash, and got the car to run in to EL ALAMEIN. On arrival in the evening at the "neck" in the 5th Sand Dune, we found it had closed up to a certain extent since our crossing the day before, and our tracks almost obliterated in the vicinity.

Monday, 11th Sept.
Having passed the night near the end of the third Sand Dune, we started for MOGHA-RA at 6.30 a.m., arriving there about 11 a.m. and reported to O.C. MOGHARA; and proceeded later to EL ALAMEIN, as the cars require overhauling before starting again on Saturday next, 16 September 1916.

NOTES
The country traversed was totally unfit for Armoured Cars, or cars larger than Fords.
     We were unable to find a guide at short notice to be of much use to us, but took a native who had been two days' camel ride S. of RAS EL BAGAR.
     Lieut. Kenny-Leveck has now found a native who is more familiar with this part of the country, and I am fairly confident that with a "dump" of water, petrol, and rations at Point D., that on Sunday next I shall be able to find a way for Ford Cars to W. of BAHARIA in the vicinity of EL LUBBAQ by striking due W. for about 30 kilos after leaving Point D., and then proceeding S.W.
     Tracks of 2 men and 1 camel were met with about 35 kilos S. of RAS EL BAGAR— going W. towards BIR LUBBAQ, 5 days old. O.C. MOGHARA already know of this, however, from his camel patrols.

(sgd) L. V. Owston, Capt.
Light Armoured Cars.

EL ALAMEIN,
13/9/16

Report on a Reconnaissance South of Moghara, Sunday 17th to 20th Sept. 1916

Sunday, 17th

Left MOGHARA at 6-30 am arriving at the dump marked "D" on the map at the end of the fifth Sand Dune at 2 pm. Filled up here with Water and Petrol and left at 3 pm, proceeding South West until 10 Kilometers South of GARET-EL-MIZAWAG, arriving there 5 pm and camped for the night.

On the previous day Lieut. Davidson, with his six Patrol Cars left Moghara at 6.30 am with: one Officer, eight Men, 2 Lewis Guns, 1,656 rounds, and rations for 18 days. We had with us: four Ford Box Cars, six men, Lt. Kenny-Leveck (Intelligence Officer) and one Native, 24 tins Petrol, 24 tins Water, 4 skins of Water, 2 Machine Guns, and 2,000 rounds, 1 box Mills Bombs, rations for 6 days, a few spares, and a soldering outfit.

Monday, 18th

Started at 6.30 am keeping South West and tried to reach the main BAHARIA-SIWA road at GHARD EL-QEZZEN. There was a soft sandy Wadi which stopped any attempt to get across. We returned to our tracks two kilometres and then describing half circle East-South-East, and South round some sandy hills, we went due South for ten kilometres and then South-South-East for five kilometres over very bad sandy going, and finally struck the main BAHARIA-SIWA road at 12.30 pm in the vicinity of QABR EL-FAIDI. Here we found tracks of 3 camels and 6 donkeys ridden West, two days' old; and a convoy of 25 camels and 12 men going West 6 days old. We then went on in a South-South-Easterly direction to see if we could strike the second track to SIWA from G. QALA SIWA, but after proceeding nine kilometres, soft sand stopped us. We then returned to the main road where we had previously crossed it arriving at 2.30 pm and lay up for the night on the chance of catching a convoy. At 7 pm when darkness came on we drew the Machine Gun Cars straight across the track, but nothing was seen.

<u>Tuesday, 19th</u>

At 6.30 am we started off due South to try and strike the second road, but going was very bad. We went 16 kilometres, within which we should easily have struck the road. On arrival at the two little hills, just above the R in BAHARIA (ref. map ALEXAN-DRIA 1 to 1,000,000 sheet North H 35) we decided to return to the Dump. I did not consider it worthwhile lying up on the main road for another night, although our water supply could easily have permitted it. But as the last 30 miles of the going had been so bad, I thought it advisable to have plenty of water in hand in case of cars breaking down. We arrived back at the Dump at 4.30 pm. The going from the Dump to within 20 miles of the main BAHARIA-SIWA road is fair, but some very bad soft sandy and treacherous places. At the Dump we buried:

    110 gallons water
    180 gallons petrol
    1 drum lubricating oil
    1 drum hub grease
    110 lbs biscuits
    1 case bully beef
    1 case food

so as to be ready for any future expedition South.

<u>NOTES</u>

I should like to suggest that if permission could be obtained for me to spend a week in the vicinity of HEIT-GUBRAN, which is above 50 miles (80 km) West of where we struck the main road, that I am fairly confident we should catch one or two convoys and despatch riders. Lieut Davidson with his patrol cars would be able to keep us supplied from the Dump.

I should patrol the road in the vicinity of HEIT-GUBRAN every day, and get well away from the road at night so as to rest the men.

I should patrol with my four Ford Cars and two Maxim Guns. Additional cars would be more of a hindrance than a help owing to the bad going in the vicinity of the main road, with the continual pushing out.

The whole of the going throughout is absolutely impossible for the Armoured Cars, or any other car heavier than a Ford. The going over the whole distance ALAMEIN to BAHARIA-SIWA road is not good enough for me to guarantee to get to a certain place at a certain time on a certain date if ordered to do so, but if I had three clear days to get to a certain point on the BAHARIA-SIWA Road as long as it was not too far West, I ought to be able to do so.

(sgd) L. V. Owston, Capt.
Light Armoured Cars.

ALAMEIN,
22/9/16

APPENDIX 6:
'THE ENGLISHMAN'S HOUSE'

'The Englishman's House' on Jebel Ma'asera, Baharia

D r Ahmed Fakhry (1905–1973) was a distinguished Professor of Ancient Egyptian History who spent years working in several of the oases mentioned in this volume. In his *Bahriyah and Farafra Oases*, published shortly after his death, is a single sentence which mentions a ruined stone house atop a 50-metre-high hill (Jebel al-Ma'asera) in Baharia Oasis from which one has a good view of the Depression.

> On its top stand the ruins of a house built by Captain Williams, commander of the troops defending the oasis from the threatened invasion of the Sanusi troops toward the end of the First World War.[96]

With all due respect to the memory of Dr Fakhry, the sentence contains several errors. For example, Williams was never commander of troops defending Baharia; the Sanusi did not threaten to invade Baharia, they *did* invade Baharia, and they held the Oasis for seven months; and that invasion (February 1916) occurred not towards the end of the war—it was closer to its beginning. But the principal error is the statement that the

---

[96] *Bahriyah and Farafra Oases* (1974), p. 37.

ruined stone house was built by Captain Williams, assuming Dr Fakhry meant Captain Claud Williams of the Light Car Patrols. The sources used for this history of the Patrols make it clear where Williams patrolled and where he surveyed throughout his three years in the Western Desert; and he was in the vicinity of Baharia only twice, and only very briefly. The first occasion was when No. 5 Patrol captured the Sanusi caravan 25 miles (40 km) north of the Oasis in September 1916. The second was a month later when the Patrol took part in the futile pursuit of Sayyid Ahmad's army when it escaped from Baharia and returned to Siwa.

Interest in the Western Desert is always considerable, and in recent decades books, articles—and even travel agency websites—have perpetuated or elaborated on the errors in Dr Fakhry's statement. The ruins are now widely known as 'the Englishman's House'; and 'the Englishman' in question is almost invariably identified as

Exterior of stone hut built by No. 2 Patrol.

Inside the stone hut built by No. 2 Patrol.

Claud Williams. Nevertheless, the present writer is certain that neither Williams nor the Light Car Patrols had anything to do with the building of this house.

It is possible that the confusion over the origin of the ruined house on Jebel al-Ma'asera is due to the fact that No. 2 Light Car Patrol, which was based in Baharia from October 1916 to April 1917, did build a stone hut. Two photos from the album of Harold Morton show the structure from inside and outside. It was about 6 ft high, a single room with at least two windows, presumably without glass, but with wooden shutters. The ceiling/roof consisted of grass-matting. Morton's captions do not mention the location, but it is likely to have been Baharia.[97] By contrast, the house on Jebel al-Ma'asera was a rather luxurious construction, with much finer masonry. The dilapidated walls are 9 or 10 ft high, and the footprint of the house is large, clearly indicating multiple rooms.[98]

[97] Likely to have been Baharia because 2 Patrol was in the Kharga/Water Dump A area for just a few weeks—too brief a period for such a project; and was otherwise mainly based at Matruh or Sollum, both of which had much better facilities for soldiers, which, one imagines, would have made the hut unnecessary.

[98] At the time of writing there is a website online called OasisPhoto.com by Ahmed Badr with good photos of 'The Englishman's House'. Offering an alternative explanation for the house's origin, Ahmed Badr claims it was built by an English officer after World War 2, but he does not mention his source for that information.

BIBLIOGRAPHY

Anonymous, 'A Military Asset', *Ford Times*, Ford Motor Company (England) Ltd., May, 1915, p. 306.

Badcock, G.E. (1925), *A History of the Transport Services of the Egyptian Expeditionary Force, 1916-1918* (London: Hugh Rees, Ltd).

Bagnold, Ralph (1931), 'Journeys in the Libyan Desert, 1929 and 1930', *The Geographical Journal*, Vol. 78 (1) Jul., pp. 13–39, (6) Dec., pp. 524–533.

—— (1933) 'A Further Journey through the Libyan Desert', *The Geographical Journal*, Vol. 82 (2) Aug., pp. 103–129; (3) Sep., pp. 211–235.

—— (1935), *Libyan Sands: Travel in a Dead World* (London: Hodder and Stoughton).

Ball, John (1927), 'Problems of the Libyan Desert', *The Geographical Journal*, Vol. 70 (1) Jul., pp. 21–38; (2) Aug., pp. 97–128; (3) Sep., pp. 209–224.

—— (1917) 'Desert Reconnaissance by Motor-Car: Primarily a Handbook for Patrol-Officers in Western Egypt', unpublished typescript, Royal Geographical Society.

—— (1916) *Military Notes on Western Egypt* (London: Ministry of Defence).

Briggs, Martin S. (1918), *Through Egypt in War-Time* (London: T. Fisher Unwin, Ltd).

Bird, Anthony (1966), *The Model T Ford*, (Leatherhead: Profile Publications, Pamphlet No. 13).

Caton-Thompson, Gertrude (1983), *Mixed Memoirs* (Gateshead: Paradigm Press).

Cosson, Anthony de (1935), *Mareotis* (London: Country Life Ltd).

Fakhry, Ahmed (1974), *Bahriyah and Farafra Oases* (Cairo: AUC Press).

—— (1973), *Siwa Oasis* (Cairo: AUC Press).

Fletcher, David (1987), *War Cars: British Armoured Cars in the First World War* (London: HMSO).

Goudie, Andrew (2008), *Wheels across the Desert* (London: Silphium Press).

Harding King, W.J. (1912), 'Travels in the Libyan Desert', *The Geographical Journal*, Vol. 39 (2) Feb., pp. 133–37.

—— (1913), 'The Libyan Desert from Native Information', *The Geographical Journal*, Vol. 42 (3) Sep., pp. 277–83.

—— (1925), *Mysteries of the Libyan Desert* (London: Seeley, Service & Co. Ltd) facsimile repr. Darf Publishers.

Harold, Jim (2005), 'Deserts, Cars, Maps and Names', paper published in the University of Glasgow online journal *eSharp*, issue 4 (spring).

Hassanein, A.M. (1925), *The Lost Oases* (London: Thornton Butterworth Ltd).

Inchbald, Geoffrey (2005), *With the Imperial Camel Corps in the Great War* (UK: Leonaur).

Jarvis, C.S. (1931), *Yesterday and To-day in Sinai* (Edinburgh and London: William Blackwood & Sons Ltd.).

—— (1936), *Three Deserts* (London: John Murray).

Jones, E.H. (undated), 'The Motor Patrol', MSS 209, AWM 224, personal account of No. 1 (Australian) Light Car Patrol available on the Australian Light Horse Studies Centre website.

Kelly, Saul (2002), *The Hunt for Zerzura: The Lost Oasis and the Desert War* (London: John Murray).

Kemal el-Din, Prince Hussein, 'L'exploration du Désert Libyque', *La Géographie*, Sept–Oct 1928, pp. 171–83 and 320–36.

Lancey Forth, N.B. de (1930), 'More Journeys in Search of Zerzura', *The Geographical Journal*, Vol. 75 (1) Jan., pp. 48–59.

MacMunn, G. and Falls, C. (1928), Military Operations: Egypt & Palestine (London: HMSO).

Massey, W. T. (1918), *The Desert Campaigns* (London: Constable and Co. Ltd).

McGuirk, Russell (2007), *The Sanusi's Little War: The Amazing Story of a Forgotten Conflict in the Western Desert, 1915–17* (London: Arabian Publishing).

Murray, G.W. (1950), *The Survey of Egypt 1898–1948* (Cairo: Ministry of Finance.

—— (1967), *Dare Me to the Desert* (London: George Allen & Unwin Ltd).

—— 'The Work in the Desert of the Survey of Egypt', *Bulletin de l'Institut Fouad 1er du Désert*, Tome II, No. 2, Juillet 1952.

Penderel, H.W.G.J. (1934), 'The Gilf Kebir', *The Geographical Journal*, Vol. 83 (6), Jun., pp. 449–56.

Shaw, W.B.K (1945), *Long Range Desert Group* (London: Collins).

Vivian, Cassandra (2000), The Western Desert of Egypt (Cairo, AUC Press).

Walker, W. Seymour (1921), 'An Outline of Modern Exploration in the Oasis of Siwa', *The Geographical Journal*, Vol. 57 (1) Jan., pp. 29–34.

Williams, Claud H. (1919), *Report on the Military Geography of the North Western Desert of Egypt* (London: HMSO).

ACKNOWLEDGEMENTS

I owe thanks to many people for their kind assistance and encouragement. First and foremost among them is Claud Williams' own family, who gave unstintingly of their time and effort to provide the author with scans of photographs, family letters, and hundreds of pages of assorted documents relating to the Patrols and to their family history. This movement of information from the Antipodes to London was deftly 'orchestrated' by the family musician, Derek Williams, with most of the scanning being done by his brother Keith Williams. To these two grandsons of Claud Williams I am much indebted, but also to Edward Williams, Anne Patricia Pilkington and Stella Overbye (Claud's son and two daughters); and to Adrian Pilkington and Brian Williams.

Family members, close and distant, of other participants in the Light Car story also deserve special thanks: Bill Lindsay, who made available the superb collection of photographs from his grandfather's album, and the late Jack Lindsay; Mary Mill (Llewellyn Partridge's great niece), Liz Seymour, Patricia Gravill, and Michael Gravill; Ian and his brother Keith Morton (grandsons of Harold Morton); John and Adam Gordon (great nephews of Leycester Owston); Owen Davidson and Diane Davidson.

I am grateful to: Charles Messenger, Dr Saul Kelly, Professor Andrew Goudie, David Fletcher, Margaret Ashby, Martin Cassell, Nicholas Peacock, Aled L. Jones, Henry Keown-Boyd, Archie Hunter, Yvonne Neville-Rolfe, Jasper Scovil, Michael Martin, David Finlayson, Rev. Peter Rutherford McKenzie, and Chris and Wendy Cundy; Andrew Lewis at the Brooklands Museum Trust Ltd., Major Ian Riley at the Liverpool Scottish Regimental Museum Trust; Capt. J Preece MBE at the Fife and Forfar Yeomanry Museum; Rusty MacLean at Rugby School; Chris Barker and the late David Skinner at the Model T Ford Register of Great Britain; Amanda Rebbeck at the Australian War Memorial; Sara Bevan and Rita O'Donoghue at the Imperial War Museum; and Lianne Smith and Patricia Methven at King's College London. We are grateful to the Michael Sedgwick Trust for their interest in the Light Car Patrol Project and offer of support.

To Alasdair Macleod, Head of Enterprise and Resources at the Royal Geographical Society, I owe special thanks for his constant support throughout the duration of this project. I am also grateful to his colleagues at the RGS, in particular, Ted Hatch, who drew three maps while still recuperating from a compound fracture; Eugene Rae, Jamie Owen and David McNeill.

My sincere thanks are also due to the Society for Libyan Studies, especially the Publications Manager of Silphium Press, Dr Victoria Leitch; but also to past President Professor Claudio Vita-Finzi, who encouraged me to approach Silphium Press; and to the Society's Chairman, Dr Robert Morkot and its Treasurer Philip Kenrick.

Lastly, I wish to thank my wife Sheila, who staunchly supported me throughout four years of research and writing, despite never quite getting used to my living in the wrong century.

SOURCES OF ILLUSTRATIONS

INTRODUCTION AND PART I

Pages 7, 9 and 13: author's private collection; page 16: Lindsay family; page 17: Royal Geographical Society; page 18: Morton family; page 19 (left): author's private collection, page 19 (right): Dr Faraj Najem; page 21: Royal Geographical Society; page 22: Lindsay family; page 23 (left and right): Archie Hunter; page 25: Lindsay family; page 27: National Portrait Gallery; page 29 (left): National Archives (Kew), page 29 (right): Adam Gordon; page 30: Williams family; page 32: Imperial War Museum; page 33: Adam Gordon; page 35: Williams family; page 36, 37, 39: Imperial War Museum; page 40 (left): Liverpool Scottish Regimental Museum Trust, page 40 (right): Rugby School; page 41 (left & right): Lindsay family; page 42 (top & below), page 42 (right): author's private collection; pages 43, 44, 45: Lindsay family; pages 46, 47, 48, 49: Morton family; page 51: David Finlayson; page 53: Adam Gordon; pages 54, 55: Imperial War Museum; page 56, 57: Lindsay; page 58: Mary Mill; page 61: Royal Geographical Society; page 62: Williams family; page 63: Davidson family; page 64 (left & right): Morton family; page 65 (top): Imperial War Museum, (below): Lindsay family; page 66: Lindsay family; page 67 (top): Lindsay family, (below) Morton family; page 68: Lindsay family; page 69: Morton family; pages 71, 73, 74: Australian War Memorial; page 77 (top & below): Lindsay family; page 81: Fife and Forfar Yeomanry Museum; page 87 (left): Imperial War Museum; (top right): author's private collection, (below right): Lindsay family; page 88: Lindsay family; pages 89, 90, 91, 93 (top & below), 95: Morton family; page 103; Williams family; pages 104, 105: Lindsay family; pages 106, 107: Morton family; page 111: Lindsay family; pages 115, 116, 117, 118, 119: Lindsay family; pages 124, 125: Royal Geographical Society; page 127: Williams family; page 149: Ahmad Badr; pages 150, 151: Morton family.

PART II

From page 160 onward all photographs are from the Williams family collection, except for those on page 198 (from *Half a Life*, by C.S. Jarvis, 1943), page 201 (from the Lindsay family collection) and pages 234 and 237, which are from the *Illustrated London News*, March and April 1919.

Copyright of the painting 'The Ridley Tragedy' by Stuart Reid, now at the Imperial War Museum, is held by the Estate of Stuart Reid. Every reasonable effort was made to contact the painter's Estate via the IWM for permission to use the image in this book, but there was no reply.

PART TWO

LIGHT CAR PATROLS IN THE LIBYAN DESERT

BY CLAUD HERBERT WILLIAMS

I suppose everybody is sick of tales of the Great War, well, this is not a tale of the Great War at all but in fact not all but simply, a few recollections of & impressions and impressions as we out of the way little known part of the world, the great Libyan desert

The desert is suggestive of mystery and romance but though in the fussy little Ford cars we penetrated into almost every corner of the country we found little that was mysterious and still less that we could describe as romantic. Perhaps we were lacking in perception and perhaps the lady novelist knows better

There is a curious paradox. The desert is hateful, cruel, pitiless. God has damned the land by withholding water. Hunger and thirst are the portion of those who travel; the few scattered inhabitants of the more favoured parts are poor, squalid, miserable looking specimens. There is literally nothing to recommend this country and yet it exercises an intense fascination. You curse it and rate it and yet you want to go back to it. It has something to offer which you can get nowhere else, yet nowhere where men jostle men and trams whistle and birds twitter and trees rustle their leaves. I cannot pretend to explain the urge of the desert but there is no doubt of its existence

The desert is not lacking in beautiful scenery but most of it isn't there & mirage effects are a daily experience. You see a lake which isn't there & pine trees which are really mere tufts of scrubby & graceful castles which, when approached, dwindle into small tombs or magnificent Bedouin camps ... They exist however, the intensely blue, palm girt ...

This account of the work of the Light Car Patrols was written by Captain C. H. Williams M.C. after World War I but never published. Captain Williams sent it to me from New Zealand in 1946 and with his permission I gave it to the Library of the R.G.S.

W.B. Kennedy Shaw
2.8.46

Claud Herbert Williams (pictured left) wrote 'Light Car Patrols in the Libyan Desert' in two drafts. The first was written in longhand shortly after the First World War. The second was a typescript, corrected by hand. In reproducing the text for this volume, the publisher has used the corrected typescript given by Williams to W.B. Kennedy Shaw, and by the latter, with Williams' permission, to the Royal Geographical Society. To retain the authenticity and character of the original, the text is presented virtually without editing, with the exception of occasional clarifications by means of footnotes. The original spelling, punctuation and grammar have been retained.

CHAPTER I

INTRODUCTION

The Light Car Patrols in the Western desert of Egypt attracted less public attention, probably, than any of the many novel military formations brought into being by the force of circumstances during the great War. They were operating on a quiet front, their numbers were insignificant, their casualty lists were almost nil, and their work was not spectacular. But the Libyan Desert is an out-of-the-way, little known part of the world and there was a great deal, both in their work and in the scene of their operations, that was of interest.

The following pages contain a few of my own experiences and impressions gathered in the course of three years' duty with the Patrols.

The nature of the country was, no doubt, responsible for their formation, for they were peculiarly well adapted for their duty of protecting the Military outposts against surprise attack and of preventing illicit traffic between the Delta lands and the enemy.

The Patrols were seven in number,[99] each consisting of six Ford cars with a personnel of thirty men; they were formed not long before I joined them in 1916 and though three were subsequently sent to Palestine, the remainder continued their work in the Western desert until Armistice Day and beyond it. As time went on we were transferred from post to post and consequently, during the period, I had the

---

[99] Patrols No. 1 to No. 6 operated in Egypt's Western Desert; No. 7 was established specifically for deployment with the Egyptian Expeditionary Force in Sinai and Palestine. By summer 1918 there were two additional patrols, Nos. 8 and 9, operating on Egypt's western frontier; and during the Egyptian riots of spring 1919 *ad hoc* patrols up to No. 15 were used to police the cities in the Delta and lower Nile Valley.

opportunity of penetrating every corner of the land into which the wheels of a car could be persuaded to travel, of visiting many curious places and of meeting many strange and interesting people.

Our territory extended west for 450 miles, from fertile Egypt to the Italian border and South from the Mediterranean coast to the great trade route leading westward from the Nile through the oases of Baharia, Siwa and Jarabub to the Gulf of Sidra. Any map of Africa will show these points. Mersa Matruh and Sellum were our base ports.

The nature of our work, of the country and of its people will appear later, but a cursory description will not be out of place as a preliminary.

With the exception of a comparatively narrow strip along the sea coast the whole country is practically rainless. Population is confined to this belt and to the oases of the interior where springs from underground take the place of natural rain water.

On the Coastal Belt the rainfall though very limited is fairly regular and the sparse natural vegetation supports large numbers of sheep, goats, camels and donkeys, while in the more fertile or sheltered spots first-rate barley is grown.

Here you find the nomadic Bedouin with their moveable tent villages. These people simply occupy a tract of country until their stock have exhausted the grazing in the neighbourhood or until the local water supply runs short; then they strike their tents and move to a fresh site, perhaps putting in a crop of barley and returning months later to reap it. Their agriculture is very primitive, the plough consisting of crossed beams of wood and the plough team a couple of donkeys or camels, or perhaps one of each, but if the seasonal rain is reasonably plentiful their crops are splendid.

The country rises by easy slopes from the sea edge of the Great Libyan Plateau. For a distance of about 30 miles inland there is still some vegetation but it is evident that, in the past, conditions were much better for there are found numbers of huge underground cisterns, cut out of the solid rock, some of them capable of holding immense quantities of water. These cisterns probably date from Roman times. They are set in positions for catching large quantities of rain water which drains from a rocky catchment area through narrow circular holes in the roof. Even now the very rare rain storms will occasionally fill them and though in most cases they are in disrepair and their catchment area choked with sand, some are kept in working order by the Bedouin and serve as the final watering place for caravans before crossing the wide, waterless plateau to the oases. Small parties from various points along the coast will often make such a well a point of concentration for the long journey.

Up to this point gazelle are numerous and hares are also to be seen but further south there is practically no vegetation and no living thing. Towards Siwa oasis, which is the most important point in the interior, the Plateau stretches south for nearly 200 miles without a break. Though the country has surface variations and is rough in parts, it is almost featureless and quite devoid of hills or valleys of any size. The journey from the last well to the oasis is an easy one for motor cars but for men with loaded camels is an arduous and even dangerous undertaking. It will occupy about 7 days and the limit of endurance of the Bedouin camel is about 8 days. If man or beast falls sick he must march or die for delay may mean disaster to the whole party. Innumerable bones and stone-covered human graves dot the course of any of the larger caravan routes, bearing silent witness to the hardships of the journey.

The caravans invariably travel by well-known trade routes or "masrabs" as they are called. A map of the country with all the masrabs plotted looks like a spider's web, for every point of importance, either on the coast or inland is connected with every other point of importance. A masrab appears as a number of wavy, parallel camel tracks, in numbers according to the importance of the route. Having been trodden from time immemorial they are conspicuous, and often deeply scored into solid rock. They are, therefore, easy to follow even without the native cairns, cunningly placed to catch the eye, and the graves and camel bones which mark their course. The connecting masrab is always the shortest route consistent with good travelling between any two points but they are useful to the traveller not only as good, well-beaten roads to follow but also, when their intricacies are understood, as a substitute for the landmarks in which the desert is so deficient.

The Plateau terminates to the south in a rugged escarpment only negotiable by camels at wide intervals. This escarpment extends in a very irregular line almost from the oasis of Wadi Natrun westward to the Italian border and beyond it. Sometimes it

is possible to drive on level ground right to the edge and look down almost vertically on the low land five or six hundred feet below but for the most part the country in its neighbourhood is very rough. Descent is made by tortuous valleys or wadis which penetrate the cliffs.

At the base of the escarpment, almost throughout its length, lies a depression varying from a few feet to several hundred feet below sea level. Large areas of this depression are boggy salt marsh or sand, but at intervals springs of good water occur. The inhabited oases of Qara, Siwa and Jarabub are situated along its line besides many minor uninhabited oases.

The country rises again to the south but not to the same elevation. Another escarpment is found descending into the Fayoum and another into Baharia. The oases depend entirely upon spring water for their existence and the number of their population is governed by the number and output of their wells. Qara with only a couple of good springs has barely a hundred people, but Wadi Natrun, Baharia and Siwa have numerous and good water supplies and their population runs into thousands. The palm groves and gardens of Baharia and Siwa must be hundreds of acres in extent.

There is not a great deal of difference in the character of the country south of the depression but it is more varied in its different parts than the Plateau and much of it is covered with sand dunes. South of the neighbourhood of Siwa the dunes are continuous over a very large area and are impenetrable by cars without special contrivances, but south and south-west of Wadi Natrun they assume quite a different and very curious formation, standing isolated in smooth gravelly desert. They consist of perfectly straight ridges of fine sand serrated along the top like a saw blade; the little peaks rising, perhaps to a couple of hundred feet in height. They are no more than a few hundred yards wide and anything from a mile to fifty miles long. The lie, within a degree or two, in the same direction, sometimes miles apart from their neighbours, sometimes yards apart and sometimes actually merging with them. There are literally hundreds of these dunes scattered over a very wide area but why they assume this shape, I cannot pretend to explain. Camels can cross these ridges but with cars a very zig-zag course is necessary to thread a way amongst them.

Opposie: *Williams in his stripped-down Ford.*

Petrified forest.

There is a popular belief that the sand dunes are always on the move and certainly, seeing the sand swirling off the ridges in a high wind gives colour to this view but a similar stream of sand will be found pouring on to the dune from the open desert and I am inclined to think that for every grain that is lost another and, perhaps, two arrive to take its place. Except for increasing size, I think a dune, once established, is permanent.

This opinion was supported by finding the Great Dune, discovered and charted by the explorer, Caillaud[100] [sic] a hundred years ago, in precisely the same map position, a few miles longer but otherwise unchanged. A very remarkable sharp pointed peak, 500 feet in height in the dunes to the west of Siwa, much valued by the Bedouin as a land mark, has certainly remained unaltered for a generation.

The sand in the desert is of course the result of the disintegration of rocky cliffs and kopjes[101] by wind action. This process is very noticeable right along the escarpment and especially in the extremely rugged portion in the neighbourhood of Siwa.

The whole country, monotonous though it is to the ordinary individual, is full of interest for the scientist. There is abundant evidence of past fertility and of the existence of human habitation at various periods of the world's history. Cliff tombs, literally in hundreds and occasional cisterns cut out of the solid rock are found in many localities quite incapable of supporting human life to-day. Specimens of the flint implements of the stone age, both Neolithic and Paleolithic are to be found in large numbers and over wide areas. The neighbourhood of Siwa, for a distance of

[100] French mineralogist and explorer Frédéric Cailliaud (1787–1869).
[101] An Afrikaans word referring to an isolated hill formed by the erosion of the land around it.

fifty or sixty miles is certainly a paradise for the flint enthusiast and one M.O.[102] of our camp, who happened to be a connoisseur, made a most remarkable collection during his period of duty. After discarding at least three fourths of his finds, as too cumbrous to convey to England, he left the camp with 120 specimens, ranging from tiny arrow heads to large spearheads or adzes, and every specimen perfect.

In one or two localities we found remnants of prehistoric animals, teeth of the mastodon, parts of the jaw of the alligator and some scraps of the shell, or hide, of huge tortoises. In several places also we drove into areas of petrified forest with great tree trunks lying thickly over the ground like a recent bush clearing. These forests have no doubt been submerged by the sea for the trees are completely vitrified and as hard as stone.

Such, then, was the country over which our patrol duties took us: sand, gravel, rock, gravel, sand for ever and ever, and travelling was often very thirsty work. During the day the surface of the desert becomes burning hot, the heat strikes upwards as well as downwards and every puff of wind is like a blast of hot air from a furnace. The thirst that arises then is unquenchable and there is no relief except shade. Nature has provided none, but the travelling Bedouin lies on the ground under his white woollen robe or blanket with one corner of the covering hitched up on his staff and dozes comfortably enough till the day cools off. We ourselves used to rig canvas shelters over the cars, but in spite of such devices found the heat almost intolerable.

But, except when a Khamsin wind is blowing the nights are always cool and pleasant and more than compensate for the discomforts of the day.

During a period of the year, I think corresponding with the monsoon period, dense fogs occur and heavy dews fall, but as a general rule the atmosphere is very dry and clear and stars or moon shine with a brilliance unknown in kindlier countries.

At sunrise or sunset desert scenery is remarkably beautiful, but when the sun is high, scenery, except in mirage form, can hardly be said to exist. The novelty of the ordinary mirage wears off very quickly for it is a normal, everyday condition.

---

[102] Medical Officer.

One knows always that the water is merely heat shimmer, the castle a little heap of stones and the beautiful grove of trees a few little scraps of dry vegetation, all greatly magnified. But there is a mirage effect of much rarer occurrence, which I myself only noticed once, where the light is refracted and objects completely out of sight are made visible. Driving along a masrab from Siwa Camp we came in sight of a small camel convoy just topping some rising ground, apparently not more than a mile ahead. It was hardly necessary to use glasses to distinguish the clothing of the men and we expected to overtake them in a few minutes. When we reached the high ground they were nowhere to be seen. We followed on for over half an hour crossing several of the ridges or elevations which occur like billows on the Plateau, and finally came again in sight of the convoy looking much as they had looked before. There were at least ten miles separating us at first and even on dead level ground they would have been completely below the horizon.

Perhaps the most remarkable feature of the desert is the fascination which it exercises. In spite of its monotony, its heat, its harshness and its acute discomforts, few who have lived there for any length of time fail to appreciate this "lure of the desert" so often dilated upon by novelists, and to experience a keen desire to return to it.

When I first became connected with the patrols the huge tract of country west of Egypt proper was almost unknown and uncharted, a few explorers' routes, the better known oases and the great escarpment being about the only features on the existing maps. Naturally enough it was easy for the imagination to people it with hordes of swiftly moving Arabs who might at any moment descend upon us for a little throat cutting. It was only when our increasing radius of activity failed to disclose trace of man or beast, when we began to understand the meaning of the waterless wilderness, that we realised the enormous difficulty and consequent improbability of an enemy attack, and grasped the fact that if we wanted a fight we must go and look for it.

For this purpose a way must be found through great distances of unexplored country for our nearest known enemy was at least two hundred miles from us at this time. At first we were a bit shy about venturing very far afield. It seemed easy to get lost or to smash cars, or to run short of petrol or water; but we soon gained confidence in our ability to provide for all our needs. As a mere precaution we began to plot our course as we went. We learned to use compass and speedometer with skill and accuracy, and evolved a simple sundial device for using the sun's shadow as a means of keeping good direction.[103] Soon we found ourselves able to make a far more accurate dead reckoning than on a ship at sea; we began to chart our information and to build up gradually a fairly reliable map of the country.

The object of our first long journey was to discover a route practicable for cars to the oasis of Baharia which the Senoussi were then occupying in considerable force. Military preparations were well forward for attacking the enemy from the east side of the oasis and it was our desire to find out whether we could get our cars near enough to share in the excitement.

---

[103] For more on the 'sundial compass', developed by Williams himself, see pp. 65–70.

CHAPTER II

A LONG JOURNEY AND A LITTLE CAPTURE

My Patrol was at this time based on the oasis of Wadi Natrun (Soda Valley), which was held by a regiment of yeomanry. Wadi Natrun is a long depression, lying about twenty-five to fifty miles from the Delta lands, at a point some twenty miles north[104] of Cairo. The depression contains a string of intensely salt lakes which support a large and thriving salt and soda industry. Besides the factory people it has a population of a couple of thousand Bedouin. Its Central point, the factory of Bir Hooker, is connected by a light railway with the main Egyptian railway system.

Baharia Oasis lies about two hundred miles to the south of Wadi Natrun and one hundred miles from the Nile. It is a large and important oasis, with a considerable population, much fertile land and a great area of valuable palm groves. A force of Senoussi, estimated at several thousand, was occupying the oasis and a military railway was being pushed out across the desert from the main line at the Nile, in order to force them out of the place.

We left Wadi Natrun with four cars, two officers[105] and eight men, carrying petrol enough for four hundred miles, and food and water for five days. Everything went ridiculously smoothly from the start. In a couple of hours we were clear of the known country and we went on and on through the whole of the day, zigzagging at times through rough country but finding no obstacle worthy of the name. We plotted our course at intervals, climbed a rocky knoll here or a sand dune there, to get a view of

---

104 Wadi Natrun is about 50 miles northwest of Cairo.
105 That is, Williams and Major Llewellyn Partridge, Transport Officer for 1/1st Pembroke Yeomanry.

the surroundings, and at night-fall camped after a very easy run of a hundred and twenty miles.

The second day promised to be equally tame but after an hour's travelling we entered softer country, and at midday found ourselves still about twenty-five miles from the escarpment of the Baharia, with a great stretch of rough, treacherous looking desert in front of us. It was obvious that this country would be difficult, if not impossible, to penetrate and our supply of petrol did not admit of our exploring it at the time. Feeling fairly well satisfied with the results of our first attempt, we determined to turn back and return later to carry on the reconnaissance. We were very anxious, however, to secure a native who might supply us with information, for one of our objects was to get news of two officers of the force operating on the east side of the oasis, who had been reported missing, and whose fate was unknown. There seemed just a possibility of capturing a camel herder, for there was a little sparse vegetation about and we had noticed tracks of wandering camels. Though we had not petrol enough to run the cars about, we had sufficient food and water to stand a day's delay, so we concealed the cars, climbed a knoll with a wide outlook and settled down for a long wait.

Our chances seemed very remote, but before an hour had passed, we espied some dark moving specks in the distance. They seemed to be coming from the direction of Baharia and before long we could distinguish the shapes of camels and men. Soon we could count five of each; not a very large bunch but quite suitable for our purpose.

As I have remarked, the country in front of us was infernally rough for cars, and we were obliged to wait until the travellers entered better desert before we could deal with them. When matters looked satisfactory, I issued out with two cars and drove a long rapid detour to get between our quarry and the bad country. They spotted us immediately and started to run, throwing off part of the loads of the camels and belabouring the beasts into a trot. The other two cars now bore down upon them so they left their camels and made for the cover of some rocky hills. A rifle shot brought two to a stand-still and these we disarmed and searched. In the meantime the other three appeared to be running a paper chase for they were tearing up papers and scattering the scraps as they ran. They were rapidly overhauled and captured.

We now examined the camel loads and here we found a curious thing. Amongst the odds and ends of the usual Bedouin travelling outfit was an assortment of automatic pistols, bombs, dynamite and some detonators. A strange load to be taking into Egypt and it set us thinking. These must be very naughty men and we could not do better than secure the papers they seemed so anxious to destroy. We set to work to gather them up and though scraps were all over the place and the wind was blowing half a gale we succeeded in collecting quite a lot before dusk.

All that remained now was to make for home. We had little enough petrol, a long way to go and a dangerously heavy load. One of the cars, too, was giving trouble and if it failed us things might become awkward so we lost no time in loading up and getting away.

One of our captives we found to be a Senoussi officer,[106] an attractive, clean looking chap. I took him on my car with our interpreter and led the way for home. My passenger and I became quite chummy in no time. He shewed great appreciation of the cigarettes and the water that we offered him and was eager to do his share of the pushing and hauling when the overloaded cars stuck in the occasional patches of soft country.

He could tell me nothing about the fate of the two missing officers. Possibly his ignorance was feigned, for it afterwards turned out that both had unfortunately been killed, and he may have feared reprisals.

The return journey occupied two full days and was without incident except for the accidental explosion of a detonator by an unusually violent bump. The car took fire and we had a few anxious moments lest the black-powder bombs should explode with the heat. Sand and patent fire extinguishers, however, soon overcame the blaze and not much damage was done. We reached home with less than two gallons of petrol remaining amongst the four cars.

Our capture turned out to be an important one. The automatics and explosives were intended for use in a plot to assassinate certain important individuals in Egypt. The mail matter that we had so laboriously collected implicated many Egyptians in

---

[106] For more on this Libyan officer, Dahman bin Hayyan, see pp. 44–5.

the business, and these were promptly arrested. Much to my sorrow, my little Senoussi friend was tried as a spy by court martial, convicted and shot. Another of our prisoners was a notorious spy and a traitor.[107] He also suffered the extreme penalty, while the remainder were sentenced to various terms of imprisonment.

A couple of weeks later we set off again to carry the reconnaissance further but this time we came upon tracks of men and camels about a hundred miles from our starting point. We tracked them for nearly eighty miles towards Baharia and made a second capture not far from the scene of the first.

This time our captives were merely traders. We gathered them in, burnt their goods, shot their camels and returned home. If you like to go back there you will find thirteen perfectly good camel skeletons lying in a perfectly straight line and there they will probably lie for all time. The shooting of harmless beasts is a nasty part of the job, but orders are orders and it must be done. Burning several hundred pounds worth of excellent tea, tobacco and fancy goods is also annoying but Ford cars are not adapted for carrying a great weight of loot.

We eventually succeeded in getting right round to the rear of Baharia with a considerable force of light cars, but the birds had flown and all we found were the tracks of a large number of men, camels, donkeys, and a couple of mountain gnus, only a few days old.

We missed our fight by those few days.

---

[107] An Egyptian Nationalist named Musa Saleh.

CHAPTER III
THE SIWA STUNT

When the Senoussi evacuated Baharia they trekked westwards to Siwa, a large and important oasis about three hundred and fifty miles west of Cairo and two hundred miles inland from the Mediterranean coast. An appalling journey it must have been, too, for there are only two wells in the whole distance of two hundred and fifty miles. They arrived at Siwa much reduced in numbers by disease and with their morale at a low ebb.

We were moved one hundred miles west from Wadi Natrun to Moghara, a small uninhabited oasis about forty miles inland. Our instructions were to find a route by which the enemy could be attacked from Moghara.

A few weeks of exploration, however, were sufficient to prove the undertaking impossible. The country was very difficult for light cars and quite impossible for armoured cars; the distance, too, was great. It was, therefore, decided to attack from Mersa Matruh, a small coastal port only about two hundred miles from Siwa. So to Matruh we were sent to take part in the expedition.

The Siwa show was probably unique in this or any other war. It was purely a motor-car affair, for the great distance of barren, waterless country precluded the use of any other force. The enemy were over two hundred miles distant and were known to be encamped in rough country in a small oasis called Girba, a few miles to the west of Siwa. The only feasible approach to their camp by car was said to have been destroyed.

As things turned out the expedition was entirely successful but the actual battle developed into a regular "opera bouffe" affair; an immense amount of noise and very little blood-shed; a very safe and entertaining performance to have been mixed up in.

The cars forming the fighting column were gathered together at Matruh. The force consisted of two batteries of armoured cars of the Light Armoured Car Brigade, and three Light Car Patrols of six Ford cars each. Supply cars were collected in large numbers from Alexandria and Cairo. Officers and men of the L.A.C.B. and L.C.P.s, to give them their official abbreviations, were fairly well trained in desert work, but it was otherwise with the personnel of the supply column, many of whom had hitherto only driven on the paved streets of a city. Many were the breakages on the comparatively rough road from Alexandria to Matruh, and as the outfit of spare parts was very inadequate there was considerable delay in getting prepared for a start. At length, however, all was ready for a day fixed.

[To our horror and disgust we were all solemnly cinematographed on the preceding day, though fortunately, in the finished picture, no features can be distinguished. We felt exceedingly like clowns in a circus at the time but afterwards recognised that it was a more fitting commencement to a highly enjoyable picnic.][108]

The column moved out before daybreak, my patrol in the lead, and by dusk we had covered well over half the distance or about one hundred and twenty miles. Another eighty miles on the following day brought us, in the early afternoon, to a point about twenty miles from our objective and here we halted, for it was necessary to find a way down the cliffs to the enemy's camp. We had been surprised and disgusted at the excellence of the route to this point. All our strenuous explorative work from Moghara had been so much time wasted, for here was a solid, well defined route, which offered no difficulties whatever.

It must be understood that to reach these oases, the bases of which are below sea level, from the coast, the Libyan Plateau has to be crossed. The Plateau is a great tract of limestone country at an elevation of five hundred or six hundred feet above sea level and is excellent car country, but the southern edge, where it breaks away into the oases, is a rugged cliff-like escarpment, which can only be negotiated at a few points.

---

[108] Williams intended this paragraph to be cut, but it's of interest because the principal operator of the movie camera was the famous Australian photographer Frank Hurley. A five-minute clip of Hurley's coverage of this expedition is available at the Imperial War Museum, but the group shot at Mersa Matruh is not included.

The regular pass down into Girba having been destroyed by the Senoussi, it was necessary to find another and to this end a native guide had been brought who claimed to know a seldom-used route not likely to be guarded by the enemy. We found and examined this pass in the afternoon. It was not attractive for, though there would be little difficulty in descending it, a return would be quite impossible. However, it was a means of descent, and we returned to camp and made our report.[109]

The following morning we had no end of difficulty in getting the Fords started for the night had been cold and some of the radiators were frozen, but a little after sunrise the column moved off and at about 9 o'clock reached the head of the pass.

There was no lack of boldness in the scheme of operations from this point. We were a great distance from our base and we were to take the cars down into a hole, the only means of egress from which was known to be destroyed. We were to attack a, numerically, vastly superior force of the enemy, in country which was not likely to be feasible for car movements, and failure to defeat him might easily mean disaster. It was in fact suspiciously like entering a rat trap.

We slid the cars down the steep slope without accident, then we roared along about five miles of rough, gravelly country and finally came in sight of the Senoussi Camp, which consisted of tents and stone huts grouped on a flat ledge of rock with a semicircle of steep rugged cliffs frowning down upon it. The rocky ledge broke away in a low but precipitous bank in front of the camp and formed a very excellent protection against car attack.

We had with us six Rolls-Royce armoured cars, and these promptly advanced. Two of them, or a third of the force, bogged to the axle in a patch of half-dried swamp, and it took an hour's work to extricate them, the remainder went on and opened fire.

The enemy, taken completely by surprise, were streaming up the cliffs behind the camp; for a few minutes they offered a good target to our machine guns but they melted away amongst the rocks and by degrees took position in the rugged cliff tops and returned the fire of the cars from a height of two hundred or three hundred feet.

---

[109] In War Diary [WO 95/4438] Leo Royle is credited with finding the alternative pass.

Here is where the comic opera element shewed up. The armoured car men were quite safe inside their cars, though the tyres were being considerably ploughed up. Brother Senoussi was equally safe behind his rock, for no one could get a decent shot at him. Obviously anyone leaving the cars would be shot down in a moment. It was like two small boys shaking fists at each other from opposite banks of a river. Brother Senoussi, however, had the laugh on his side. He had five hundred men, we had about 70 actual fighters. He had several machine guns excellently placed amongst the rocks and quite invisible from below. He also had two mountain guns and could lob shells among our light cars in the rear and we couldn't hit him back. But the people who sold him the shells had the last and best laugh, for he might as well have thrown cricket balls. They were obviously faulty stuff for even those that burst nicely in the air scattered their shrapnel like the gentle dew from heaven, and it pattered quietly on the ground like so many dried peas. Most of the shells burst in the sand and their effect was nil.

We light car people left our cars and approached as near as we could to the enemy. We spent a lot of time and trouble trying vainly to see where the bullets were coming from but at last gained a target, and some amusement, in a mountain gun which we

Williams' photo of the Siwa column, February 1917.

succeeded in locating. We got the range to a nicety with a Lewis Gun and prevented the enemy from working it for hours.

The slaughter continued till dusk, by which time most of the ammunition had been shot away. Our casualties numbered three officers wounded and a dozen car tyres busted. Reports vary as to the number of Senoussi who bit the dust. Official accounts stated 150 to 200 killed and wounded, but a native doctor who served with the enemy afterwards told me there were nine casualties, all slightly wounded.

As evening approached things began to look more and more like a stalemate. There appeared to be no reason whatever for the enemy to abandon his impregnable position, and a means of retreat for the cars in case of necessity became an important question. An officer sent to examine the damaged pass out of the depression reported it quite impractical without considerable repairs. My patrol of 2 officers and 14 men was sent to make it good before dark, and after an hour's hard work I had the satisfaction of driving my car up it and of sending word to the effect that it was fit for traffic.

The armoured cars, however, held their position during the night and their plucky persistence evidently impressed the enemy for just before daybreak the Senoussi abandoned their positions and started the long retreat to the holy city, Jarabub, 70 miles further to the West. Cars had been sent beforehand to intercept the expected retreat, but the enemy were able to evade them by taking to the sand dune country and the force escaped practically intact.

The expedition was well carried out and the scheme boldly executed, for there can be no doubt that there was quite an element of risk in entering Girba Oasis at all. Having entered the place, and having found the enemy much more numerous and better armed than was anticipated, and able, at a few minutes' notice, to establish an absolutely impregnable position, it was a bold stroke to bluff him out by keeping the cars in position during the night, for a determined counter-attack, under cover of darkness would have had every chance of success. The temper and morale of the Senoussi, however, were correctly estimated and the result justified the action taken.

The Girba fight had most important results for it finished the Senoussi menace for good and all, and though there were, subsequently, frequent warnings of their returning in force, no further attempts were made.

We did not, at that time, understand the reason for their retirement from Girba. We put it down to loss of morale, due to sickness and boredom, and to an exaggerated idea of the powers of the cars. Later on, however, we found that our first attack had given us possession of "Ain Girba" their nearest and best water supply, we also found that it was actually possible completely to isolate them from any water supply. Thus their position, absolutely impregnable though it appeared, might have been rendered untenable on the following day had we possessed the necessary information to cut between them and the other more distant springs.

We spent a couple of days in the Siwa Oasis and then returned to Matruh, the whole undertaking having occupied only eight days. A few weeks later Siwa Camp, one of the most isolated outposts of the Empire, was established about twelve miles from Siwa town and in this camp we were destined to spend many weary, monotonous months during the next two years.

CHAPTER IV
SIWA AND SIWA CAMP

Siwa Camp was the most desolate looking spot imaginable. It was situated on gravelly plateau some miles from the escarpment. There was nothing to be seen but bare grey desolation, with a few rocky hills shewing up in the distance. It was grilled daily by a pitiless sun and swept by every wind that blew. On winter nights the cold was often intense. The camp consisted of bell tents, a few reed huts, a ring of barbed wire, and a stink of petrol.

Water for the camp had to be carted some ten miles from a well in the depression, and patrol duties also took us all into every corner of the oasis. We thus had many opportunities of visiting a very remarkable and interesting place.

The oasis of Siwa is situated in a long depression which stretches east and west for many hundreds of miles. To the north is the frowning edge of the Libyan plateau, a rugged almost precipitous escarpment, which is unbroken and continuous nearly to the Nile Valley in the east and away hundreds of miles into Italian territory in the west. To the south lies an immense tract of sand country, which borders the depression east and west of Siwa town and stretches for 250 miles south to the oasis of Kufra, a mysterious place almost unknown to Europeans. To the west of Siwa the nearest inhabited place is Jarabub, a small city which contains the tomb of the founder of the Senoussi faith[110]. Jarabub has a population of about 300 and is the Mecca of the Senoussi sect. There is no further habitation for nearly 200 miles further west. East of Siwa, with the exception of a small oasis, called Qara, there is

[110] al-Sayyid Muhammad bin 'Ali al-Sanusi (1787–1859), grandfather of al-Sayyid Ahmad Sharif, who invaded Egypt in 1915, and of al-Sayyid Muhammad Idris, the pro-British future king of Libya.

no sign of habitation until Baharia, 250 miles distant, is reached. Thus the isolation of Siwa is complete.

The oasis is considerably below sea level and is rendered habitable by the fact that many excellent springs of water rise to the surface from the bed of porous sandstone below. The area in which these springs occur is about 50 or 60 square miles in extent, but large expanses of swamp land reach to a considerable distance and other occasional springs are found at a distance of perhaps 25 miles from the main centre of supply. The swamp is, in parts, covered with vegetation in the shape of barren date palms, tamarisks, a prickly weed called Camel-thorn, and dense masses of reeds. For the most part, however, it is bare and with a rough, broken surface, composed of salt crystals; hard as rock in the more elevated parts, soft and boggy elsewhere. This swamp land is only fertile in the vicinity of the wells where water is available to wash the soil free of salt. The lowest-lying parts are occupied by intensely salt lakes, generally very shallow but with occasional deep pot-holes, from which, probably, water rises from below.

Owing to its isolation, it is no wonder to find that the inhabitants of Siwa differ in appearance, language and customs from those of other parts of Egypt. The permanent population is about 3000, but the heavy date crop of the oasis renders it a most important trade centre and there is a great annual influx of trading caravans from all parts of the western desert.

In appearance the Siwans are very mixed. In ancient times the oasis possessed a famous oracle, enshrined in a large temple, called the temple of Jupiter Ammon. In spite of the enormous distance and the difficulty and hardship of the journey, multitudes of pious pilgrims, amongst whom was the most famous tourist of history, Alexander the Great, [who] visited the place to consult the oracle. Many of these people came from overseas, hence you find traces of Roman or Grecian blood in the present day inhabitants. In the heyday of prosperity thousands of slaves were brought from the south. These, too, have left their mark. Siwa has absorbed them all, together with hundreds of the present day travelling Bedouin, and consequently every gradation of colour and type is to be seen. The most frequent, or what may be termed the average type, is a rather undersized, thin, wiry individual, slightly darker in colouring than the Egyptian, with a narrower, longer head and more aquiline features.

Left: *On the plateau in winter, Williams second from right. The tall man to his right is renowned soldier and future desert explorer Nowell de Lancey Forth, area commander (December 1918).*
Opposite: *No. 5 Patrol under escarpment wall, Siwa Oasis.*

Siwa is the Piccadilly Circus of the western desert and, like London or any other large centre, has its own standards of morality, but it may be said to excel all other great capitals in the art and craft of race suicide. The men are excellent workmen, fairly honest in money matters as viewed by eastern standards, but in sexual matters are absolutely unmoral. Amongst the women the oldest profession has numerous representatives, but even the respectable women will not bear children. It does not pay; for a married woman may easily find herself suddenly divorced, for no particular reason, and she is left with the burden of supporting the progeny. The birth rate is, consequently, practically nil, only about two per month in the whole oasis. Since the death rate averages about 20 per month the process of self-extermination but for the continuous recruitment of outsiders should not take very long.[111]

The young children are pretty little things but they are as timid as hares and it is difficult to get a good look at them. The little girls wear a mass of ornaments, necklaces of amber beads, earrings, anklets and bracelets of silver or brass and generally a very heavy neck ring of silver, to which is suspended the virginity plate, a large thin silver disc, worked in some fancy design. The plate is usually discarded at a very early age and the ring only is worn. On one occasion I noticed a very small girl wearing a complete set of the local ornaments. I sought out the parents and offered them £5 for

---

[111] In 2006 the population of Siwa Town was just over 16,000; the population of the Oasis has now surpassed 20,000.

the ornaments. They indignantly declined to separate the child from its trinkets but offered to sell me the whole outfit, child included, for £6.

Most of the better class people can speak Arabic but amongst themselves they use their own language, utterly dissimilar from Arabic and having a curious sing-song intonation, slightly suggestive of Chinese. The religion is Mohammedan entirely, though there are probably sectarian differences. Undoubtedly, many of them hold to the Senoussi faith, which is merely a very rigid and fanatical form of Mohammedanism. Most of the people are as lax and careless in religious matters as the average English Christian.

In temperament the people seemed to me of a kindly, peaceful nature, and though there is said to be a hereditary feud between the residents of the east and those of the west of the oasis, which occasionally leads to violence and bloodshed, I noticed no evidence of it and the treatment accorded to us was invariably courteous and free from hostility. They seemed full of gratitude for their deliverance from the tyranny of the militant Senoussi and appeared to appreciate the difference between the English, who

'Some unshaven Car Patrol officers'.

'The Garrison of Siwa Camp'.

paid for everything most generously, and their former rulers, who commandeered all they wanted, without the slightest scruple.

Cultivation in the oasis is carried on entirely by means of irrigation, for there is practically no rainfall; indeed the natives look upon the very rare rain storms as disasters, from their injurious effect on the mud houses and their inopportune watering of the crops. Wells are numerous and of good quality, and the water is utilised with great skill. As a rule the output from a good well is from 100 to 400 gallons per minute but in one case I measured a flow of over 3000 gallons per minute. In appearance the wells are great circular holes, perhaps 50 feet in diameter and sometimes as much as 20 feet deep. A narrow cavity in the bottom taps the water supply and culverts at the top regulate the outflow into the various irrigation cuts. The wells are all of ancient construction and are generally lined with a masonry wall. The great pools of crystal-clear water, surrounded by shady palms, are a most beautiful and enticing sight in that sultry climate and many a refreshing dip we enjoyed in them.

Each well is utilised to the full and each has its luxuriant gardens, varying in extent according to the quantity of the water supply. Dates and olives are the chief products but pomegranates, apricots of a tiny but sweet variety, a citrus fruit, half orange and half lemon, excellent grapes and figs, and several other varieties of fruits are grown.

'Our bathing pool at Siwa'.

Siwa dates are looked upon as being the best in the world. Their cultivation is quite a science and the varieties produced are innumerable. The date palm also supplies a heart which is used as a vegetable and from which a very potent alcoholic beverage is produced. Its timber and leaves are used for every conceivable purpose, from house-building to bird-trapping.

A small amount of grain, in the shape of barley, maize, or dhourra, is grown, and also some bersim, or lucerne, for donkey fodder, donkeys being the chief means of transport in the oasis. For grain or vegetable growing the land is divided into tiny rectangles, about 6 ft. by 12 ft. in extent, each being surrounded by a little bank to retain the water. The Siwan has not the Egyptian peasant's skill in levelling, which would enable him to make his little patches, or "hods" as they are called, larger and his system is obviously wasteful where land is so precious. The cultivation is very deep, a very curious digging implement used. It is shaped like an adze but the blade is much larger and is bent with a curve, which brings it almost parallel with the handle. The handle is short and the implement is heavy. To work it effectively the body must be bent almost to the ground at each stroke. A more clumsy or dangerous looking contrivance it would be difficult to imagine but it does excellent work and a depth of at least 15 inches of soil is turned over with it. The agricultural labourers toil at the digging like galley slaves, to the accompaniment of a weird, dirge-like chant performed by the foreman.

Trade, both with the coast and with the western Arabs is considerable. Large caravans arrive lightly laden with dress goods, fancy goods, tea, sugar, tobacco and what not, and return with heavy loads of dates and olive oil. As many as 20,000 camels may be required to lift the annual date crop, which varies from 2000 to 3000 tons. The dates are carried in large, woollen sacks, two to each camel, each sack weighing about

180 lbs. No attempt is made at cleanliness, either, in the gathering, the drying or the packing of the date crops. Several large enclosures in the city form the date markets, and in these may be seen acres of dates, piled in pyramidal heaps, according to quality or variety, and drying in the sun. Donkeys bring them into the markets, myriads of flies help to dry them; refuse from the donkeys, dust, dirt, and dead flies are all tramped indiscriminately into the sacks to make weight for the trader.

The olive oil press is a curious and interesting sight, and there is quite a large number of them in the city. The olives are crushed in a circular trough cut in a huge block of stone. The crusher is a heavy, cylindrical stone about three feet in diameter and this is rolled round and round the trough by means of a pole, the end of which is passed through a hole cut in the middle of the stone and which is pivoted to an upright set in the centre of the circular trough. The tedious process of working the crusher round and round is performed by blind men who, as in all Egyptian towns, are numerous in Siwa. The resulting mass of pulp is folded tidily into strong woollen cloths and these little parcels placed one on top of another, three or four at a time, under the "monkey" of the screw press. The monkey and the screw are both cut out of olive wood and work in a frame of palm logs. The whole system is no doubt as ancient as the city but the

'A garden laid out in "hods".'

Above right: *'Crushing the olive berries'*.
Above left: *'Pressing out the oil'*.

process is quite effective and every vestige of liquid is extracted from the mash. The refuse makes good fodder for donkeys or camels.

The town of Siwa is most picturesque and well worthy of inspection. It is built around and upon a steep, rock knoll; the streets and many of the houses being, in part, cut out of the solid rock. The buildings are constructed of stone, plastered with mud, the ceilings and door, or window frames being of plastered palm logs. The fronts of the houses may be many storeys high for they are built against the steeply sloping rock behind. You mount higher and higher through the narrow, crooked streets and alleys, climbing numerous flights of steps, and at last your guide will bring you to the roof of the top-most house and you will be rewarded by a panorama that I do not think could be surpassed in beauty in any country in the world. You look down, from a height of a couple of hundred feet, upon the roofs of the city, making an irregular chess-board pattern below you; outside the city are groups of dense, dark green palm groves, with here and there splashes of the vivid green of barley or young corn; beyond the palms, on either side of the town, are placid salt lakes, which in the still air reflect the palm groves or picturesque isolated masses of rock standing beyond them. The frame of the picture is the dark irregular line of frowning cliffs to the north and the gleaming, shimmering, white sand dunes to the south. East and west your view stretches along the depression where rugged peaks, misty with distance, purple, pink, mauve or pearly grey blend with the glowing sky.

Having enjoyed the view from the summit you will probably have a look at the date markets and an olive press; then you will visit the ruins of the temple of Jupiter Ammon a mile or two away, near the village of Aghourmi. There is little left of the temple but there is enough to shew that it must have been a large and noble building. In Aghourmi, parts of well finished, ancient masonry walls may be seen, almost concealed by rough modern hovels. Aghourmi, like Siwa, is built upon a high, rock hill, and a similar glorious view can be obtained from the summit; unlike Siwa, however, Aghourmi has, in the past, been used as a fortress, and the natural defences of the precipitous rocky sides have been supplemented by a substantial wall.

Half a mile from Siwa, in another direction, is a sharp-peaked isolated hill, evidently the ancient Necropolis. The hill is literally honey-combed with tombs, some of which are mere rectangular chambers cut in the rock, while others are of a more pretentious character, being adorned with small, carved pillars or, perhaps, with coloured hieroglyphs on the walls. Plaster of Paris has been freely used in some cases, shewing that the ancient inhabitants know how to utilise the gypsum that is to be found in large quantities in parts of the surrounding desert. Bones, skulls, bits of mummified skin and tufts of hair are freely scattered about, for every tomb has been rifled. Tombs of this description are a feature of the whole oasis and may be seen in thousands far out from the town. The methods of embalming practised hereabouts were evidently cruder than those of the ancient Egyptians and the wrappings, as a rule, are merely loose cloths tied about the corpse with pieces of twine. In many cases the body, after being thus wrapped, appears to have been enclosed in a casing of plaster of Paris, for pieces of the mould have been picked up shewing the imprint of the cloth and the shape of the body.

During or after your sight-seeing you may be invited to take tea with the leading Sheikh. If you are unlucky you may be entertained indoors, where you will spend a miserable hour battling with myriads of flies. In the garden, however, all is delightful, for you recline on excellent cushions and carpets in a sort of arbour surrounded by beautiful shrubs and palms, and with a tiny, running stream of clear water nearby.

'A street in Aghourmi village'.

Opposite: *'The village of Aghourmi'.*
Left: *'The leading Sheikh and his servants.*
Tea in the garden'.

The serving of tea is something of a function and must not be entered upon lightly or hurriedly. The Sheikh will infuse the tea himself but while it is being prepared you will be served with the most delicious fruit; fresh dates, figs, sweet lemons, or grapes. Tea is served in tiny glasses but there will be at least three, and possibly five different brews, each flavoured in a different way, perhaps with mint, perhaps with lemon leaves, but always delicious. In the meantime, peddlars will come about and you may bargain for some of the local curios, a Siwan lock, a relic of the ark, which you will have noticed in all the doors in the town; or a virginity plate and ring, or perhaps some of the little baskets woven from dried palm leaves, these last are peculiar to Siwa.

Frequent visits to the oasis merely for the purpose of bathing were of course essential to the health of the troops and the attractions of Siwa in this respect, aided by the dryness and clearness of the air, and also, above all, by the absence of red-tape which characterised the outpost, made Siwa Camp a very pleasant spot both for officers and men. After a couple of months, however, the isolation and monotony began to tell and therefore matters were so arranged that the garrison could be frequently changed to Matruh or, later on to Sellum, where the work was lighter, where cars could be thoroughly overhauled and men get the benefit of a change of scene. Let us take the road again, therefore, and get to Matruh.

CHAPTER V

A BIT OF EXPLORATION

We had been in camp at Matruh for weeks. Officers and men were thoroughly camp-sick and spoiling for a journey; cars were in good trim, having been completely overhauled after a strenuous time at Siwa Camp. It was absolutely necessary to find or forge a reason for burning Government petrol.

Mount Iskander would serve as well as anything else so a few hints must be dropped into the receptive ear of the General. Mount Iskander was a most important landmark; Mount Iskander was, unfortunately, incorrectly placed upon the map; a most important but uncharted trade-route passed close to Mount Iskander; everything connected with Mount Iskander was most highly important. We did not want to go near the place; oh dear, no! We hoped we should not be asked to undertake the difficult and troublesome journey to Mount Iskander, though we were obliged to admit that a bit of a reconnaissance in that direction might serve a useful purpose. Thus did the poor old mountain begin to assume undeserved proportions in the eye of the man at the helm of affairs, and bye-and-bye we were told that in spite of our reluctance we must damn well do as we were told, and the army was no place for damn slackers, by Gad! Mount Iskander must be found and fixed on the map.

There being two patrols at Matruh at the time, my friend L.[112] in command of No. 4 L.C.P., and I decided to make a joint patrol of it, taking two cars each. It did not take us long to figure out details of loads, weights, etc. and the following day we joyfully set forth, accompanied by a Major[113], who was keen to see what the real desert was like.

---

[112] Alfred ('Mac') Lindsay.
[113] Major C.S. Jarvis, Devonshire Regiment, in command of the perimeter at Matruh camp.

The last European to climb Mount Iskander* was Alexander the Great [*Williams' footnote: "The name Iskander is the Arabic form of Alexander"]. An old legend has it that on the long journey from Alexandria to visit the oracle of Jupiter Ammon at Siwa, the monarch lost his way. He therefore climbed the hill in the hope of some guiding mark being visible from the top. While he was gazing vainly round a raven appeared from the cliff at his feet and flew as straight as an arrow towards the south west. Alexander noted the direction, descended the hill and followed the course set by the bird, leading his followers to water and safety in the little oasis of Qara, 30 miles distant[114].

Jupiter Ammon Temple

The idea of being the next to climb the hill, after such an illustrious tourist added spice to the journey.

There was a route, known to be feasible for cars, leading from Matruh to the neighbourhood of Iskander, but in order to accomplish our purpose we wished to approach the hill from a different direction and to map the known route on the return journey. We therefore set our course to cross a wide area of unexplored country. I may mention that I had already seen Iskander in the dim distance from the other side and had fixed its position approximately on the map so we had this assistance in laying off our course.

---

[114] Jebel Iskandar is to the northeast of Qara and near the northern escarpment of the Qattara Depression. The legend of the raven(s) is told by Arrian in Book III of the *Anabasis*: '...Aristobulus, whose account is generally admitted as correct, says that two ravens flew in front of the army, and that these acted as Alexander's guides. ...The place where the temple of Ammon is located is entirely surrounded by a desert of far-stretching sand, which is destitute of water.' [translation by Edward Chinnock.]

For about 120 miles the country we traversed was good and all went smoothly, but at that point we suddenly found ourselves at the brink of a cliff, several hundred feet high and reaching to the right and left of us as far as the eye could reach. At the base of the cliff was an apparently interminable stretch of rough, hummocky country, not by any means attractive for cars.

In a case of this sort you simply alter your course and follow the line of least resistance. We drove along the cliff top for miles until at last we came upon a "wadi" or water-course, which seemed to offer possibilities. A distant sight of the top of our mountain made us too impatient to do the safe thing and test the wadi on foot before taking the cars into it, so we slid them down a steep slope into the gully and followed its windings down into the mess below. We had burned our boats now, for the wadi was far too steep and soft to tackle on an up-grade.

The low country was far worse than we had anticipated. The hummocks were rough rock and the intervening flat land was composed chiefly of great slabs of gypsum, cracked and fissured and lying at every conceivable angle. Between the slabs was a soft, powdery, white material, partly sand and partly decomposed gypsum, into which the cars ploughed to the axle. Man-handling loaded cars through soft country is never very pleasant, but with clouds of this plaster-of-Paris dust combining with the acrid petrol fumes from the red-hot exhaust pipes and helping to choke the lungs of the sweating men, it was most cruel toil. The joy-riding major was having a really choice experience of the desert. Though it was nearly the worst country we had ever crossed we of course assured him that it was quite usual. He needed no encouragement, however, to do his full share of the pushing. There was no possibility of retreat so we plugged along until dusk, having accomplished about a couple of miles in two hours.

In the morning things looked better. Iskander was still nearly 30 miles distant but we studied out the lie of the country and learned the trick of getting through it. Zigzagging along ledge after ledge of gypsum; wriggling amongst the hummocks; pushing and hauling through many unavoidable soft patches, we emerged at last from the beastliness to see our hill standing up in front of us like a tower with only 20 miles of nice, undulating, gravel country intervening.

Major Claude Scudamore Jarvis, 1st Devonshire Regiment. In command of the perimeter guards at the British camp at Mersa Matruh, Jarvis joined Williams and Lindsay on their trip to Jebel Iskandar.

This we crossed before lunch and had the satisfaction of verifying the old legend for, at our approach, a couple of ravens fluttered out of a cliff at the base of the mountain. Alexander's bird had found a mate.

After lunch we climbed the hill and put in some good work with the theodolite on its wide, flat summit. At night we nailed it securely to the map by the aid of the stars.

At day-break we started for home, anticipating no difficulty for, though the same line of cliffs which we had already descended had to be penetrated on the up-grade, the route we intended to follow, a native caravan-route, or "masrab", was known to be feasible for cars and had already been once travelled. As luck would have it, however, we hit upon the wrong masrab and followed it for a mile or two before we could be certain of the error.

Now the demon of exploration entered into us. Here was a beautiful masrab, obviously important, judging by the number of camel tracks, unsullied by the foot of white man and undefiled by the wheel-mark of the desecrating Ford car. Its direction was towards Matruh, so of course we followed it. The other could wait and form an excuse for another joy-ride. Better the ills you don't know than those that somebody else has proved to be non-existent before you.

We hummed over good going, recording our route as we went and before mid-day reached the base of the steep country. The tracks of the masrab here led into a promising looking wadi, which seemed to offer every chance of an easy ascent, and between the precipitous jaws of this gully we halted for lunch and rested awhile before proceeding.

The wadi proved to be one of those wretched, enticing passes that draw one on and on by offering considerable but surmountable difficulties at intervals. For about five miles we followed its windings, sweating blood at the occasional steep pinches but finally reaching what appeared to be an almost impassable obstacle near the top. This was a very steep sand slope, up which it was obviously impossible to push or haul the loaded cars. Loads would have to be carried up and the cars hauled up empty.

We set to work on the first car, but the heat in the narrow valley was appalling and the effort was too much for all of us. Fearing heat or sunstroke for some of the party we decided to rig the sun shelters, boil the billy and rest until the day cooled off. In the meantime I ascended the remainder of the gully on foot and found, to my dismay, that the next mile was completely sand-choked and a palpable impossibility for cars. I cast round for a way out of the difficulty, searching the rocky ledges in every direction with my glasses, and finally saw what appeared to be a feasible route. This involved leaving the wadi and tackling the successive rock ledges seriatim by means of long zig-zags.

I returned to the cars, announced the result of my observations at the head of the pass and then set off with one car to try the only possible alternative. The attempt was crowned with success. After a couple of miles of horribly rough climbing, grinding gradually up and up on low gear, rushing the gallant little Ford at the fearfully steep but solid limestone slopes, from ledge to ledge, a man on each running board to nip off and shove when required, I had the satisfaction of looking down on the little group of cars and men from the top of a sheer cliff, almost above their heads. It did not take long for the reminder to join me and our troubles seemed at an end.

Bad luck was in store, however, for this part of the plateau turned out to be horribly rough. Again and again we had to collect all hands and heave the cars through soft ground. We only made about five miles before dark and camped, utterly exhausted, with the prospect of more trouble on the morrow.

The position now was a little bit disquieting. We measured our petrol and water and found we had none too much of either, the intense heat having seriously reduced the latter, and the unusual difficulties of the country having increased petrol consumption abnormally. We were still 100 miles from home and of this distance half at least was through unknown country. However, there was no sense in borrowing trouble. We got our position fairly well fixed on the map, made our plans for next day and turned in.

The men were soon snoring, but I could not sleep for fatigue and worry. There was a bright moon shining so I got up and set out on foot to find a way through the first few miles. I tried every direction in turn and at last, towards daylight, hit upon a curious, narrow causeway of solid rock winding through the shattered country. It was very rough but looked hopeful. I returned and roused the sleeping camp.

At the first peep of daylight we had a good breakfast, loaded the cars, and started with the rising sun.

My rock causeway proved friendly and, after a few miles, crawling over the boulders at an incredibly slow pace, we saw good desert in front of us. For the remainder of the day we made good pace and towards nightfall reached a well-known road which would lead us into camp.

Up to this point our journey had been most successful. We had met and overcome exceptional difficulties without any damage to the cars. We had acquired a mass of useful information, for though our new route was too difficult to be much use for cars, it was quite a good camel-route and its existence had not previously been suspected. We all felt thoroughly well pleased with ourselves and our exploits and we bowled along the road to camp discussing what particular brand of drink we would send hissing down our parched throats when we got there. The Major and I were driving together and we were positively gloating as we tried to get a tongue moist enough to lick a lip with. Suddenly, a few miles from home, my engine began to cough. Thinking it was carburettor trouble, I jammed into low gear. It wasn't carburettor trouble, but an empty petrol tank, and the low gear acting as a brake, the car stopped dead. We were driving fast, the other cars were too close, my signal was too late, and the whole four-cars telescoped in a second.

My brother officer in the second car cursed me for stopping, I cursed him for driving too close, then we walked along the line and began to laugh. Nobody was hurt and the whole twelve of us, weary, unshaven, disreputable looking figures, staggered with laughter at this most amusing spectacle. My friend's car was the worst, for the body of it was a sort of patent of his own designing, and of rather flimsy construction. Jammed before and behind, there seemed to be nothing left intact. When we dragged the mess apart, it leered at us like a disreputable drunk. One side of the frame was bent up, the other down, lamps and radiator leaned back at a ridiculous angle, the latter vomiting water. The radius-rod had a most appropriate resemblance to a corkscrew, the two front wheels eyed each other suspiciously from about a foot apart, the body was a confused jumble of tin, and sticks, blankets and haversacks.

We soon got busy, and here is where a Ford car begins to shew its real qualities. Things get bent crooked, but you can bend them straight again, and our men were experts at road repairs. The still desert air soon echoed with the clang of picks, crow-bars and hammers. Heavy stones acted as heavy hammers and heavier stones as anvils. Wire, rope, tyre-levers, and bits of the broken car were pressed into service to splint the broken wheels and springs. Chewing rum reduced the leakage in radiators from gallons to pints, and inside an hour we were moving along the road.

I rode in my friend's car, as a matter of curiosity. She moved in a series of ungraceful curves, but it was possible, with luck, to keep her on the road. Just as darkness fell we reeled into camp under the disapproving eye of the sentry, and finally crawled painfully into our own yard.

Then Bacchus reigned.

CHAPTER VI
A SAND STORM

A first class, made-in-Africa thirst is a luxury when you have the means of satisfying it: when you have not, it is the devil. Travelling in the desert, one is always more or less thirsty. The air is so intensely dry that evaporation from the body (especially in a sand-storm or when travelling fast, as in a motor car) goes on far more rapidly than one realises—to test this, place the palm of the hand against the cheek, and both will drip sweat. Large quantities of water are, therefore, necessary to keep up the proper proportion of moisture in the body. When one becomes thoroughly parched, and the throat is one-dry, and the lips crack, all the water in the world will not completely relieve the thirst: one must simply grin and bear it.

On our long car journeys we were always obliged to economise rigidly in drinking water, for it was impossible to carry it in large quantities. We soon found, however, that economy could be carried too far, and that it did not pay to get to the parched stage. Our remedy was the frequent issue of weak tea, for the drinking of tepid water only wasted the precious fluid. I need not say that washing or even shaving, was strictly taboo, except after a dewy night, when a little water could be mopped up from the car-bodies with a piece of rag.

Except at night, therefore, a feeling of thirst was the normal condition, but only once during my three years' experience in the desert, did I have an opportunity of appreciating its agonies in the acute stage, and this is how it came about.

On one of our journeys westwards from Siwa Camp, we had come within sight of the Senoussi holy city, Jarabub. By our rough and ready methods we had found its position, as shewn on the existing maps, to be seriously in error, and I stated this fact in my report of the journey. The matter was thought to be of considerable importance, and an expert from the Egyptian Survey Department was sent out to set it right. Incidentally, he was to take the opportunity of fixing basic positions in various parts of the neighbourhood, upon which fairly accurate maps could later on be built up by our comparatively rough methods.

These basic positions were to be fixed by astronomical observations, and the expert was a keen astronomer and a wonderful mathematician; as a matter of fact he was an eminent scientist of more than Egyptian reputation, with whom I shall always consider it a privilege to have been associated. Being a Doctor of Science, and a man of small stature though of a big heart, he was always known endearingly as "The Little Doctor."

I was given the job of taking the little doctor round the country, and we had already had several very interesting journeys. This journey was likely to be particularly interesting, for our objective, Jarabub, was a "terra incognita" to Europeans. There was, at the time, a treaty with the Sheikh of the Senoussi, by which we were precluded from entering the city or even from closely approaching it, and our orders were very definite upon the point, but I felt no doubt that the orders could be twisted to allow, at all events, a fairly close look at the place.

We took five cars, for we were carrying a wireless receiving set and lots of instruments, theodolite, chronometers and what-not, in addition to our ordinary loads of rations, water, petrol and arms. The weather was splendid for a start. We drove to within sight of Jarabub, halted, measured a base-line, triangulated the dome of the famous tomb, the most conspicuous point of the city, erected our half mile of copper aerial, and treated ourselves to a square feed. We spent the evening with star observations, tapped the Berlin time signals at 2 a.m. and then turned in.

In the morning we drove as close as our consciences permitted to the city and examined the approaches and the possibilities of attacking it should the necessity ever arise. The doctor was mad keen to go right in and introduce himself to the local Sheikh, but abandoned the idea when he was assured that if we escaped being shot by the Senoussi, I should most certainly be shot for flagrant disobedience of orders.

The job was now finished except for the necessity of checking the results by a second set of observations from a different direction. For this purpose I proposed to drive to another point, from which I knew a good distant sight of the city could be obtained.

Just at this stage the Egyptian spring climate took a hand and a "Khamseen" sprang up. A Khamseen is a sandstorm and is so called because the period when these storms are likely to occur (roughly from the middle of April to early in June) extends to about 50 days, "Khamseen" being Arabic for "fifty".

In the desert a khamseen is the last thing in beastliness. It may last for, anything from one to five days, and while it blows earth and sky are completely obscured by driving, blinding, cutting sand. For car travelling nothing can be more vile for you can't see bumps or holes or obstructions, nor can you see the sun to keep your direction. To reach the desired spot we had 15 or 20 miles of rough country to traverse under these conditions but by dint of carefully estimating which corner of which eye was the most painful and keeping at that, I succeeded in reaching the place.

We rigged the best shelters we could with car covers and settled down to wait for a clear sky. Our position was on high land, close to the edge of the almost precipitous slopes of the escarpment; from the base of the cliffs a great depression, swampy for the most part and containing many little salt lakes, stretched away westwards to Jarabub. Nothing of this could we see at the time, of course, for the limit of visibility was about the length of one's nose.

Waiting was far from pleasant, for the gale was strong enough to blow the mosquitoes up from the swamp lands and these settled in myriads under the lea of our shelters. Reared on scraggy Bedouin meat, the succulent blood of good, well-nourished British soldier was, I am sure, a pleasant change for the poor little things. In the meantime, the temperature was steadily rising and it became evident that we were in for the father and mother of a storm.

After two days in which we could do nothing whatever, for neither sun by day nor stars by night were visible; in which we breathed sand, scraped sand continually from eyes, nose and ears, ate sand with every meal, and all the time sweated in the sweltering heat, I found that our water supply was getting low. I told the doctor we must make for camp and refill. He was much disappointed and begged for another day. All would

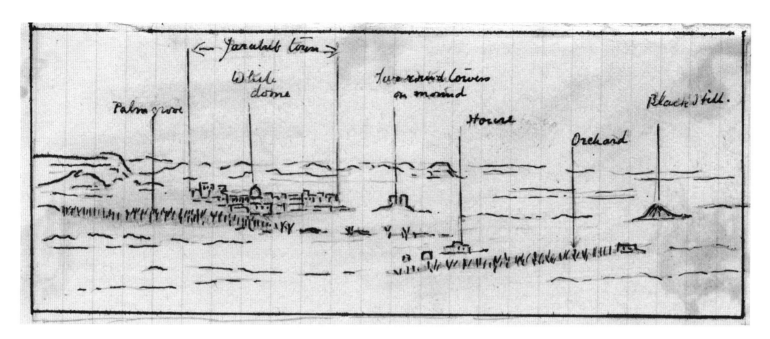

'Sketch of Jarabub by the Little Doctor'.

be well to-morrow, he thought, sun, moon and stars would shine, the air would be clear enough to see Jarabub, it was slacking to turn and run; yes, certainly, he would drink radiator water.

At the time the weather certainly did look better and the air was clearing so I yielded to his wishes. I sent a sergeant with two cars to fetch a supply of water from the camp and resolved to live on the rusty mess from the radiators until his return. I allowed 24 hours for the cars to be absent, for it was 70 miles to camp, and the track was none too good. It took nearly all our remaining water to equip the party safely for the trip.

No sooner had the sergeant started than the devil himself seemed to get into the weather. It thickened up again worse than ever and it became obvious that it would be no boy's work to find the way to camp and back. I felt fairly easy in my mind about the safety of the party for the sergeant was a man in a thousand, and would certainly not get lost. He might be delayed, however, and in case we should be obliged, eventually, to bolt for home, I determined to get some salt water from the lakes below to replenish the radiators.

The nearest lake was only a couple of miles distant, so four of us set out, carrying a rifle and an empty two gallon tin each, and a quart water bottle of drinking water to keep us going till our return.

The walk down was a joke, but we found the heat in the depression intense. Struggling through the mile or so of dense, swamp vegetation towards the lake, I found I had been mistaken in thinking that all the mosquitos in the oasis had gone visiting. After the walk the clear water of the little lake was too enticing to resist and we stripped for a bathe.

We now made the acquaintance of another pest of the oases, the camel fly. He came in his thousands to attack us as we stood naked on the bank of the lake. He has a nose like a bayonet and in a moment we were all streaming with blood. We took to the water immediately, of course, and thoroughly enjoyed the dip, but the water was as dense as pickle, and the salt tickled up the stabs of the fly in a most uncomfortable manner. After the swim we filled our water tins and started back, and here our troubles commenced. The awful heat, the dust laden air, but above all the dip in the intensely salt water brought on a terrible thirst, and I soon realised that our quart of drinking water was not half enough. The two little miles back to the cars began to look like twenty. We reached the foot of the hill without much difficulty but when we began to climb we found a rest necessary every couple of hundred yards. Our drinking water was soon exhausted; the rifles and water tins began to weigh tons, and the hill to grow steeper and steeper. At last I began to know real thirst, the dry throat, the cracking lips that seem too small for their job, the swelling tongue that grows and grows, from the size of a golf ball to a pillow and then to a balloon; the starting, bulging eyes; the throbbing head; the jumping, pumping heart.

When still a quarter of a mile from the cars all four of us were done to a turn and the air was too thick for our friends at the top of the hill to see our predicament. I told the others to wait, and I struggled on. I was seeing curious things when at last I flopped down behind the wind shelter, and could only mumble and point down the hill to indicate what was required. A mug of tea made from the beastliness out of the radiator, with a tiny dash of rum in it was soon forthcoming and by-and-by my heart stopped bumping and things got normal. The same mixture had been taken down to the others and in half an hour, all four of us were lying stark naked in the sand, streaming with sweat, but happy, for though we had all suffered, and had been within an ace of serious heat-stroke, we had made a unique discovery, no less than the recipe for nectar. Here it is. Take of plain water six parts, of oil two parts, of rust two parts, season with paint and tar, paraffin and petrol; mix and boil 50 times in a rusty tin, add tea leaves to taste and stir into the mixture one part of liquid fire or ration rum; serve boiling hot.

The following morning the weather was as bad as ever and there seemed no sense in persisting. We determined simply to wait for the completion of the 24 hours for the return of the absent cars and then, in any case, to return to camp. The time would be up at 9 o'clock.

At 5 minutes to 9 we were all ready with engines running. Three minutes later the two cars loomed up through the swirling sand, on time to the minute. At 9 o'clock we had our noses into the coolest, clearest nectar that ever came from a chlorinated water tank. Yes, nectar! I was wrong about my recipe.

The sergeant's performance was a fine one and I do not think there were many men in Africa who could have done it. He had covered 140 miles of desert in the time, in a blinding sand storm, and his only guide was a very ill-defined trail of car tracks. The trail was confused, too, by hundreds of intersecting or diverging tracks, very confusing even in clear weather but under the existing circumstances, most bewildering. He had been at fault occasionally but he kept his head and worried through. I take off my hat to him for a stout fellow.

The storm continued for another couple of days and was the worst I have known. We all enjoyed the experience, I think, but I for one don't want to repeat it. The desert is always there, however, for anyone who wishes to know the full delights of the khamseen, but—clean and refill the radiators before starting.

CHAPTER VII

STAR OBSERVATIONS AND THREE STAR OBSERVATIONS

It is a fine thing to see a man really keen on his job and there is no doubt the little doctor was such a one. The enemy might be gathering round, or worse still, the Maconochie[115] might be getting stone cold, but as long as the particular star he was observing did not do the shooting star act and drop out of the field of the telescope, he cared nothing. Precision in his observations and calculations was almost a mania with him and the fact that the position of Matruh was in doubt by some few hundred yards almost approached to a calamity in his mind.

We had just completed several very strenuous weeks' work; the days full of the incessant struggles between the Ford cars and the various desert difficulties or obstacles; the nights full of astronomical observations, during which meals or sleep became matters of no importance whatever.

I had been booking for the doctor and on account of his partial deafness, part of my work had been the difficult and delicate operation of taking the Berlin or Paris time signals at the wireless receiver, to ascertain the chronometer error. Extreme accuracy was necessary in this matter, for it was desirable to estimate the error to within 1/10th or, at all events 1/5th of a second. This job had been almost a nightly occurrence with us for weeks and I had naturally become expert at it; the doctor therefore asked me to help him with a final night's observations at Matruh to set right this little matter of its latitude and longitude.

---

[115] Tinned meat and vegetable stew.

I might explain that it is the custom for wireless time signals to be sent out from Berlin at midnight, or about 2 a.m. by our Egyptian time. Paris follows from the Eiffel Tower a few minutes afterwards but the German signals are considered to be the most accurate in the world. When far out in the desert, by keeping our wireless operator on duty for an extra hour or two, we had often also secured the German Official War intelligence hot and strong from Berlin, and had it served up with the breakfast, to be translated by the doctor. This always seemed to me a curious anomaly when we were completely out of touch with our own people, and I take this opportunity of cordially thanking the German military authorities for their courtesy.

I was pleased at the doctor's request, for mere humanity urged me to help. It seemed horrible to think of the poor devils at Matruh being perhaps half a mile out to sea without even being aware of the fact.

We dined at headquarters that evening, and the general[116] was naturally curious to know what was afoot.

"Doctor," he enquired, "please tell me just exactly what is the purpose of your work at Matruh."

"Well, General," was the reply, "I am investigating an abnormal, lateral displacement of the zenith due possibly to refraction."

"Er, er, yes certainly, quite so", stammered the general, "er—I beg your pardon, what did you say?"

The lucid explanation was repeated mildly but distinctly by the doctor but the bewildered expression of the general's face was too much for the rest of us and there was a roar of laughter, in which the latter could not help but join. The bewildered expression then transferred itself to my little friend who sat, the picture of discomfort, with his hand making a scoop behind his ear, politely and attentively awaiting a reply.

"I say, W. --", said the doctor to me afterwards, "did I say anything wrong at dinner? You see, I don't understand the military people, and the general has been very kind to me; if I said anything that was not quite the thing, I should like to apologise."

---

[116] Brig.-Gen. Ralph M. Yorke, CMG, DSO, GOC Coastal Section, Western Frontier Force. Wherever Claud Williams refers to 'the General' in this memoir and in his home letters, he is referring to General Yorke. Cf also the letter from Yorke to CHW in Appendix 4.

"Calm yourself, doctor" I explained; "it is the military people who don't understand you; it is translations the general wants, not apologies."

Having dined well we were ready for work. The doctor had prepared an elaborate programme of 12 or 14 pairs of stars which would keep us going at intervals till 2 a.m.; the time signals would then occupy us for half-an-hour or so and the evening's entertainment would conclude with one final and important observation.

A little after 8 o'clock we had everything prepared, theodolite adjusted to a nicety, level perfect; books, lights, pencils, etc. all ready to hand. A few minutes before the first star was due, small clouds began to chase each other across the sky and it blotted out at the critical moment. The first observation was spoilt.

"Malaish (never mind)" said the doctor, "we can spare some of these sets; the next will be a beauty."

We lost the next and the next after that; Gamma this and Delta the other thing, were in turn chased by scud and obliterated, until by 10 o'clock, the doctor, though persistently optimistic, was getting worn out by the strain of trying to observe the invisible. We adjourned for a "tot", for, knowing what was coming, I had provided some brandy.

We hurried back for the next observation, lost it and hurried back for another "spot"; hurried again to the theodolite, with the same result, and thereafter continued to hurry back and forth, from failure and disappointment to comfort, and back again until at midnight we had finished nothing except the bottle of Hennesey, and I had to draw another cork. We were both so dog tired that the good "Three Star" seemed to have little effect except to increase the doctor's optimism and my pessimism.

"Malaish" from the optimist after about the tenth failure. "Malaish; it is excellent practice for to-morrow night. To-morrow night Beta, Gamma, Epsilon and the rest of them will march serene and glorious across a clear and cloudless firmament. It will be superb."

"To-morrow night be damned!" from the pessimist. "To-morrow night I can't help you. I'd like to, I would indeed, but I have duties, many and very important duties, military necessiduties."

"What a pity!" he went on, "but never mind, I'll rake out some morning stars and we'll work till daylight."

"But the brandy will not last till daylight, doctor," I wailed, "leave the blessed place out at sea; The people are all Greeks, and you can't kill a Greek. Let the blighters swim ashore."

At 2 o'clock we took the time signals and staggered from the wireless instruments to the theodolite for the last crowning observation. The star we wanted was beautifully visible to the south east, so was its mate to the south west. You must understand that these two stars had to be observed at equal altitudes, and within a few minutes of one another, the one rising and the other setting.

The first we caught beautifully, and the results were booked to a tenth of a second. The telescope was switched round to the other just as a cloud began to chase the little twinkling dot. Would it catch it? The doctor glued his eye to the telescope.

"It's in the field, W--" he cried. "Two minutes will do it; damn! I can't see; yes I can; no I can't; there it is; no it isn't."

Then came the doctor's prayer.

"Oh, God" he breathed. "O God, I do not ask to see all the marvels of Thy handi-work, nor all the wonders of Thy firmament, but only one little star, one little fourth magnitude star, O God, and only for a minute."†

We reeled mournfully back and finished the brandy.

"I honestly believe," said the doctor vindictively, apropos of my expressing an overpowering desire for sleep. "I do firmly believe that some of you fellows would rather sleep, or even eat, than take an observation."

Next night was splendidly clear and the stars shone like searchlights. I postponed my imaginary duties, and the programme went like clock-work. We saved Matruh by fixing its position firmly on dry land.

The following day I drove my string of cars away into the kindly desert, far from wandering astronomers, and slept, and slept, and slept.

† Perhaps I had better admit that the doctor's prayer was a quotation.

Note The "Little Doctor" is obviously Dr. John Ball, once Director of Desert Surveys in Egypt. This chapter gives an excellent idea of Ball's unswerving devotion to his work. W.B.K.S.

Greek fishing vessels, Matruh

CHAPTER VIII

A LONG JOURNEY INTO THE WEST

A very long desert journey may often be singularly devoid of incident but, to the car traveller himself, the interest never flags, for he never knows the moment when serious and perhaps insurmountable obstacles may be met with. In spite of the most careful preparations and most complete and well-considered equipment, accidents to cars, especially in rough country, are always liable to occur, and situations may arise where only skill and resource will avert failure or even disaster.

Orders to escort a military mission on a journey 500 miles to the west, promised something out of the common, beyond the mere traversing of unexplored country, for we should be almost wholly in Italian territory and we knew their bounteous hospitality of old. We should also pay a visit to the desert chief, Sayed Idris, Sheikh el Senoussi, and would have an opportunity perhaps of seeing the wild, free, untamed Bedouin and the gentle, beautiful, gazelle-eyed Bedouiness in a proper environment. The total distance of the journey would be well over 1000 miles so a successful expedition, especially as the column would include armoured cars, would be something of an achievement. There was, naturally, keen competition amongst the men to be included in the force.

I had better say at the outset that the journey was, on the whole, a disappointment. The difficulties were not sufficient to try our powers very hard, and things ran too smoothly right through. The only difference between the Bedouin we visited and those we had previously seen was that the former were dirtier, more squalid, and uglier. The ladies in common with their more easterly sisters, seemed to suspect any white man of a desire to make an assault upon their affections. They were quite unaware that their dirt, their livestock, and their lack of personal charm formed an ample safeguard. I came to the conclusion, probably erroneous I must admit, that the wild, free, etc. etc. Bedouin man and the gentle etc. etc. Bedouin girl exist only in the imagination of the novelist.

Nevertheless, we saw some very interesting things. We saw flies hungrier and more prolific than any we had seen before; mosquitos more numerous and more venomous; bugs greyer, fatter, and yet more fleet of foot than we had believed possible. Except for the mosquitos, however, with which no fault could be found, we thought the insects badly trained and lacking the rudiments of military intelligence. The flies gathered in groups of dozens on a single grape, forming a perfect target for the leather fly-flap: the bugs were easily outwitted and kept at bay by the simple expedient of spreading a ring of insect powder, one inch thick and two inches wide, completely round the body before trying to sleep.

We made the acquaintance of the Italian military chauffeur, a marvel at his craft. When he sees a right-angled bend in front of him, especially if there is a stone wall on the far side and fairly crowded traffic, he does not slow down. He accelerates: the car takes the bend neatly on one wheel, missing the wall by a microscopic margin. A couple of native donkey carts may be overturned and possibly an odd pedestrian or two may be smashed up in the process, but the chauffeur still calmly puffs his cigarette as he proceeds on his way to the next bend. I aged about a year per minute while under his protecting care.

In respect of Italian hospitality, we had under-rated it. We were their guests from the time of our arrival at the first Italian outpost and right royally did they

Rolls-Royce Armoured Cars and Ford Light Cars of the British Military Mission about to depart to visit Sayyid Idris, July–August 1918.

entertain us. Whether in camp or in the desert, everything we could reasonably desire was always forthcoming.

The purpose of the mission, a joint undertaking of Italians and British, was to visit the Senoussi chief, Sayed Idris in his own territory. Sayed Idris had remained neutral during the recent troubles fomented by his uncle, the usurper, Sayed Achmet,[117] and it was hoped by means of personal conversations to adjust existing misunderstandings and sources of friction and to cement a firm friendship with him. The British and Italian representatives were to join forces at Benghazi, a town on the coast 400 miles west of Sellum.

Our column consisted of a couple of Rolls-Royce box cars for the accommodation of the officers of the mission, one F.I.A.T. car for the local Italian liaison officer and his attendants, two Rolls-Royce armoured cars, and ten Ford cars, four of which were carrying small portable wireless sets. Drawn up ready for departure in front of the fort at Sellum, in the dawn of a bright July morning, the force looked quite imposing, for in addition to the 15 cars of the mission, there were an extra half dozen carrying petrol to fill us up at the end of the first day's run. All cars were loaded to the utmost capacity, for 400 miles means a lot of spare tyres, petrol, oil and etcetras.

The first 150 miles was all plain sailing over a well-known route and we ran it out on the first day. The following morning we said good-bye to the returning convoy cars, left the road and entered the unknown.

Here is where we expected enjoyable trouble and did not get it though we certainly had a gruelling day and had to run a most devious course to avoid bad country. To a certain extent we were tied to the programme, and in an unsuccessful attempt to keep to time table, drove for fully ten hours, with the result that we were all done up when we halted.

On the next day, realising the impossibility of carrying the journey through in the time specified we took matters more easily and devoted a reasonable time for rest in the heat of the day. We succeeded in reaching Solluch, an outpost some 40 miles short of our and destination, Benghazi.

---

[117] Sayyid Idris and Sayyid Ahmad were, in fact, first cousins. The latter was not a usurper. He was chosen by the elders to become Grand Sanusi in 1902 because Sayyid Idris, the rightful heir to the position, was too young.

Of course we were asked to dine with the officers of the garrison and had our first taste of Italian hospitality. A long car journey is always a great strain, and feeding is naturally rather scrappy, it is therefore doubly enjoyable to sit down to a perfect meal with all the liquors in the world within call. We returned very happy to our bivouac, late in the evening, accompanied by our new-found friends, mostly arm in arm with them for the sake of balance, and trying our best to be polite in a language of which we had no knowledge.

Early the following day we reached Benghazi and were met and welcomed some miles outside the city, by leading officers and officials. On arrival at our destination, the cars were parked in a barrack square; the men were shewn to excellent quarters in the barracks and the officers were conducted to the best hotel in the town.

Benghazi is a well-built, well-laid-out city of about 20,000 inhabitants, and is the seat of the Italian Administration of the province of Cyrenaica. A small proportion of the population is Italian but the great majority of the people are a sort of polyglot

Italian column escorting the British Military Mission to Libya, July–August 1918.

Sayyid Muhammad Idris al-Sanusi.

mixture of all shapes, colours, and descriptions, such as one would expect in a Mediterranean sea port. It was here we made the acquaintance of the wonderful insects I have mentioned. It was in joy-riding about the town that I lost so many years of my life by reason of the idiosyncrasies of the Italian automobilista; but Benghazi had more to offer for our entertainment than I have mentioned. There were delicious fruits; more kinds of liquid refreshment than I thought existed; excellent sea-bathing; and above all, the sight of the trees, gardens and flowers, very luxuriant by contrast with the barrenness to which we had been so long accustomed, for I may mention that our base, Sellum, was almost completely devoid of anything of this nature.

We remained in Benghazi three days, and during our stay saw much that was of interest. We saw the process of turning the local Bedouin into soldiers. They are put through a course of instruction which, besides riding and military matters generally, includes a rudimentary education in arithmetic and in reading and writing Italian. The instruction is well carried out and the pupils are keen and intelligent. Later, we saw some of these Bedouin horse-soldiers on parade. They drilled and handled their horses excellently.

This parade included practically the whole of the garrison. Besides the Italian and Bedouin troops there were three battalions of Eritrean or Abyssinian infantry. These are wonderful fellows and are said to be fine soldiers. Their strong point is endurance and speed in marching. They move at a sort of jog-trot and we were told that they are capable of covering 40 miles a day in full marching order and of keeping it up indefinitely. Looking at their keen, dark, eager faces, wiry bodies, and long lean shanks, strangely like the legs of gazelle, it was not difficult to believe it. We ourselves saw them march fully three miles a brisk double in the heat of a midsummer mid-day. They marched past their general at the double in most perfect formation and afterwards, as if they had not already had exercise enough, they begged permission to perform a "Fantasia". They grouped themselves round the headquarters party and began the maddest and most energetic dance you can imagine, chanting and shouting the while with voices gradually growing more and more raucous with the

dust and sweat. In their picturesque uniforms of white and bright scarlet, the dancing thousands made a most barbaric picture. The fantasia lasted fully half an hour before they appeared to have had enough of it.

Curiously enough Benghazi, out-of-the-way little place though it is, possesses a small but very choice art museum. The ruined, ancient city of Cyrene is situated near the coast, about 100 miles to the east. It is said that the ubiquitous Alexander the Great established an art school at Cyrene, and certainly many very valuable specimens of marble sculpture, as well as brasses and bronzes, have been unearthed there. The finest of these, the famous Venus of Cyrene, has been removed to the Vatican, and only a plaster cast is to be seen at Benghazi, but many very beautiful statues remain.[118] A feature of the statuary is its perfect state of preservation due, perhaps, to the dryness

[118] See footnote #72.

Opposite: *Claud Williams (far left, back row) commanded the Light Cars escorting a British Military Mission to Muhammad Idris (centre front in white robes) in Benghazi, July 1918. Idris became king of Libya in 1951 and was toppled by Colonel Gaddafi in 1969. The heads of the mission were Capt. Leo Royle (front left) and Maj. Mervyn MacDonnell (front, second from right). Royle, who featured prominently in the Sanusi Campaign, was an RFC/RAF pilot. He was killed over Palestine two weeks after this photo was taken.*

of the African atmosphere, or perhaps to the fact that it has been embedded in a water deposited material of very fine texture and quite impervious to air or water.

As is the case further east traces of Roman occupation remain in the shape of deep wells or "sanyas", narrow holes cut through solid rock to a depth of sometimes over 100 feet; and also huge underground cisterns, which in many cases are capable of holding as much as a million gallons of water. The water supply of Benghazi is obtained from an enormous cavern, partly excavated and partly natural, in which, we were told, it was possible to row a boat for several hundred yards; a veritable subterranean lake.

Leaving Benghazi, and accompanied now by the Italian part of the column, numbering 15 cars, we had an easy and pleasant run of about 100 miles southwards to Zuetina, the base camp of the Senoussi chief. We had now an opportunity of criticising Italian methods and I must admit that both then on easy country, and later on, in rough country, we found them most efficient, and we could certainly learn as much as we could teach; a painful shock to self-satisfied Britons.

Zuetina is a small group of insignificant buildings encircled by barbed wire, and situated in sandhill country, half a mile from the sea. Numerous Bedouin tent villages are scattered about near it, in the hollows of the dunes, where good water lies only a few feet under the surface. Sand prevented our driving quite close to the buildings, and we set our camp on hard country at as near a point as possible. Some of Idris' officers, dressed in Bedouin fashion, and riding gaily caparisoned Arab ponies, came across the sand to meet us, bringing spare ponies, and an invitation from the Sheikh to visit him forthwith.

The next three days were occupied by the chiefs of the mission in hob-nobbing with Idris over political affairs, for in the east diplomacy is a tedious business. We others amused ourselves by bathing, sleeping, and cursing the flies.

The position amongst the Senoussi was briefly as follows: the rightful Sheikh el Senoussi was our friend, Idris. The title was claimed, however, by his uncle, Sayed Achmet, who had held the reins of power of the sect during Idris' minority. Achmet was hostile to Egypt and his claims were supported by Turkey and by Germany. Achmet's country lay to the west of Idris's, and upon his defeat at Girba, he was permitted to pass through the latter's territory; Idris, however, refused to allow his neutrality

Opposite: *The public square Benghazi, 1918.*
Left: *Italian general and Staff in Benghazi, 1918.*

to be again violated by a re-entry into his country. Thus, the two Senoussi tribes or factions, though not actually fighting, were at loggerheads, and Idris was keeping a comparatively large force in scattered outposts along his borders. For thus acting as a buffer state he was receiving money from Italy and certain trade concessions from Egypt. Achmet, on the other hand, was receiving support from our enemies in the shape of money and arms, shipped by submarine to his chief sea-port town, Misurata.

Whether Achmet desired to unsheathe the sword again and invade Egypt is a moot point, but there is no doubt that he was under constant pressure from the Turks and Germans to do so, and as [such] constantly responded to the pressure by promises of action. One can almost see the wily old chap chuckling as he made his blood-thirsty but empty promises while he patted his well-filled pockets.

Part of our programme was to visit these out-posts of Idris's and our great hope was that in doing so we might come in contact with the enemy. We set off, therefore, with a fairly strong column of both British and Italian cars, to drive to the main out-post camp, Tebilbo, situated on the coast about 50 miles south west of Zuetina. Alas! the journey was abominable. The further we went the rougher and sandier the country became and we had actually to travel 80 miles to reach Tebilbo. It was abundantly clear that to try to penetrate beyond this point was simply to invite disaster. This was the crowning disappointment and after inspecting the few hundred ill-clad, ill-fed troops in the camp there was nothing left to do but return.

Williams captioned his photo of the gallows in Ajdabia 'An important feature of the city.'

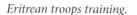
Eritrean troops training.

On our way back to Zuetina we were able to visit Idris's Capital City, Jedabia,[119] a miserable, squalid place, with a few fairly pretentious buildings, but chiefly consisting of mud huts. The most interesting feature of the place was the gallows, and the most interesting figure, the hangman.

We had now to settle down to several more days of wearisome waiting, the monotony being relieved, however, by several banquets, to which we were invited by the Sheikh. At these feasts the food consisted of many and various very delicious Bedouin dishes, served, I regret to say, on a distinctly up-to-date Italian dinner service.

In the meantime flies were multiplying apace and, fearing an outbreak of fever, I requested the chief of the mission, if possible, to cut short the diplomatic conversations and let us get away.[120]

---

[119] al-Ajdābiya.
[120] Major Mervyn Sorley MacDonnell. Leo Royle was still a captain.

Claud Williams visiting Roman ruins near Ajdabia.

At length we were able to bid good-bye to our Italian friends and start on our homeward run. This time we were not tied to programme and we made a joy-ride of it. We were still accompanied by the one F.I.A.T. car that had been with us all the time and this car was the cause of numerous stoppages, for it was well stocked with antidotes to thirst. It was only necessary to halt the column, stroll along to the Italian car, salute, shake hands and pass the time of day in bad French, to receive a pressing invitation, also in bad French. After a little drink of some nameless liqueur, mixed with iced soda water, one would again shake hands, salute, return to one's car and start again. Thus halts were frequent, but we improved vastly upon our outward route and, in spite of delays, ran the distance in three days.

We had accomplished nearly 1200 miles in all without any serious accident and almost without damage to the cars.

Speaking generally, the country we had travelled through differed little from our own; the same high plateau land, desert and uninhabited, the same narrow, semi-fertile strip of coastal belt with its flocks of fat-tailed sheep and its patches of barley cultivation, the same frequent evidences of ancient Roman or Grecian occupation in its ruins and sanyas and cisterns. The great drawback of the whole of this coastal belt is the unreliable rainfall. Now-a-days the Bedouin gets a good crop in about two seasons out of five; in the other three he is lucky if he gets back the equivalent of the seed. The climate in the distant past must have been much better, for everything points to a much larger population in Roman times than exists to-day.

The main result of our journey was to lay to rest any fears of a renewal of the Senoussi trouble. Hitherto, reports of Sayed Achmet's bellicose intentions had been constantly sent through by our agents. The fact that it paid him handsomely in good German gold and rifles, to express these intentions, whether true or false, did not, of course, enter into our agents' calculations, and even if it did, it was no part of their business to spoil their own market by discounting their news intelligence. In view of such constant and alarming reports from the west it had not been considered safe to deplete to too great an extent the protective force on the western side of Egypt. Now, however, the enormous distance between us and our potential enemies was more fully appreciated, while the heart to heart talks with our ally, Sayed Idris, had given our people a truer estimate of the possible dangers of the position and a more favourable opinion of the solidarity of the intermediate buffer state.

 At last there seemed a chance of the Car Patrols getting to some part of the world where it would not be necessary to drive 500 miles to find an enemy.

Soon the chance became reality. Two Patrols were ordered to Palestine.[121] They reached the front on Armistice Day!

---

[121] No. 2 Patrol left Sollum for Palestine 11 October 1918. It was in action against the Turks before the end of the month. No. 3 Patrol left Egypt on 15 October and arrived in Palestine the next day. No. 4 Patrol was in Syria before the Armistice.

CHAPTER IX
THE DWELLER IN THE DESERT

In the foregoing chapters I have not betrayed any great admiration for the Bedouin, and it is certainly a fact that we all looked upon then as, in the average, dirty, treacherous, lying, lazy and cruel. This estimate is hardly fair for the conditions were all against a favourable impression; at all events, it is only just to consider the conditions.

Here we were, intruders into his country; enemies with whom he had only recently been fighting; obliged by the nature of our duty to poke round his villages and into his tents in our search for hidden arms. We had deprived him even of his old flint-lock fowling-piece and had bound him down by all sorts of restrictions in his behaviour and in his trade. What wonder that we were greeted always with scowling looks and with scant courtesy.

Even under ordinary conditions the country does not lend itself to the production of a cheerful, genial people. The Bedouin never sees nature's gifts in superabundance; hunger and thirst drive him perpetually from pillar to post. He does not travel because he wants to but because he has to, for he exhausts the possibilities of each locality in turn in respect of food and water. Enough, one must admit, to make anyone peevish.

Under existing conditions the country was in a particularly bad way, and though most of the destitute people were gathered in camps in the military centres and fed, it was no uncommon thing for us to meet with half-starving people out in the desert. For a whole family to make their daily meal off a couple or three small rats does not add to their love of humanity in general and of the intruding unbeliever in particular.

The Bedouin is undoubtedly dirty. Chasing and killing the livestock on his own body is the normal occupation of the lower class villager or traveller in his idle moments, and I have more than once seen amongst our occasional prisoners, a man whose white, woollen robe appeared grey by reason of the innumerable black specks moving upon it. All the idle moments in eternity would not suffice to chase down all those moving dots.

Yet this condition is more readily understood when one considers what water means to these people. Water is the Great Good and they almost worship it. It is much too valuable to wash with. It is as difficult for us fully to realise this as it is for the Bedouin to picture a land of runny streams, where grass and vegetables grow without laborious watering, and where each man's morning bath would suffice to keep life in a desert family for a month. He has got so accustomed to a lack of water that he does not think of using it overmuch for washing even when he has it in plenty. We Patrol people have no right to throw stones, for washing was never permitted with us, when on patrol in the desert, and I leave you to imagine our condition after a week of toil in dusty weather.

As to the treacherous nature of the Bedouin, my evidence is chiefly second-hand and based on the warnings we always received from those who knew him well, to trust no Bedouin but a dead Bedouin, and to make quite certain he was in that desirable condition. Once we neglected their excellent advice when a small party raised their hands above their heads in token of surrender. We remembered it when they suddenly grubbed in the sand, produced concealed rifles and opened fire upon us. They got one of our men and should have got more before we reduced them to the condition recommended by our advisers.

I think the Bedouin lies to us as a matter of course, simply because we are foreigners and unbelievers, but nevertheless he is rather a pleasant liar and as a rule tries to tell you what he thinks you would like to hear. Sometimes, of course, this may be truth but that is not his fault. I used to notice this trait in any native guide we happened to have out with us. Sometimes being anxious and impatient to reach a certain point I would ask the guide how far it might be. "Karib" (near) would be the reply, accompanied by an indescribable gesture of the hand, indicating that it was just over the horizon, just out of sight. The short distance would be like a Scotchman's mile, interminable, and the question and answer would be repeated at intervals during the next hour or two. In the end, finding the distance to be 20 miles or so, if I cursed him he would naively remark that no one could call 20 miles anything but a short distance, in fact no distance at all. "Karib, karib ketir" (very short).

Except in one particular the Bedouin is a lazy beast, and that one particular is walking. A Bedouin will walk for ever and ever, amen, and his long, lean body seems incapable of fatigue. Give him a daily ration of water, bread and dates, and I have no doubt he would circumambulate the globe, but shew him a job of work and he would put 50 miles between himself and it rather than tackle it. To be sure he is quite ready to flog his wife or child into performing it, but himself, O! la, la, la! (no, no, no).

On one occasion as I was passing a Bedouin tent, some 12 miles from Siwa town, I was hailed by the owner, who on approaching, informed me that his daughter was ill, and begged me to see her and if possible prescribe for her. I told him that I was no doctor but would be pleased to do what I could. He uttered a hail and a small child emerged from the tent. This was the sick daughter and sick she certainly was and a very piteous spectacle. A tiny, emaciated, wizened little old woman of about 8 or 9 years, pallid and trembling with weakness. I immediately offered to take the child on my car to Siwa Town, where there was an Egyptian doctor and a hospital.

"Impossible, quite impossible", said the loving father, "who would chop my wood and draw my water and cook my food?"

The next day I drove the Egyptian doctor to the place. He was a qualified man and an excellent doctor and when he told me there was nothing wrong with the little thing but over-work and under-feeding, we simply kidnapped her and took her to Siwa, threatening the expostulating parent with a beating if he made too much noise. A week of rest in the Siwa hospital made a new creature of the little patient.

The Bedouin is cruel, too, to his animals, in fact to anything that is in his power. He overloads and underfeeds his camels and his donkeys and beats them unmercifully. His only excuse is that everything in that harsh country is underfed. You have read of the Bedouin and his well-beloved Arab steed; well, examine the sides of his horse and then see his stirrups; they are, very often, rectangular iron trays, like flat shovels, and the corner of each has a prolonged angle that cuts like a knife; this sharp corner acts as a spur. Look also at his bridle and bit; the latter is provided on one edge with great, sharp thee like a cross-cut saw. The bit normally lies flat on the tongue but when he uses his curb it turns sideways. You will see the pony's mouth streaming with blood when its rider displays his skill by drawing from a gallop to a standstill in a few yards. A right noble sight!

I turn with some relief, to the more engaging side of the Bedouin's character as it appeared to me.

First, there is his piety. At certain times of the day, as a matter of course and without ostentation, every Bedouin spreads his blanket and kneels in prayer, bowing his forehead to the dust. Even our prisoners, often men of the lowest type, would ask permission to perform this duty, and if they were bound, we used to loose them for the purpose. All through the desert adjacent to the masrabs, you may see occasional patches of ground swept clear of gravel and with an image of a mosque outlined on the ground with rows of stones. These are praying places and no Bedouin traveller will pass one without saying a prayer. Whether his prayers were sincere or not his behaviour was an impressive lesson to us.

Again, he is possessed, in some respects, of great self-restraint, a quality I often had an opportunity of admiring. All trading convoys were obliged to report at Siwa Camp to have their passes examined. If travelling towards Siwa these wayfarers would always arrive thirsty, for the camp was near their destination, and it used to please me to treat them to a really good drink of water. I never saw a Bedouin take the first cup from me and drink it himself. Even though he was almost fainting from thirst, he would invariably pass it on till it reached the farthest away of the party. Nor would any of the party drink without the short and solemn "el ham do lillah" (thanks be to God)[122]. When they had done all that politeness and piety required it was a sight to see the quarts following each other down their throats, and their paunches swelling in their lean bodies, like calves overfed on skim-milk.

A quality that is often remarked on in the Bedouin is his marvellous sense of direction but this attribute is the subject of a good deal of exaggeration. I have sometimes heard officers describe how they were guided over trackless desert for 50 miles, as straight as a line, to some spot they wished to reach. More than once I have followed

A young Siwan.

---

[122] 'Praise be to God.'

the route afterwards with compass and speedometer, and plotted it. It was certainly as straight as an extremely crooked line and it was evident that the guide had been feeling his way until he reached country that was known to him. Naturally enough, unless the compass were watched, the officer would not notice the deviations.

Nevertheless, in one case I was able to put a native to the test, with rather astonishing results. We had tracked a convoy very rapidly for over 50 miles and lost it eventually in stony country. I had kept track of the course and knew our position within a mile or two. After plotting the position I took off bearings to several well known distant points and then asked the guide in what direction these places lay; he pointed to each in turn, correctly almost to a degree. This man was exceptional, however, and it was quite common to find the native utterly bewildered the moment he got off a route that was familiar to him.

In appearance Bedouin are often very striking, generally they are tall and lean (you never see a fat Bedouin in the desert) hawk-featured, and with a high narrow brow. Their colouring is darker than that of the Egyptian. Amongst their women an attractive face is a rarity, though possibly this impression may be due to the fact that just as in Egypt or in Siwa, the young girls are kept out of sight of the unbeliever and one only sees the old, and haggard.

A very curious little community of people is found in a small, unimportant and completely isolated oasis, called Qara, about 80 miles north-east of Siwa. These people have the same origin as the Siwans whom I have briefly described elsewhere and they speak the same language, quite distinct from Arabic. They have, however, evidently been separated from the Siwans for many generations and have evolved a somewhat different type, shorter in stature, darker in colour and much less intelligent.

The little oasis is not more than 5 or 6 miles in diameter: that is these people's world and the edge of it is their horizon.

The interesting point about the people, however, is this. The oasis produces food enough to support 100 people and no more; the population must never exceed that number; whenever there is a birth there must be a death. How do they do it? I don't know, but we were led to believe that the population has never been less than 90 or more than 100 for perhaps hundreds of years.

Another interesting community inhabits the Coptic monasteries in Wadi Natrun. There are about half a dozen of these places, very strongly built, the largest of them accommodating, perhaps, a hundred monks. These people are most simple minded, hospitable folk, taking a great pride in their buildings and keeping them scrupulously clean. They display with reverence the bones, or rather the mummified remains of their patron saints, and perhaps an old picture or two, sometimes quite good, sometimes mere daubs.

One venerable father told me of their system of testing novitiates. A very reliable old monk is sent in charge of a few lads to Cairo. He takes his charges to the most notorious street he can find and turns them loose at the mercy of the painted temptresses that swarm like bees about them. Some of the boys forget their years of teaching and the monasteries know them no more. Many return to the old priest and journey back with him across the desert to a permanent home.

Both amongst the Bedouin and amongst the inhabitants of the oases, many aliens may be noticed, especially is this the case in Jarabub, where there is a considerable slave population. There you will find people from the Soudan, from Timbuctoo, from the Gold Coast, from almost anywhere in Africa. In Siwa you may find a few Greek or Egyptian traders carrying on very profitable businesses. Doubtless many of the aliens are fugitives from justice—or injustice. The desert is wide and offers a secure haven for such. I often think of going back there myself.

Caravan starting with dates from Siwa.

CHAPTER X
THE RIOTS IN EGYPT

This little collection of sketches would be incomplete without some mention of the disturbances which occurred in Egypt in the early part of 1919, for the light car patrols were mixed up, to a certain extent, in the trouble.

I was in Cairo at the outbreak of rioting and happened to pass the little mob of students who were the initiators, just before they commenced window breaking. I did not know anything unusual was afoot, which was perhaps unfortunate for I am sure the presence of one British officer, armed with a cane, would have been sufficient to prevent the beginnings of trouble.

The lads got busy with the windows of one of the main thoroughfares, and finding excitement and pleasure in the exercise of smashing, naturally proceeded with the sport. They were not interfered with and in a short time the toll of damage ran into thousands of pounds.

This was the beginning, and in a few days Egypt was ablaze. British officers had been murdered when en route from Luxor to Cairo. Communication by rail with Alexandria, with Ismailia and with the Fayoum was interrupted, and there was widespread destruction of Government property, with much burning and slaying. All military leave was stopped.

Some explanation of the causes which led up to the outbreak may be of interest for the storm was long a-brewing and if the students' window-breaking experiments had been nipped in the bud the ferment would, no doubt, have broken out in some other direction.

The mainspring of Egyptian unrest is undoubtedly the spirit of Nationalism, a very strong element in the educated or cultured class; but this class is a very small proportion of the total population, and though repeated attempts had previously been made to stir the people into open rebellion, such attempts had failed for the simple reason that the great mass of the people were happy and contented under British rule.

Well over 90% of the Egyptian people consist of the Fellahin, or agriculturists. Nearly all of these are illiterate and so long as they could get ample water, a market for their crops and freedom from acute oppression, they could not but look upon the British control of affairs as a vast improvement upon their old-time conditions under their own rulers.

As the war went on, however, the Fellahin were furnished with grievance after grievance, which rightly or wrongly they attributed to the British. When the first few months of peace failed to remove these grievances, the mass of the ignorant Fellahin arrived at the ideal state of discontent for the purposes of the agitator and sedition-monger.[123]

I will try to describe some of the more burning grievances without vouching for the correctness of my statements, for the information was gained from scattered conversations with various Egyptians whose knowledge of the subject may have been very superficial.

First, there was the forced recruiting for the Egyptian Labour Corps. In the later years of the war it had been found necessary to conscript this labour, and through a fair wage was paid to the men and every reasonable care taken for their comfort, a way was unfortunately left open for all sorts of abuses in the actual incidence of the compulsion. The selection of the men was left to the local village magnates, or Omdehs, who greedily seized the opportunity of resuming their former "Backsheesh" methods. Incidents of the David and Uriah type also were not uncommon; and though the quota required from each village was doubtless scrupulously fair there was room for gross injustice in the selection of the individuals.

---

[123] Egypt was occupied by the British in 1882; martial law was imposed November 1914, when Turkey sided with Germany in the war. Before the war the rural population, used to being oppressed whoever was in power, had been relatively indifferent to the fact that control of the country was now in British hands. As the war went on forced recruitment into the Egyptian Labour Corps was a cause of wide-spread complaint. By contrast, according to British Intelligence, the urban population of Egypt generally disliked the British before and after the outbreak of war.

A Cairo tram guarded by soldiers, spring 1919.

Again, the authorities were obliged to exercise the power of commandeer, both in animals and in foodstuff. The prices paid for these things were generous to the verge of extravagance, but here again the Omdeh and his satellites had a glorious chance of feathering their own nests. The immediate result of the high commandeer prices and the depletion of the local supplies was to send local values soaring up to a still greater height. The Omdeh could commandeer other people's grain at the Army price and sell his own at the inflated local price, or even commandeer more than necessary and sell the surplus.

All this was nobody's fault in particular. The Army Authorities could not spare the men to watch every part of the country and they naturally trusted the local authorities, but Backsheesh and the Egyptian are two heels of the same mule, and the result was inevitable.

Another cause was the mere operation of the law of supply and demand. Camels, for instance, were commandeered at, perhaps, £20 a piece, the local value at the time being only about £12. The resulting scarcity, however, sent the latter up to over £30 and at the close of the war camels sold at public auctions by the military would naturally fetch this price. A Fellah might then buy back, perhaps, his own camel several years older and much the worse for wear, for half as much again as he had received for him.

Lastly, there were the railway employees, State servants. These men were granted a cost-of-living bonus after much agitation, but when the time came for each man's automatic increase of pay due for long service, he was given his rise in wages, minus the bonus. Such an injustice seems incredible and there is doubtless another side to the question, but whether or no, the side I have described was the view of the lower classes in Egypt, and to that injustice may be attributed the strike of railway servants, a circumstance which contributed largely to the gravity of the situation; for these men, when they went on strike, took their tools with them. Thus, they had the necessary experience and the necessary implements for the uprooting of lines, which was soon a feature of the disturbance.

The circumstances which set ablaze the mass of inflammable material was the arrest and deportation of four prominent Egyptians; Zaghloul Pasha and three others. These men had been prominent in demanding representation for Egypt at the Peace

Conference, but whatever their office, they were suppressed and spirited out of the country, as far as I know, without public trial. Zaghloul was immediately elevated to the status of a martyr and became a popular idol.

It is quite unnecessary to discuss the merits of the case. The foregoing are some of the causes of the unrest as they appeared to the man in the street, and one cannot avoid sympathising with the Egyptian view. He had the chagrin of seeing most of the profitable billets in Government service going to the foreigner and intruder. He had also the maddening experience of hearing his people referred to as dogs or carrion by many of the said intruders.

It seems almost incredible that otherwise sensible English people should make the error of expressing, almost in public, their supreme contempt for the Egyptian people, especially at a time of tension, yet I myself heard the opinion offered both by English civilians and by officers, within the hearing of a dozen or more educated Egyptians, that Allenby should machine gun the mob and shoot them down like the dogs they were. This was with reference to the mob taking part in the perfectly peaceful and good humoured demonstration I am about to describe. One can imagine the intensity of the hatred generated in a patriotic mind by hearing such remarks. Not all the tact and generosity shewn by the splendid English gentlemen holding responsible positions in the Egyptian service could counteract the bitterness caused by such grossly insulting epithets.

The release of the four exiles by Lord Allenby gave rise to a unique spectacle. Cairo was turned from a city of gloom and riot into a city of joy. Practically the whole population was on the streets. All the accessible trees were stripped of their branches to furnish banners for the excited populace to wave. An immense procession was formed which snaked through the city miles in length, and without ceasing through two complete days. The procession was entirely good-humoured, and a European child of ten could have entered the stream of people at any point in perfect safety. Every here and there at irregular intervals, local orators were addressing the crowds from the roofs of Arabiehs[124] or from donkey carts or from anything else available. A strange and

---

[124] Wheeled vehicles, here probably motorized.

interesting sight was the sumptuous carriages of the wealthy jostled amongst the foot passengers, hand carts or donkey carts; from the carriages, in many cases, the ladies of Cairo, clad in the inevitable black, and wearing the white, gauzy yashmak,[125] would harangue the crowd, for all the world like English Suffragettes. They spoke well and forcibly did these women who, we had all supposed, were mere down-trodden, useless dolls of the Harem.

Seditious cries were the order of the day but delivered with smiles and great good-humour. "Egypt for Egyptians! Down with the English!" from the orators and echoed by hundreds of thousands of people who did not even know the meaning of the words.

Unfortunately, on the concluding evening of this colossal demonstration there was shooting in the streets and the ugly side of the business became once more apparent. In Cairo there are an immense number of vagabonds, thieves, murderers, and such like outcasts. This element comes to the top like scum on a pot whenever there is disturbing heat; They seize the favourable opportunity for loot, and a little blood-shed matters nothing to them. I think in Cairo itself most of the sinister work must be ascribed to this element, for the people as a whole are a docile and rather genial crowd. In the provinces the power for evil of the malefactor element would be supplemented by the profound ignorance of the peasantry.

As is usually the case in times of riot and agitation, a favourite pastime of the rioters was massacring the Armenians, of whom there are quite a number in Egypt. I came to understand the reason for the peculiar fascination of this sport. The Armenians are the money lenders of Egypt. They occupy the same relation to the native population as do the Jews in Europe and they are unscrupulous and pitiless creditors. When law and order are at a discount, what simpler method can be imagined of settling one's debts than by slitting the throats of one's creditors?

Ford cars were of great use, both in the large cities and in the provinces. There were no organised patrols in Cairo itself and I was given instructions to get several into running order out of the wreck of a number of ambulance cars from Palestine. The Citadel Garrison was drawn on for officers and men and before daylight on the same

---

[125] Turkish for 'face-veil'.

night we had a brand new patrol of six very staggery old cars on the road, armed with Vickers guns. They were in the thick of a mess before breakfast and I fear many native families have reason to regret their formation.

Patrolling the city was one of our duties, but with the exception of bedroom crockery (not empty) from upstairs windows, we had no actual firing.

One of the old patrols was shut up in the Fayoum with the small garrison there. They were for a time completely isolated, but with some of our ambulance cars we succeeded in driving across the open desert from Cairo, and getting in touch with them. The cars were also useful in getting into communication with our former quarters at Wadi Natrun and with other points along the west side of the delta lands.

An amusing incident occurred on a journey of this nature. We had been sent via the open desert to a place called Abu Ghalib, about 20 miles north of Cairo, to rescue a certain medical man who was isolated at his residence there and whose position was far from safe. I was anxious to know beforehand whether he was in safety or not, and also to find out which was his house. Just before reaching the place I noticed a small Bedouin youth herding a few sheep across the desert so I bore down upon him to get the information. He was full of terror, however, and took to his heels. There was nothing for it but to head [off] the poor little beggar, and the spectacle of a small, very naked little darky, running and doubling like a hare, with three cars full of soldiers cutting figures of eight all round him, would have drawn full houses at a cinema theatre.

The little chap kept going for quite a while but at last fell down exhausted. I picked him up and tried to soothe him sufficiently to answer questions but it was no use; he was too terrified, so we let him go and he sailed away over the sand like a scalded cat. We found that the doctor had left his house for Cairo by boating up a canal. He reached the city safely before we arrived back.

Quite soon the acute stage of the disturbance passed away; leave was again available and eventually I was able to bid good-bye to Cairo, to Egypt, to the beloved Ford Cars and to the great expanse of grey desolation which had been my home for over three years; the sandy, gravelly, waterless waste; the Desert.

Demonstrations in Cairo, March 1919.

CHAPTER XI
THE WORK OF
THE CAR PATROLS

One of the questions of the future is going to be "Daddy, what did you do in the great war?" It may well be asked with reference to the Light Car Patrols, for few people outside of Egypt and Palestine even knew of their existence, and they never figured at all in the public eye.

What did the Car Patrols do in the great war? Why were they kept continuously on the western desert of Egypt? Why did not their personnel get themselves transferred to other units and shift to a more exciting sphere of action?

These questions are easily answered, and I will take the last first. We stuck to our job because we damn well had to. Again and again many of us tried for a shift but without success, and to understand this it is necessary to realise the nature of the work. A fleet of cars in the western desert is not unlike a fleet of ships at sea. If you substitute a grocer or a farmer or a politician for an experienced navigator, in the case of the ships, you are asking for trouble. Thus, also, navigators for the cars were not made in a day, nor yet in six months. So much for patrol leaders, but it took months to train any officer or man to a stage of reasonable efficiency in patrol work. He had to be something of many things; soldier, chauffeur, mechanic, blood-hound, surveyor, signaller, astronomer, and a few hundred other trades and callings. On most of our journeys only 2 or 3 men could ride in each car, in case of accident; therefore, gunners must be able to drive and drivers to gun, in fact all jobs must be interchangeable. Each N.C.O. and private must be thoroughly reliable, for it might at any moment become necessary to split a car force into little groups of two or three or even of single cars, each group acting independently. The senior soldiers in a car cannot refer to a leader who is travelling at 20 miles an hour in a contrary direction. To put the matter in a nutshell, the officers and men of the patrols had developed into highly skilled and versatile specialists, who could not be displaced or replaced without spoiling the efficiency of the units for a considerable time.

Furthermore, it was the misfortune of several of the Patrol leaders to have acquired too comprehensive a knowledge of the western desert. The very best and most intelligent native guide knows only a comparatively small area of the country; his journeys have been confined to well marked routes and he knows little or nothing of the vast intermediate spaces, especially as regards suitability for motor traffic. Here was a country as large as England; here were men who could take Ford cars to almost any part of it; who knew which areas were suitable and which were unsuitable for light cars or for armoured cars. Obviously, they must make the best of it and mind their own business for it was not difficult to see in what direction their duty lay.

Why were we kept in the Western Desert? Well, as a matter of fact, we were not *all* kept on the western front, for three of the original patrols were sent to Palestine early in 1917 and did splendid service there.[126] We others used to hear of their doings and were proud of them. We worked and strove and trained for the day when we too should get our chance of honour and glory. Though all our training was modified to suit the conditions of the western desert, we nevertheless felt sure we could give a good account of ourselves under other conditions and we bitterly resented the fact that opportunity was denied us.

It was these conditions, peculiar to the Western front that tied us to it, for they were ideal for Light Car operations. We had evolved a system by which we could work cars like cavalry. We could bunch several patrols together and handle them as one unit under one leader. A few waves of the signalling flag would split the force into sections, advance them, retire them, wheel them, shift them from position to position, and bring them, in short, into almost as great a variety of formations as can be done with a squadron of cavalry. On that fine open country such a force, able to strike, and to strike hard and often at a distance of hundreds of miles; self-contained for a radius

---

[126] Williams is presumably referring to (i) the Australian patrol, (ii) some members of Lt Harding's No. 4 Patrol, and (iii) part of Lt Lindsay's original No. 1 Patrol.

of several hundred miles and for weeks at a time, formed the best possible protection against further trouble with the western Arabs.

The Senoussi had been ousted from Siwa by cars and had a wholesome respect for them whether armoured or not. Thus, it came about that while nearly all the armoured cars were sent to the east, and while the various garrisons on the west side were reduced to a minimum, we were kept on for month after month, eating our hearts out, with only the doubtful satisfaction of knowing that our presence enabled many times our manpower to be released for service elsewhere.

We worked hard to get all our knowledge of the desert into map form so that it might be used by anyone, and so that our own services could be dispensed with; we charted every car route, camel route, pass, lake or water supply, and our maps were almost as complete as we could make them when Armistice Day arrived. Gone forever were our chances of putting our beloved car patrols to the test, and bitter, bitter was the disappointment, for though many of our number had seen hot fighting in other units, all were equally proud of the patrols and were equally eager to prove their value as a fighting force.

Now, what did the Patrols do to justify their existence?

From the foregoing pages, it might appear that our chief end in life was to burn petrol in joy riding. This was not so, for no car journey was ever undertaken without a reasonably good object.

The main purpose of the patrols was to be prepared to resist any hostile incursion by the Senoussi, to detect and prevent any illicit traffic or communication with them, and incidentally to act as eyes and shield for our own outposts; the subsidiary purpose was to acquire and to chart topographical information as a present or future aid in the accomplishment of the main object.

Well, we prepared, to the best of our ability, for finding and fighting the enemy if he should invade the country and it is highly probable that our presence there deterred him from making the attempt. Looking at the relative cost of forcing the Senoussi out of Baharia by means of railway blockhouses, infantry and camel corps; and of expelling the same people from Siwa by means of cars; looking at the enormous expense of using any other type of force than a car force in a country such as

I have described, it must be clear that the mere prevention of trouble justified our existence over and over again.

The prevention of illicit traffic between Egypt and the western Arabs, though it entailed a great deal of wearisome work, provided us also with much amusement and excitement. Travelling day after day and week after week, over the same monotonous stretch of desert, with our noses to the ground, as it were, did certainly lack charm but every now and then the sight of fresh tracks of men and camels would reward our industry. In a moment cars and men would collect like flies round a honey pot. Perhaps we would have a native tracker with us, perhaps not. In any case the age of the tracks would be learnedly discussed. Were they days old or only hours old? A scrap of camel dung would be pounced upon as if it were a precious stone, for to the amateur sleuth this clue gave up its information much more readily than impalpable marks in the sand. But the contraband traffic was very profitable to the smuggler and he grew cunning. Camel dung several days old would be carried and strewn from the convoy as they crossed the tracks of our main patrol routes. Sometimes a large convoy would be split into parts. Of 50 camels, forty would travel in one block, five would travel parallel with the main lot and a mile or two to the right, the remainder a mile or two to the left. The Patrol on duty would be drawn away on the tracks of one or other of the smaller lots and probably make a capture, but in the meantime the rest would get through to Italian territory or to the populated coastal areas and safety. Small convoys would dodge and double on stony ground to delay our pursuit and would often succeed in tricking us and escaping.

On the other hand, we also grew cunning and were not so easily eluded. We would spread our cars out fan fashion. The leader's car would follow the tracks with a flag hoisted; if he lost them, down would go the flag and the others would begin to search as they drove straight ahead. Presently one or other of the flanking cars would hoist its flag, the leader's car would swing over and again take up the running and the original formation would be resumed. Thus, no time would be lost and I have often seen an exhilarating chase of 30 or 40 miles with hardly a check. With luck we would eventually come up with our quarry, perhaps still travelling, perhaps camped in a hollow thinking themselves safe. As a rule they would surrender quietly enough, but occasionally they would put up a fight and on one occasion succeeded in getting a couple of bullets into a driver, and half a dozen more into his car, before the Lewis gun, which had already been sent to a flank, got to work and reduced them to a more peaceable frame of mind and, incidentally, to a more suitable condition for burial.

If a capture were made, pigeons would be sent off with information as to their numbers and the route by which we proposed to escort them into camp. Spare cars and men would be sent out to meet them and the escort would return to its beat. In the meantime, the remainder of the Patrol would be off north, south, east or west, hunting for possible tracks running parallel to those we had followed.

So it went on. Often we were out for a week or 10 days without making a capture; sometimes we would gather in half-a-dozen convoys in as many days. Sometimes a capture would be made 3 or 4 days camel march from home and the escorting of the convoy into camp would be a tedious and troublesome job. Sometimes it might be still further afield and our duty then was to shoot the camels, dump their loads and carry the prisoners into camp. I can give you latitude and longitude of several tons of sugar, tea and tobacco still waiting in the sand for an owner.

On many occasions we were warned to intercept more important people than mere traders. One, for instance, whom I will call Mohammed Ali (Anglicée John Smith) was to leave Egypt on a certain date with information for the enemy. Our orders were to stop him *at all costs*. He might cross our line anywhere so we had to watch, not only the 200 miles between the coast and Siwa, but also the edge of the sand dunes for a hundred miles east and west of Siwa, for he might enter or leave the dune country at any point. We had, consequently, fully 400 miles to patrol and much of it was difficult country.

Three solid weeks we were at it, with all available cars, and to add to the enjoyment a most pernicious heat wave chose to pass at the same time as Mohammed. Three weeks are associated in the minds of readers of light literature, with occupations of a sort other than 21 days' looking for a needle in a dozen haystacks. We were well cursed for missing the blighter. What were the Patrols for? we were asked, and was one lousy

Arab a match for 18 Ford Cars? Later on it transpired that Mohammed Ali was a myth and the whole thing the outcome of false intelligence.

The most satisfactory part of our occupation, from my own point of view, was the exploration and cartography, for it provided a source of interest to every journey and was of more than passing value to Egypt. But for the war and the consequent establishment of the car Patrols the greater part of the Western Desert must have remained a blank for generations, for the country is well nigh valueless and could never justify the expense of proper surveying. The opportunity was unique and it enabled a valuable return to be secured for thousands of gallons of petrol that would otherwise have been burned, with only negative results. Though, from the very nature of the country the sum total of results is meagre, the old feeling of doubt and mystery has been dispelled, and any menace from the western Arabs can never, in the future, assume the importance it has had in the past.

In this branch of the work, too, there was the satisfaction of knowing that the whole thing was our own invention, for no one had ever thought of using cars for such a purpose before. Most of our work was done off our own bat, in the course of ordinary patrol duties and without specific instructions from anyone, the resulting patrol maps were, therefore, our own in every sense of the term.

At first our car-traverses were rough-and-ready, and slowly carried out, but later on we evolved more correct methods; we learned to check our compass by the North Star; to find our speedometer error to a minute fraction and to carry traverses through with fair accuracy almost as quickly as the cars could travel. We spider-webbed the whole country with these traverses and though each was in itself necessarily only approximate, one controlled and checked another until, helped by occasional theodolite observations, they form a great part of the present "Survey of Egypt" maps of the north-western desert. The gradual filling up of the blank spaces was, I am sure, a source of pleasure and interest to the humblest private, in spite of the extra and arduous work it often entailed.

It may be asked whether there was any danger to life and limb in the work. Well, for inexperienced men, yes, certainly there was very great danger; for experts there was practically none. Had we been asked, or ordered, to do in the early days what we had to do later on, I have no doubt danger and disaster would sometimes have been the result. It is the easiest thing in the world to get "rattled" in the desert. There are few, if any, landmarks to help you to get right again when once you have gone astray; you are utterly dependent on your cars and on what can be carried on them, and the situation, if you don't know where you are, and some of the cars break down, is most gloomy. To a new hand these things may easily occur and a horrible death from thirst stares him in the face, for he can never be found unless there are some experts handy to find him.

As a matter of fact, the possibilities in case of trouble were so gruesome that we were always very careful about sending doubtful men in charge of cars, and a new officer did many a trip as a looker on before taking a job in hand himself.

We used to provide against the results of breakdowns by always taking cars enough to bring the party home if we should lose one, but in this respect the Ford car stood us in good stead, and though we frequently had to drag one ignominiously home at the end of a tow rope, it was only very rarely that we had to leave a car out in the desert. The Ford has as many lives as a cat, and I am sure the sight of some of our Patrol cars after makeshift road repairing, would have given the average motor mechanic a blue fit. Imagine, for instance, the engine swaying in a cradle of twisted wire because the attachments for fastening it to the frame had given way; imagine leaky radiators plugged with chewing gum, broken wheels spliced with bits of petrol cases, a crank case with a couple of bullets rattling round like dice in the inside and holes plugged with corks. No, you can't kill a Ford car!

Thus, with experience as a guide and helper and with the right type of car, the perils of the desert may be said to be non-existent.

The rank and file of the Light Car Patrols were a good lot of fellows, indeed, for my part, I was given the pick of my regiment. The work was monotonous and strenuous, there was little or no comfort while on duty, and the base camps were isolated, far from civilization and lacking in most of life's amenities, yet the men stuck to their jobs, taking the rough with the smooth, and their only serious grouse was at being kept from the more active fronts, and at the Armistice for coming just at the time when their hopes of a move were about to be realized. They are all no doubt at their various homes now, and busy at the old prosaic occupations. I wonder how many are like the writer and pine sometimes for the great open spaces, the glare of the heat, the sweat, the toil, the thirst and the stink of petrol, for the busy days; the peace and beauty of the calm starry nights?

"Daddy; what did the Light Car Patrol do in the Great War?"

"Little enough, my son, little enough, but like most of the rest, they did what they were told to do, and did it as well as they could."

Who can say more?

CHAPTER XII
CONCLUSION
[WRITTEN BY CLAUD WILLIAMS IN THE 1960s]

The foregoing chapters were written in 1920 and on the whole I think they present a fairly true picture of conditions ruling during the First World War. I am adding a concluding chapter nearly half a century later for two reasons: first, that while I wrote rather scathingly and perhaps unfairly of the Bedouin I said little of the inhabitants of Egypt proper, the fertile Nile Delta. In view of the drastic change in political relations I wish to record my impressions of the Egyptians as I knew them. Secondly, I want to refer to some of the work of the Light Car Patrols which only became significant long after they were disbanded; without concluding remarks their story is incomplete.

During my three years in Egypt I came in contact with nearly all social grades from the humble Fellaheen to the high-class intelligentsia. I met with many surprises; gratitude for small services, generosity where one would expect greed, courage in place of fear and honesty instead of guile. A few actual personal experiences may be worth repeating.

On my first visit to Cairo in 1916 I employed a guide, an oldish man, M'Barak Hassan by name. After a full day with him I paid him off and watched him walk away down the street until he stopped to talk with a policeman. A few minutes later I was told that a small boy wanted to speak to me and had given his name as "Ali Hassan". His story was that his father had been put in prison for molesting tourists near Shepheard's Hotel and would be glad of help. It appeared that the policeman had demanded "Baksheesh" and, regarding Hassan's refusal as a criminal offence had arrested him. I went with Ali to the prison, got an interview with the Chief of Police, proved the charge false and watched a grinning M'Barak brought to the office. Before leaving I asked the Chief what would happen to the rogue who had jailed my guide: "He shall be thrashed" was the reply and within moments the poor devil was held face down on the floor and the first stroke of the murderous "kourbash" administered. I called a halt at that and the surprised victim got to his feet and disappeared. On reaching the street old Hassan expressed his thanks thus: "I guide you anywhere you wish for nothing and when I am gone Ali will guide you anywhere for nothing. It is not only because you got me out of prison but because you had that policeman thrashed". One stroke was a mild dose but enough to satisfy everyone, especially the rogue.

M'Barak was as good as his word and better. On my duty visits to Cairo I never got him to accept a piaster more than out-of-pocket expenses and when I was given "Luxor leave" I was approached by a fine looking young Egyptian who told me that his uncle had written asking him to get in touch with me and attend to all my needs. For a week I was treated like Royalty; a superb riding camel for distant sights and a wonderful little donkey for close at hand, above all a keen intelligent guide who knew his subject from A to Z, introductions into the homes of several local farmers and an insight into their way of life. My little service was repaid ten times over.

Another rather similar case came after the Armistice in 1918. I had paid a visit to a friend and after a chat invited him to dine with me at Shepheard's. He agreed and proceeded to hail a gharry.[127] On arrival at the Hotel the driver flatly refused even to name a fare, with the following explanation. "Last week I win big money on the horse you ride, so I drive you anywhere in Cairo for nothing and your friend also". My guest was a sheep-farmer in New Zealand who owned horses, raced them, rode them himself and followed the sport in Cairo.

A man I came to admire and to respect was the young Egyptian doctor at Siwa referred to in a previous chapter, who told me that he would not leave his Siwan patients until a substitute was appointed by the Government which might be months or years in the future. Since his qualifications were sufficient assurance of a lucrative career in any large city his attitude meant genuine self-sacrifice.

---

[127] Horse-drawn carriage.

To ascend the social gradient a stage further: During the course of the riots described earlier I was summoned to Headquarters and asked whether cars could be driven across the open desert to Fayoum, sixty-five miles south of Cairo. I had not been over that particular area but I assured them that there would be no difficulty. It appeared that [an] Egyptian, resident at the time, was in danger of his life at the hands of advancing rioters. I was ordered to rescue him without delay. Taking three cars and a dozen men I drove almost a bee-line to the oasis. A gap in the low cliff was easily found and cars driven down a sandy slope to the edge of the fertile plain. It was easy also to spot our objective, a fine house among cottages. Taking half our force we walked to the house where we were received by the astonished owner. When I asked him to get ready to leave as quickly as possible he thanked me for the offer of a lift to safety but refused quite definitely to accept it. He knew all about the approaching rioters, he said, but he would not leave his people; he would not go. This put me in a quandary since I had no authority to use force. I tried argument without success though the suggestion that his people would be safer without his presence seemed to shake him, but he countered it by saying that they were free to go, that some had already gone. I then explained that my orders were explicit and that if he persisted in his attitude I should be obliged to put him under arrest. This settled the matter; we walked to the cars, drove up the slope and halted to let the radiators cool. Not a word had been spoken until he and I walked to the edge of the escarpment. Looking down on his abandoned property he said, "I am glad, Captain, that you threatened to arrest me; if you had not done so I should surely be a dead man before morning". I was, and I am, quite sure that he spoke with sincerity. The outcome for me was an invitation to dine with him at his palatial Cairo residence and a glimpse of millionaire luxury of the Middle East.

These few instances were selected from many because the spoken words remain fresh in my memory; they serve to confirm my general impression that the Egyptians were at that time a kindly, genial people with little or no animosity towards the British; then why the reversal? The spirit of Nationalism, world-wide in recent years, is undoubtedly the main cause but is it not probable that the high-class, cultured leaders got tired of hearing their people alluded to as "Wogs" or "Dogs" and themselves relegated to a level of permanent inferiority in their own country?

In speaking of the Light Car Patrols I am obliged to confine myself to No. 5 Patrol of which I had the command and the task of sending periodical reports to Cairo. But there were always two Patrols allotted to the Siwa area on account of its isolation and lack of amenities. Men could not endure more than a couple of months of Siwa Camp without detriment to health so the location of each Patrol would alternate between Sellum and Siwa. Much of the exploration and mapping of the rough country included in the oasis was done by my opposite number, Captain Lindsay, O.C. No. 4 Patrol.

Before leaving Egypt it was suggested by the General Staff that I should put all I knew of the North-Western Desert on paper and offer it to the War Office in London. This I did and submitted it to the proper authority in the form of a Report. I fully expected it to find its way into a pigeonhole and remain there indefinitely; but it was published all complete with our patrol maps and a couple of copies sent to me in New Zealand. I had included anything that might have future military value: caravan routes, water supplies, notes on Car Equipment, etc. etc. Two items in this last category, the sun-compass and the water-economiser came immediately into use as standard for motor travelling in the desert. The genesis of the former was a nail in a board but it was soon elaborated into a useful surveying accessory as described in the Report. Major Bagnold adopted it for his desert explorations with the addition of further refinements adding greatly to its accuracy and the convenience of its use. Even as we knew it, however, nearly 4,000 miles of traverses were plotted and mapped with the speedometer and the aid of a never failing sun. Since the compass was always used and since our total mileage amounted to nearly 70,000 miles the value of the device can be imagined.

Concerning the topographical efforts of No. 5 Patrol there were no developments until the outbreak of World War II. Reading the description of General Wavell's attack on Benghazi it appeared that he had followed the desert route pioneered and mapped by us twenty years earlier. Later on our investigation of the Qattara Depression may have been of use in the defence of Montgomery's southern flank. In both cases aerial photography had probably superseded our laborious groundwork for actual survey by this means had come into use before I said goodbye to the desert in 1918. Planes had been sent to Siwa Camp with orders to photograph the whole area of the oasis. I was pleased when the Lieutenant in charge asked me to accompany him on a preliminary flight with a view to pointing out emergency landing grounds, but rather disgusted to recognise in an hour tracks that had taken weeks of sweaty toil for our cars to imprint on the ground.

The first intimation that we had contributed anything of real value was in 1945 when I read "Long Range Desert Group" by Kennedy Shaw who wrote very kindly of the L.C.P. work in general and of the War Office publication in particular. The book may be described as a Super-Thriller and should be read by every New Zealander. The almost fantastic exploits of the group under Brigadier Bagnold made a significant contribution not only to the success of the Eighth Army but to the prosecution of the war as a whole. The extent to which our soldiers were concerned is indicated in Appendix 3 of the book where the figures speak for themselves. The list of Honours and Awards contains one hundred names, all volunteers carefully selected for both physical and for mental qualities, drawn from twenty-one army units. Due to the fact that large numbers of N.Z. troops were available in Egypt at that time, 2 N.Z.E.F. with forty names outnumbered greatly any other single unit. Headed by a D.S.O., an O.B.E., an M.B.E., 4 M.C.'s and 3 D.C.M.'s, their contribution is impressive.

The origin of the L.R.D.G. was a small group of enthusiasts who, at their own expense, set about the task of extending vastly the knowledge of the Libyan Desert gained by the Light Car Patrols. Major Ralph Bagnold was the leader and recorded the experiences of the party in this book "Libyan Sands"; his greatest achievement was the conquest of the Great Sand Sea lying to the south of Siwa, almost as dangerous an enemy as Hitler's Africa Corps, and a vital factor in subsequent tactics against the enemy.

The services of N.Z. soldiers in desert warfare as described by Kennedy Shaw, bear out an opinion expressed to me by one of the finest Englishmen I have ever met. Colonel de Lancy-Forth was the last Commander of the Sellum-Siwa area and it fell to my lot to show him over his territory, a ten day's job. He had a wide experience in Palestine of troops from many countries including Australia and New Zealand. Asked what he thought of these Dominion troops his reply was, "They are the finest soldiers since the Roman Empire". Asked whether there was anything to choose between them he said: "It would depend on the job; if I wanted extraordinary dash, I would use Australians but if I wanted men who would stick their toes in and cling till the last man was killed I'd pick New Zealanders".

And so from small beginnings, the T Fords of World War I, through the 1930s and culminating in the agonies of World War II, gradually the mysteries of the Desert have been exposed until the advent of the aeroplane has stripped bare to the public eye the whole of Libya and its vast neighbour the great Sahara Desert.

REPORT ON THE MILITARY GEOGRAPHY OF THE NORTH-WESTERN DESERT OF EGYPT (excerpts)

BY CLAUD HERBERT WILLIAMS

REPORT ON THE MILITARY GEOGRAPHY OF THE NORTH-WESTERN DESERT OF EGYPT

PREFACE

The object of this report is to place on record any information in my possession, gathered in the course of desert patrolling during the past three years, that may be of military value in the future.

The report is supplementary to "Military Notes on Western Egypt," which was compiled from a variety of sources in 1915–16. Since 1916 patrol duties have taken us over such a large proportion of the area reported upon, that it is possible to amplify considerably the information given in Military Notes, and to fill up certain other gaps as regards the outlying places of which information was scanty, and sometimes inaccurate. I propose to confine myself to such outlying parts.

The report is limited in its scope by the necessity of subordinating exploratory or cartographical work to ordinary patrol duties, and by the impossibility of penetration by cars of certain large areas.

It must be remembered that the whole subject is dealt with from a car point of view, and with the underlying idea of using cars as a military weapon. Cars have been our means of visiting and examining the country, and we have only very seldom had the advantage of being accompanied by men with expert knowledge outside of military matters. Maps names have presented a difficulty, for it has often been impossible to carry native guides with us, and even when they were available they were found to differ in their statements in this respect. We have been obliged to adopt any names that occurred to us at the time as a means of identifying localities, and many places will, therefore, be found on the map, of which the native names have been superseded by new names.

In the carrying out of exploratory work, thanks are due to other patrol leaders, Captains Lindsay and Davidson, to Lieut.-Colonel Llewellyn Partridge, who was largely responsible for earlier work carried out by No. 5 Patrol; and to Lieutenant Kennett, of the Frontier Districts Administration Camel Corps, who has supplied some very necessary information about the sand country south of Siwa, inaccessible to cars.

In the cartographical portion of the work, Dr. Ball, of the Survey of Egypt, has been instrumental in putting the material collected into a form to be of practical use, and also in devising simple methods of measurement and calculation suitable for patrol conditions. Some of these methods are described in a handbook entitled "Desert Reconnaissance by Motor Car," which has been found an invaluable aid on the patrols.

I wish also to thank the non-commissioned officers and men who have worked with me. The collection of cartographical data has often involved much extra work of an arduous character, and such work has always been carried out in a cheerful and efficient manner beyond all praise.

INTRODUCTION

The area dealt with is, roughly speaking, defined by the sea on the north, the Nile Valley on the east, the Baharia-Siwa caravan route on the south, and the Egyptian frontier line on the west.

When the car patrols started work in 1916 good maps existed of Baharia, Fayoum, Wadi Natrun and the coastal belt from Alexandria to Sellum for a distance of about 10 miles inland. The Oases of Siwa and Qara were partially mapped and the positions of Siwa town and Qara village were known from Mr. Wade's astronomical observations of 1912. The remaining information on the maps available at the outbreak of war was of a partial character, gathered from the reports and observations of explorers, and was of a widely varying degree of accuracy. The use of the speedometer has provided us with a very simple means of measuring distances with a fair approximation to accuracy, and has enabled us to verify or correct existing information which was largely gained by the less accurate process of estimating distance by the pace of camels.

The maps included are the result partly of speedometer and compass traverses and partly of a plane-table survey, in both cases controlled by astronomical observations for latitude and by theodolite triangulation where possible. The whole of the mapping is based on a series of positions astronomically determined by Dr. John Ball of the Survey of Egypt, who accompanied the patrol in two long journeys in October, 1916 and May, 1917. The chance of serious error was thereby greatly minimised, and the maps may be relied on as approximately correct in all important features. All cartographical detail shown is embodied in the latest maps compiled by the Survey of Egypt. Detail relevant to the report, which is not contained in the route map, will be found in the smaller map of the oases […]

RAINFALL AND WATER SUPPLY

Rainfall is, generally speaking, scanty. On the coast the annual average is about 6 to 8 inches, and is confined to 3 or 4 months of the year. At Siwa it is said to be only a fraction of an inch, but, as far as I know, reliable records do not exist. It is a diminishing quantity from north to south, and may be said practically to cease at about 40 miles inland. The rainfall in the practically rainless areas appears to consist in very rare, but occasionally very heavy cloudbursts, and the eroding effect of the resulting sharp showers on a ground surface unprotected by any form of vegetation, especially in the steep country, is so apparent that it is often difficult to credit that their occurrence is so rare. In January, 1919, a cloudburst of this nature occurred sufficient to convert every depression between Sellum and Siwa into a temporary shallow lake and to prevent all car traffic for a week. A heavy rain storm at Siwa is looked upon as a disaster from its injurious effects upon the houses and its interference with the irrigation system by watering the ground at inopportune times […]

POPULATION

Population being entirely dependent on water supply, any approach to settlement is naturally confined to the coastal belt or the extreme north edge of the plateau, where the rainfall is sufficient to support a sheep raising industry and where barley can be grown in season; and to a few of the more favoured oases where the wells supply sufficient water for irrigation. The coastal population is of a semi-nomadic type and moves from place to place according to the amount of vegetation available for the flocks or to the supply of water in the local cisterns. That in the oases is of a more permanent character and the people live in fairly well-built stone or mud houses and carry on the cultivation of dates, olives and other fruits by means of irrigation.

The population along the coast is Bedouin but the oases of Siwa and Qara are inhabited by a race apart. They are different in language, customs and appearance, from the inhabitants of the coast or of Egypt proper […] The Siwans are described in "Military Notes" very much to their disadvantage, but our experience of them has been distinctly more favourable […] They have seemed to us of a kindly nature, for during the two years that the military outpost has been in contact with them, no friction of any importance has occurred, while the leading Siwans have shown a good deal of genuine hospitality to the garrison.

ANIMAL LIFE

Game is scarce over the whole country and the sportsman will find little encouragement. Gazelle are fairly numerous in some parts and a few hares are to be seen occasionally. Quail are numerous along the coast at certain seasons. The oases are remarkably deficient in animal or bird life. In addition to a few gazelle the only other wild animal I have seen is a species of wolf or large jackal, a grey beast about the size of a large dog. A few flamingos are to be seen and the migratory crane pays the oases a yearly visit. There are wild geese on some of the lakes but they are not numerous […]

Other points of interest in studying the north-western desert are the existence in certain places of fossil bones of animals. A number of good specimens were found near Escarpment Post, at Moghara, by the garrison of the outpost in 1916, and a few were noticed on the top of the Barrier Scarp. Fragments of the shell of tortoises and bones of crocodiles and other animals are numerous.

THE PLATEAU

The Libyan plateau consists of a great tract of limestone country, stretching from the Nile Valley in the east to the Gulf of Sidra in the west.

It is waterless except for occasional rain-catching cisterns of ancient construction; and is uninhabited except to a very small extent on its northern edge, adjacent to the coastal belt.

The average altitude is about 500 feet, but it is several hundred feet higher between Moghara and Qattara. It varies in width from about 30 miles, south of Alamein, to about 170 miles, south of Sellum […]

The northern portion of the plateau, a belt of 15 or 20 miles wide, has fairly abundant vegetation, and depressions are filled with loam, which supports good camel grazing and is cultivable. The surface, generally, is covered with rough stone, and though it is everywhere feasible for cars, it is too severe on tyres and mechanism to be styled good car country […]

As one travels further south, and vegetation disappears, the surface of the desert for car traffic improves, the rough stone giving place to finer gravel. The soil is practically devoid of humus, and depressions are filled with a hard pan of water-deposited material, which sets like cement and presents a smooth surface, delightful to drive over […] Broadly speaking, the whole of the plateau is feasible either for light cars or for armoured cars; though with the latter, it is well to keep as much as possible to the masrabs, or caravan routes, which are harder, and much less extravagant in petrol consumption than the unbeaten desert […] Except on the beaten tracks, car travelling on the plateau almost resembles navigation at sea; for the monotony of the surface is almost unbroken by conspicuous features and in many places cars can be driven in a straight line for as much as 100 miles without encountering a serious obstacle.

CAR ROUTES
General Remarks

NATIVE GUIDES
Good native guides accustomed to motor travelling are rare, and may not always be procurable, and an unreliable guide is worse than none at all. A native guide may be very familiar with a camel route and yet, if unused to cars, will become confused by the deviations that are so often necessary to get good going. The pace also of a car, in comparison with that of a camel, will lead him to misjudge his distances. A guide does not like to acknowledge himself at fault, and the result is that he may take one many miles in an entirely wrong direction […]

OLD CAR TRACKS
Old car tracks are a fruitful source of trouble and are likely to remain so for a very long time. In certain types of country they will probably last a lifetime to form pitfalls for the traveller. Where the car patrols have been working, tracks exist in hundreds, crossing or diverging from the recognized routes in every conceivable direction and leading to nowhere in particular.

USE OF THE COMPASS
In following a compass course it should be remembered that correct readings cannot be made from a car; nor is the compass error constant on the car, for it varies according to the pace at which the engine is running. It is, therefore, necessary, if accuracy is required, to leave the car and take readings at some yards distance. In country where there are no distant landmarks to provide direction points, this involves constant stops, but this difficulty can be overcome by using the sun's shadow as a means of keeping the direction […]

WEATHER

Wet weather is very detrimental to desert travelling. All types of country, excepting pure sand, are adversely affected to a surprising degree. Depressions become lakes or quagmires, and quite elevated country is often difficult to get through. Even on hard, well-beaten tracks the petrol consumption is greatly increased.

Remarks on the use of Ford Cars in the Desert

The Ford has been the only type of light car extensively used in the north-western desert, and though there are, no doubt, other makes that would serve the purpose, the Ford has qualities that render it very suitable for desert conditions, and it has passed the experimental stage. As it seems probable that Ford cars will be largely used in the future, some observations, based upon our experience of them in the past, may be of value.

Desert conditions involve very great wear and tear and general depreciation, partly because of the constant wearing effect of sand on the working parts; partly because the surface conditions are such that driving power is continually being heavily called upon; and partly from the nature of obstacles which cars are required to overcome in the shape of sand or rough, broken country, or declivities up which they often have to be hauled or pushed by main force.

The qualities required in a car are, therefore, lightness combined with strength and high power, convenience in the procuring of spare parts and simplicity in fitting them.

The Ford has these qualities combined with the very important one of cheapness, both in the initial cost and in the subsequent cost of the duplicates.

The system of transmission also, which I believe is peculiar to the Ford, is particularly adapted to desert requirements. It is possible for even an inexpert driver to change from top gear to low gear with an ease and rapidity impossible in a gate-change, and this point is very important when stretches of sand have to be crossed where it is a matter of doubt whether the car will ride over the surface or not. A too great loss of pace in changing down will often cause a car to stick, and a strenuous push will be the result.

A great drawback to the Ford is the difficulty of getting the engine started, especially after a damp night or a sand-storm, and the spectacle of cars being towed round the desert in the morning, to start the engines, is a common one. It is almost always necessary to jack up a rear wheel and crank the engine while in gear. This disability could probably be overcome by the provision of a stronger electric current by means of a supplementary battery. It is worth experimenting in this direction, for the drawback may be very serious where only two cars are out, and both give trouble.

WORKSHOP ATTENTION

It is difficult to put a Ford car out of action and makeshift road repairs of a most drastic nature can be carried out, but the internal parts of the engine or of the rear axle are matters for the workshop. A new power unit may run under desert conditions for 7,000 miles before requiring its first overhaul, but after that it will probably need workshop attention after each 3,000 or 4,000 miles. Engines should be carefully examined before and after every long journey.

Defects in the rear axle assembly are sometimes very difficult to detect. It should, therefore, be completely taken down and examined after each 5,000 or 6,000 miles. A rear axle breakage is about the most serious accident that can occur, for it is often impossible to tow a car in such a case, and the cost of retrieving may be almost as much as the car is worth. As a rule, a few minor replacements in the workshop will make everything safe.

COMMON ROAD BREAKAGES

SPRINGS
Spare springs should always be carried, but a rear spring is very heavy and cannot always be accommodated. A good makeshift expedient is to carry some clamps, by means of which a piece of plate, a tyre lever, or a piece of old spring leaf can be spliced across the break.

CAR ATTACHMENTS

THE SUN-DIAL

This attachment is of great use as an assistance to cartographical work, but it is so useful for keeping a correct direction in all desert travelling that it almost approaches a necessity.

The device consists of a horizontal plate, in the centre of which is fixed a vertical style about 3 or 4 inches high; at the base of the style is a pointer so adjusted that it will move stiffly round upon the horizontal plate. This is affixed to the top of the dash-board so that the vertical style is exactly central in the car. All that is required is to set the car in the direction it is required to travel, move the pointer to coincide with the sun's shadow cast by the style and drive as nearly as possible so that the two continue to coincide.

A development of the above consists in the addition of a circular plate figured round its circumference like a protractor, but with the figures in the contrary direction to compass figures. (The plate need not be more than 6 inches in diameter, and it is easy to mark it for each degree, figures being for each 10°.) This plate lies horizontally on the base-plate and under the pointer. It is arranged to move stiffly, like the pointer, round the central style, but the two should move independently of each other. To set the sundial, observe accurately the direction in which the car is pointing, by a bearing on some definite object. Set the movable plate so that the shadow falls upon the corresponding figure. Then move the pointer to the figure or bearing on which it is desired to travel. When the car is started, drive so that the shadow coincides with the pointer. It will be clear that any figure on which the shadow is resting will be the bearing on which the car is at the moment travelling, and this will be correct for 10 to 20 minutes according to the time of day, when the movement of the sun makes a resetting necessary.

The addition of a figured dial is useful as it enables a rough record of a devious course to be kept without the necessity of constant stops for taking fresh bearings.

The sundial attachment can be very easily made with sheet tin or brass. Figuring can be for each 10°, and can be done with mapping ink on a white-paint ground.

CLAUD HERBERT WILLIAMS:
A BIOGRAPHICAL SKETCH

BY RUSSELL McGUIRK

Claud Williams in late middle age.

CLAUD HERBERT WILLIAMS: A BIOGRAPHICAL SKETCH

Claud Williams was born in Auckland, New Zealand, on 18 February 1876, the third of five consecutive sons. His parents were Henry Edward Williams and Isabel Annie Connell, who later had a sixth child, a daughter named Violet Isabel Williams. During the Great War she was the recipient of Claud's letters from Egypt. Violet was in her thirties and married at the time, but the letters, so often quoted in Part I of this volume, invariably open with terms of unconcealed affection, such as 'my dear little girl' or 'dear little soul'.

Around 1880 the family moved to Dunedin, on South Island, where Claud was raised and educated. Given his intelligence and inquisitive mind one would guess that he was a good student; what is known for certain is that he was a talented musician. From an early age Claud took lessons at a violin school run by a German immigrant to Dunedin, Herr G.H. Schacht. By 1891 fifteen-year-old Claud was performing in public several times a year. He continued to play at local concerts and *soirées musicales* for many years. In 1913, a reviewer for a local newspaper wrote of one of these events: 'The instrumental soloist was Mr Claud Williams (violin). There is an entire lack of affectation about this musician… and although his manner is quiet, his tone is full of sympathy and his technique is becoming brilliant…' He had a considerable repertoire, including works by Mendelssohn, Handel, Bach and Beethoven. During the last year of the war Claud was loaned a violin by Dr Ball, and his favourite pieces quickly came back to him, much to the delight of music-starved soldiers, like the British Army doctor assigned to Siwa Camp.

Young Claud with violin and sister Violet.

After 'high school'[128] Claud became a farmer. He worked as a farmhand and eventually became a farm manager. In 1905, he moved to Gisborne on North Island, where he and his brother Carleton acquired some 4000 acres of land at nearby Muriwai with a view to becoming sheep farmers. Within a few years they were managing 5000 sheep per annum.

Around 1913, as war clouds began to gather, Claud joined a local militia, part of an unofficial British defensive organisation called the Legion of Frontiersmen. The Gisborne section of the Frontiersmen was established by a Boer War veteran named Francis Twisleton, who ran a 'military training camp' on his own farm. Its members, known as C Squadron, were instructed in the soldierly arts and generally endeavoured to keep fit. When the war began, Twisleton unsuccessfully tried to get the New Zealand Expeditionary Force to accept C Squadron as a fully-equipped and functioning unit. Some of the Gisborne Frontiersmen, including 38-year old Claud Williams, then tried to enlist individually but were rejected. In Claud's case, the reason appears to have been a combination of bad eyesight and being over the age limit.[129]

Undeterred, he decided to go to England in order to enlist in the Royal Army Medical Corps; and having made this decision, he seems, like Phileas Fogg, to have journeyed half-way round the world in a remarkably short time. On 1 April 1915, he sailed from Wellington on the Royal Mail Steamship *Marama*, bound for San Francisco. He then crossed the USA by rail in six days. In New York, again like Phileas Fogg, he discovered his plans had gone awry. He had booked passage to the UK on the White Star Liner *Megantic*, but the British Government had just requisitioned that vessel as a troop transport and sent it to Canada. Consequently, he was held up in New York for a week. On 6 May, he began a long letter to Violet relating the latest adventures

[128] Claud's words on a British Army form.
[129] Twisleton was killed in action in Palestine in November 1917.

of his journey and the following day, before he finished it, the *Lusitania* was torpedoed by a U-boat near Ireland with the loss of well over a thousand lives—including many women and children. A few days later Claud sailed on the Cunard's S.S. *Transylvania*. As the *Lusitania* had also sailed from New York, the Transylvania's passengers must have spent an anxious week on-board, before arriving safely in Glasgow on 17 May. In fact, the voyage was apparently not without incident, as is indicated by the following item which appeared in Gisborne's *Poverty Bay Herald* some weeks later:

> Frontiersman Claud Williams, who went to London with the idea of joining the R.A.M.C., after having an interview with a German submarine off the North Coast of Ireland, has entered for a cavalry regiment.

The 'cavalry regiment' was the 1/1st Pembroke (Castlemartin) Yeomanry. Claud enlisted in late May 1915 and was gazetted second lieutenant on 10 June. The question arises: why did Claud Williams change his mind about joining the RAMC? Did he choose to join a fighting regiment instead because of the *Lusitania*'s fate? Or because of his own close encounter with a German U-boat, enigmatically mentioned in the *Poverty Bay Herald*? There is a six-month gap in the letters home at this point (May to December 1915), so it's possible that his written explanation for the change never reached New Zealand. In any case, the question remains unanswered.

Claud's first surviving letter after joining the yeomanry is dated shortly before Christmas 1915. His regiment was then billeted at Bacton, near Norfolk. A month earlier it had been part of the South Wales Mounted Brigade; since then it had been 'dismounted'. In other words, the Pembroke Yeomanry had become cavalrymen without horses. The yeomen were thoroughly discontented and Claud was no exception:

> … I am wondering what malevolent fate let me into this cussed regiment. I believe the South Welsh Brigade [is] about the only 1st line regiment left in England. The thing is getting a positive nightmare, and the worst [is that] one cannot exchange. I shall surely die of old age in Norfolk & be buried in one of their damp untidy church yards. Verily I am fed up.

By his next letter two weeks later Claud's tone was more positive. Aware already that the regiment was going to Egypt, he was residing in a comfortable boarding house in Surrey and taking a course in the use of explosives.

> It is a Grenadier course where one learns all about explosives, trench fighting, etc. It is almost as dangerous as the real thing as we juggle with high explosives in large quantities as if it were sea sand. We shy fully loaded hand grenades about like marbles. Yesterday, just by way of amusement we exploded some mines, one consisting of 25lbs of guncotton, another of 20lbs of TNT. The whole thing is very enjoyable. I have another week of it yet & fully expect to get blown into small pieces before the end of it. If that happens you will of course [hear] of it by cable & you have my sincere sympathy.

Claud passed the course and qualified as a 'Bombing Officer'.

On 3 March 1916, the Pembrokes embarked at Devonport on HMT *Arcadian*, part of a convoy of three transports and four destroyers bound for Egypt. Also sailing that day were the yeomanry of Shropshire, Cheshire and Glamorganshire. Dozens of future Light Car Patrolmen were on those ships, which reached Alexandria on 14 March.

Already forty years old when he arrived in Egypt, Claud mentioned over and over again in his letters that he was not cut out to be a soldier. In fact, it is perfectly obvious that his qualities were such that he excelled at his work in the Western Desert. His letters reveal a man of character. For all his intelligence and inventiveness he was invariably self-deprecating. His appealing sense of humour would bubble up even when he was fulminating against everything and everyone. He had an impeccable sense of duty and responsibility. He was not afraid to improvise, to think laterally (as we say today) in order to overcome obstacles. Apart from his work, his interests seem to have been limitless: fossils and petrified forests in the desert; astronomy; ancient monuments and artefacts wherever he found them: Cairo, Luxor, Benghazi, Ajdabia…; how Siwans made olive oil and managed their date crop. He was fascinated by it all. He liked Egyptians—poor or wealthy, it made no difference. He befriended the Libyan prisoner Dahman bin Hayyin, with whom he could scarcely communicate—and his visit to Dahman's cell inside the old Citadel speaks volumes.

The one conspicuous exception amidst all this enthusiasm, as Williams admits himself, was his antipathy for the Western Desert Bedouin, not so much because they had sided with the Sanusi, but because he felt the men were sullen, lazy and cruel, tending to lord it over their womenfolk and children and work their animals half to death. We have seen that in old age he revisited this subject and conceded he may have been unfair in his memoir, considering that the Bedouin live in such extreme conditions that it is wrong for those who lead easier lives to judge them.

*   *   *

At the end of May 1919 Claud Williams arrived back in England to be demobilized from the British Army and repatriated. In high summer he left for New Zealand aboard the SS *Friederichsruhe*, a German steamer, which was later awarded to France as part of war reparations. The voyage took over seven weeks, so it is possible that Williams wrote the first draft of his memoir aboard ship.

Claud Williams was nearly forty-four years old when he finally reached Gisborne. He may have felt old, but in fact he lived for another half-century. He returned to sheep farming on his land at Muriwai. In 1920, he married Dorothy Lesley Egerton, who at that time was exactly half his age, and they had a son and two daughters. Apart from actual farming, he was for many years actively engaged in local farming and civic organisations. In addition to serving as the national president of the New Zealand Sheep-owners Federation for several years, he was on the County Council, the District Highways' Council, the Harbour Board, the Power Board, the Catchment Board, etc. Indeed, he was chairman of most of these bodies at some time or other.

Williams never returned to Egypt, but the country had left its mark on him. He knew that his work there had been important, and that he had a good story to tell. He typed up a new draft of 'Light Car Patrols in the Libyan Desert' and tried to get it published in New Zealand. The publishing company returned it with the comment that the reading public was sick of hearing about the war. The story's rejection was unfortunate but perhaps understandable. The Sanusi campaign had had its brief time in the limelight—a few days' headlines about armoured cars and Model T Fords, about the Duke of Westminster and the rescue of the Tara crew—but it was soon forgotten, cast into the shadows by all the publicity given to Lawrence of Arabia and Allenby, the defeat of Germany, the Versailles Conference… People could scarcely take in the enormous cost of the war or remember the endless sequence of great battles on the Western Front. What had happened in the Western Desert was a mere 'side show'.

What *is* surprising is that the memoir was not published after the Second World War given that Ralph Bagnold and W.B. Kennedy Shaw had each called for the Light Car Patrol story to be told.

Claud Williams died on 5 August 1970 in Gisborne.

The house at Muriwai.

INDEX